Marketing and the bottom line

FT Prentice Hall
FINANCIAL TIMES

In an increasingly competitive world, we believe it's
quality of thinking that will give you the edge – an idea
that opens new doors, a technique that solves a
problem, or an insight that simply makes sense of it all.
The more you know, the smarter and faster you can go.

That's why we work with the best minds in business
and finance to bring cutting-edge thinking and best
learning practice to a global market.

Under a range of leading imprints, including
Financial Times Prentice Hall, we create world-class
print publications and electronic products bringing our
readers knowledge, skills and understanding which can
be applied whether studying or at work.

To find out more about our business publications, or
tell us about the books you'd like to find, you can visit
us at **www.business-minds.com**

For other Pearson Education publications, visit
www.pearsoned-ema.com

PEARSON
Education

Marketing and the bottom line

The marketing metrics to pump up cash flow

Second edition

Tim Ambler

FT Prentice Hall
FINANCIAL TIMES

An imprint of **Pearson Education**

London ◆ New York ◆ San Francisco ◆ Toronto ◆ Sydney ◆ Tokyo ◆ Singapore
Hong Kong ◆ Cape Town ◆ Madrid ◆ Paris ◆ Milan ◆ Munich ◆ Amsterdam

Reviews of *Marketing and the Bottom Line*

"Measuring marketing performance is consistently one of the biggest issues faced by senior marketing executives. Without effective measurement, they cannot show that marketing is an investment for the firm. I highly recommend this excellent book as the most comprehensive and helpful one on the subject."
Andrew Abela, Managing Director, *Marketing Leadership Council*

"No topic has more immediacy for marketers than improving and monitoring our effectiveness and productivity. Marketers need to be far more accountable and this excellent book shows them not just how to provide the measures of success but also how to achieve top management consensus about marketing investment. I love the idea of the CFO taking over responsibility for marketing measurement. The more that financial people understand our markets and marketing, the better we will perform."
Kevin Bishop, Director of Marketing, *IBM United Kingdom Limited*

"This is a succinct, witty and mould-breaking book on a very important topic, and the second edition is a further improvement. It should be read by all senior managers and marketers."
Professor Hugh Davidson, *Cranfield School of Management*

"No topic has more immediacy for us than improving and monitoring marketing productivity. No other book so well communicates the importance of marketing metrics, still less doing so with a touch of Monty Python humor. Outstanding! I will be giving copies to all my colleagues."
Mike Duffy, Director of Analytic Modeling and Database Services, *Kraft Foods Inc*

"This book is a big step forward in assessing marketing impact – an area which is short of regular performance management."
Sir John Egan, President, *Confederation of British Industry*

"Since procurement people are getting so involved in our industry. I'd like to see them working much more closely with their colleagues in marketing. Let's see them take joint ownership for the investment programme for the brands they control. The collaboration should shift to a greater focus on added value, rather than cost reduction, and a more professional emphasis on the proof of effectiveness. This book gives them a route map to do this."
Bruce Haines, President, *Institute of Practitioners in Advertising*

"One reason why marketing does not always have CEOs' full attention is that there is no generally accepted set of metrics from top management review. The second edition of *Marketing and the Bottom Line* marks significant progress on this most vitally important marketing topic. Brilliantly conceived and highly entertaining, Amber provides marketing with both the measures of success and the means to achieve top management consensus about marketing investments."
Kevin Lane Keller, E.B. Osborn Professor of Marketing, *Amos Tuck School of Business, Dartmouth College*

"Companies and their investors now need a larger set of metrics to measure their progress and forecast their future. Tim Ambler provides the best discussion that I have seen of the metrics that companies need to guide their planning."

Philip Kotler, SC Johnson & Son Distinguished Professor of International marketing, *Northwestern University*

"If marketing wants a seat at the table, it has to be more accountable and provide measures of success that can sit right beside traditional financial metrics and make sense to the CEO. This insightful book charts the way for marketing managers who are ready to accept this challenge."

Alyssa Kuhn, Vice President, Global Brand Management, *VISA*

"Marketers are experiencing huge pressures on budgets. This excellent book gets the debate away from confrontation and towards constructive appraisal of forthcoming and completed marketing programs."

Lord MacLaurin of Knebworth, Chairman, *Vodafone PLC.*

"I encourage public company directors to take a closer look at the sources of cash flow and at marketing as the generator of customer preference. They both need to be regularly measured. This admirable book shows the way."

Sir Michael Perry GBE, Chairman, *Centrica PLC*

"Marketing will only move forward when evidence supports the value that it has provided. Marketers need metrics to do so, and this is the definitive book, in providing measures on how to do so."

Raoul Pinnell, VP Global Brands & Communications, *Shell International Petroleum Company Limited*

"Marketers need to be far more accountable. I have frequently recommended this book which shows marketers how to provide the measures of success but also how to achieve top management and board consensus about marketing investment."

Professor John Quelch, Senior Associate Dean, *International Development, Harvard Business School*

"This book drives the thinking at the heart of marketing's credibility (or lack of it). If we cannot effectively measure what we do or directly connect marketing investment to profitable growth and bottom-line contribution, then marketing as a function will never be seen by CEOs or CFOs as 'core'."

Simon Waugh, Marketing Director, *Centrica PLC*

PEARSON EDUCATION LIMITED

Edinburgh Gate
Harlow CM20 2JE
Tel: +44 (0)1279 623623
Fax: +44 (0)1279 431059
Website: www.pearsoned.co.uk

First published in Great Britain in 2000
Second edition 2003

ISBN: 0 273 66194 9

British Library Cataloguing in Publication Data
A catalogue record for this book can be obtained from the British Library

10 9 8 7 6 5 4 3

Designed by Sue Lamble
Typeset by Pantek Arts, Maidstone, Kent.
Printed and bound in Great Britain by Biddles Ltd, King's Lynn, Norfolk

The Publishers' policy is to use paper manufactured from sustainable forests.

Contents

Acknowledgements

This second edition turned out to be a substantial development of the first, partly a reflection of how quickly this world is changing. I am extremely grateful to all those who provided case histories especially as the great majority had to be rewritten after just two years.

The book first came from a research project sponsored by the Marketing Council, The Marketing Society, Institute of Practitioners in Advertising, Sales Promotions Consultants Association and London Business School. The key members of the Steering Group were John Stubbs (TMC), Nick Turnbull and then Mike Detsiny (TMS), Peter Field, Janet Hull and then Hamish Pringle (IPA), Barry Clarke (SPCA) and Professor Patrick Barwise (LBS). A number of these organizations additionally sponsored the marketing glossary – see Appendix A. Dr Flora Kokkinaki was the key researcher during the first 18 of the 30 month project. Ben Sear (then Diageo), Shashi Halve (British Airways) and Tim Harris undertook key interviewing.

Additionally, James Best, Tim Broadbent, Frank Cokayne, Hugh Davidson, Mike Fisher, Gareth Hill, Nick Kendall, Sarah McMahon, John Mayhead, Peter Mitchell, Raoul Pinnell, Angus Slater, Robin Stotter, Steve Willis and Gerald Wright kindly read drafts of the first edition. Valuable contributions to particular chapters came from (with the second edition chapter numbers) Jonathan Knowles (BrandEconomics) and Professor John Lynch (3), Bettina von Stamm (6), Kevin Thomson and Lorrie Arganbright (MCA – 7), Doug Ross (Watson Wyatt – 7), Professors Patrick Barwise and Chris Higson (8), and Philip Kleinman, ACNeilsen and Ruth McNeil (Research International – 10). Laura Mazur provided innovation interviews as well as valuable and insightful editing for the first edition.

The star for the second edition was Ian Hannah who critiqued every chapter and brought together most of the crucial case histories. The contacts for these histories are named in the text and I am glad to thank them collectively here.

Sir Peter Davis and then Professor Don Lehmann were able to contribute the Forewords despite the pressures on their time and I am delighted by the endorsements for this book which bring together the contributions of so many busy people.

Finally, the FT Prentice Hall team were very helpful and supportive and especially Richard Stagg and Stephen Partridge. From the first edition thanks also to Jacqueline Cassidy, Lisa Nachtigall, Angela Lewis and Gill Harvey and to Lesley Felce and Penelope Allport for the second.

When I completed the manuscript for this book the eminent marketer Professor Peter Doyle kindly agreed to provide the endorsement printed on the cover. Since then we have learned that he has died. Professor Doyle was Britain's leading academic researcher, teacher and marketer; this is a great loss.

Foreword to the first edition

Sir Peter Davis, CEO J. Sainsbury, PLC

MEASUREMENT IS THE COMPANY'S nervous system. Financial measurements are communicated backwards and forwards, yielding the gross data on a company's well-being, the equivalent of pulse, heart rate, calories taken in and spent, in short the evidence of life, and healthy equilibrium. But even our most eminent accountants agree that financial metrics alone can be misleading and are often incapable of explaining either cause or effect.

Nowadays the unremitting demand for organic growth has led chief executives to turn to the measurement of intangibles for precise evidence of success. Marketing can be described succinctly as 'winning customer preference'. It is critical to competitiveness and wealth creation.

Marketing metrics have the power, as a short scan of the book reveals, to throw light on many of the key questions that beset business leaders. What is our company really worth? Do we have competitive strengths in innovation and branding? Have we achieved sustainable growth based on sound customer strategies?

Too many executive boards have relied too much on the financials. At worst their view of the company can become one-dimensional and *trompe l'oeil*. If marketing metrics are absent, marketing must admit failure. For without credible metrics marketing is isolated and such isolation has no place in a modern company.

To promote the measurement of marketing effectiveness both to the profession and to the executive board we first need facts, best practice models and a common language, which we may use to describe and evaluate our marketing assets.

For these reasons The Marketing Council agreed to take a leading role in the work which underpins this book. The project team and Tim Ambler of the London Business School have exceeded expectation and must take credit for promoting the role of science in marketing, and for encouraging the broad uptake of marketing metrics at the level of the executive board. This book represents an advance for marketing and potentially for our national competitiveness.

Foreword to the second edition

Professor Donald R. Lehmann, Columbia Business School

MARKETING HAS RECENTLY SUFFERED from a distinct lack of respect and 'clout', which is only partly due to economic recession. Marketing's role has been either subsumed in other areas and functions (e.g. new products by design and R&D, customer relations by IT and operations) or marginalized (i.e. to ad copy and promotion planning). This shift has been abetted by the tendency of marketers to think both small (i.e. at the individual product or brand level) and in terms of goals (metrics) such as awareness and attitude which are relevant to those involved in hands-on management (e.g. brand managers) but not to others in the rest of the organization in general and those in finance in particular. This has led the Marketing Science Institute (MSI) to label 'metrics' as a top priority for the past three two-year priority setting periods, including 2002 to 2004. Indeed, a 2002 research competition on 'Linking Marketing to Financial Performance' produced the largest number of proposals and papers of any competition in MSI history. Into this turbulent area steps Tim Ambler, who happens to be both a 'real' accountant and a marketer, as well as an expert in the area. In doing so he not only provides valuable information but also offers a distinctive and provocative perspective.

The reader of this book should not expect to find a simple, neat tool kit. As Ambler points out, there can be no simplistic one-size-fits-all answer. Rather, the book, through logic and numerous examples of current practice, provides the reader with the opportunity to consider what combination of metrics is most useful for different purposes and different companies. In doing so, it makes many great points, including:

◆ Measuring long-term assets is critical if they are to be considered in conjunction with short-term financials (profits)

◆ Metrics are a means, not the end

◆ A slavish devotion to specific metrics will lead to distortions and suboptimal behaviour (i.e. focusing on the percent of revenues from new products may lead to churning of marginally new products)

◆ Multiple measures are needed for the purpose of guiding decisions and these measures differ somewhat across firms/businesses

The book also makes points which at least some readers may find disquieting. Some of the more provocative suggestions include:

◆ Since finance people don't trust market research or market information, give the responsibility for them to finance so they can't routinely dismiss the results

◆ A certain fuzziness helps the firm to achieve a great future

◆ Shareholder value is not the appropriate sole goal of a business

While the primary thrust of the book revolves around brands, Ambler also has interesting chapters on metrics for new products, employees (a frequently neglected determinant of firm success) and the marketing mix, each of which make sense on their own. One intriguing aspect was the discussion of reporting transparency, which points out the pros and cons of reporting information (and correctly suggests that stated concerns over revealing secrets to competitors are exaggerated).

In summary, the book addresses a critical but little discussed issue for marketing in particular and business in general, namely how to measure the impact of marketing on the bottom line. At the conclusion the reader may wish that a simple solution had been offered. However, this would have been neither consistent with the author's philosophy nor beneficial (as opposed to pleasing) for the practical manager.

While I have many quibbles (e.g. I would place relatively more emphasis on output vs process metrics), I learned a lot from reading this book and suspect many others will as well. Given the style is engaging (not an easy feat for a potentially ponderous topic) and the content valuable, I am happy to recommend the book. I am also curious to see if others find the same points of agreement and disagreement that I did.

Executive summary

TOP MANAGEMENT IS NATURALLY preoccupied with its firm's wealth. You might expect it to be equally preoccupied with generating it, but the astonishing fact is that, on average, meetings of top UK management devote nine times more attention to spending and counting cash flow than to wondering where it comes from and how it could be increased.[1] The monthly accounts commonly have just one line for the sales revenue from immediate customers. The rest concerns spending and storing it. The source of the cash flow – the end users – does not even get a mention.[2] The same pattern characterizes many other firms in the USA and around the world.

Accountants seem to imagine that a pile of money will grow if only you count it often enough. Large companies are understandably concerned with certainty, but re-counting the same money does not make it any more certain. The same profit and loss account numbers are planned, budgeted, forecasted, then reforecasted, without getting the company any closer to the marketplace. The point is simple: if you want to know what your future cash flow will look like, investigate where it comes from – the market. A farmer whose livelihood depends on a river flowing through his land will be concerned with the upstream situation, especially if the river could be diverted to a neighbour's property. Companies should be just as concerned with their upstream wealth, and whether their competitors are diverting it. Our research shows that companies that look to the sources of cash flow – those that think about the market – are more profitable.[3]

Understanding where corporate wealth comes from involves questions like: 'Why do consumers buy now?' 'Why might they buy more (often)?' 'Which other kinds of people might buy these products for other reasons?' In industrial or business-to-business sectors, who are the 'consumers' or 'end users'? The train driver has quite different interests from those who buy the trains.

Over the last 30 years, large firms have kept ahead through acquisitions (spending cash again) but not through organic growth.[4] In other words, these leaders, such as Unilever, have been paying too little attention to their consumers. They have been looking at the bottom line – net profits or shareholder value – rather than at what generates it. Analysts today are looking a little closer: survival depends on basic wealth creation. And wealth creation is exactly what marketing does.

The first edition of this book summarized a 30-month research project into 'Marketing Metrics' and this second edition updates that with research in the USA. Similar work has also taken place in Australia, China, Scandinavia and Spain. Our purpose has been to report best practice in marketing performance measurement, to show how it could be better and to share these concepts and language. The project sponsors[5] recognized that, unlike accountants, marketers are divided by their understanding of even common words such as 'marketing' or 'brand'. As well as clarifying the financial aspects of marketing, the project sought to pinpoint the non-financial factors that lead to business success.

While this book takes a wider view of marketing, renewed pressures to justify marketing expenditure require a thoughtful response. In the USA particularly, corporate financiers are looking for new standards of proof:

These new standards are driven in part by the current economic climate but are also a function of growing corporate intolerance for the lack of ROI discipline that has traditionally characterized much of brand spending.[6]

Also in the USA:

While companies have struggled for years to quantify the effects of marketing activities, the urgency to do so has recently increased as firms reevaluate spending levels in the face of tightening economic conditions. Driven by the need to demonstrate the impact of their activities on their companies' financial performance, [Marketing Leadership] Council members today attach far greater importance to measurement than they did one year ago.[7]

This book is not a paean of praise for marketing. What it does, uniquely, is to provide a complete guide to making marketing fully accountable. Some marketers may find this greater transparency uncomfortable; others will find that the professional use of metrics will give marketing its rightful place in top management councils. To see if you need this book, ask yourself these eight questions:

1   Does your firm routinely research consumer (end user) behaviour (retention, acquisition, usage, etc.) and why they behave that way (awareness, satisfaction, perceived quality etc.)?

2   Are your external market indicators (customers and competitors) aligned with your strategy and with your internal market metrics covering employees and innovation?

3   Can you quantify what 'success' for your firm would look like and the metrics or milestones on the road there?

4   Do you have a quantified business model that connects marketing activities, market results and the bottom line?

5   Are these metrics routinely reported to top management, annually or semi-annually, in a format integrated with financial marketing metrics?

6   In those reports, are the results compared with the levels previously forecasted in the business plans?

7   Are they also compared with the levels achieved by your key competitor(s)?

8   Is the assessment of marketing performance adjusted according to the change in your market-based asset(s), usually known as brand equity or reputation?

If the answer to any of those questions is 'no', then your system is not good enough. Read on. An overview of the rest of the book is followed, as is each chapter, by recommendations for immediate action.

1 Is your metrics system good enough?

Too many companies dismiss the importance of marketing merely because they do not understand what it is. Take the Confederation of British Industry, for example. In their 1999 Fit for the Future campaign,[8] innovation and competitiveness are rightly extolled, but marketing and customers of any kind barely get a mention. Alec Daly, the campaign chairman, says, 'We want companies who find it difficult to innovate talking to those where innovation is inbred; companies who find it difficult to control cash, talking to those who find it second nature; and companies who need and want a step change in their competitive performance, exposed to those who have already done it.' This is all admirable, but it is also production oriented and ignores the outside world – the market.

To evaluate marketing performance, we first have to clarify what marketing is

When people say 'marketing', they may mean any one of at least three things: 'pan-company', 'functional' or 'budgetary' marketing. The first, perhaps ugly, expression describes a holistic view of marketing: it is what the whole firm does, not just the 'marketers', to secure customer preference and thereby achieve higher returns for the shareholder. According to the UK publishing company EMAP: 'Marketing is central to our business here. This is a total marketing company and everyone is interested in marketing.'[9] Consciously or not, every business in the world engages in marketing in this primary sense and would be bankrupt otherwise.

Pan-company marketing is not an option but a necessity: firms engage in it whether they recognize marketing or not. The difference lies between those who consciously espouse this customer-oriented philosophy and those who market by happenstance.

'Functional' marketing is what marketing professionals do and this varies from business to business. It limits marketing to the activities of one department. Few small companies have marketing departments and even large firms, like the Unilever beauty products subsidiary Elida Gibbs, are dispersing their marketers throughout the organization. In terms of responsibility, some marketers are not accountable for profits whereas others see this as their main charge. Some have charge of product specification, pricing, sales and trade marketing functions, whereas others are seen as staffers, outside the main direction of the business.

The third definition sees marketing as expenditure which means largely advertising and promotion. When people talk of the 'return' on marketing, this is the marketing they generally mean. But the incremental gains from advertising and promotional expenditures should be evaluated in the context of the wider meaning of marketing.

The first definition of marketing is the most important. Only a minority of companies have separate marketing departments or separate marketing budgets, but they all have end users to satisfy. We shall address the secondary meanings, but we are going to focus on maximizing marketing health throughout the whole company's business in order to maximize corporate wealth. 'Marketing' needs to include employees (the internal market) and innovation that impacts customers because these, possibly more than advertising and promotion, create new cash flow.

Even not-for-profit organizations, such as charities and national governments, have to be concerned with marketing in this sense. Without inward cash flow they would not be able to achieve their objectives. Marketing, in short, is the creation and harvesting of inward cash flow and this chapter looks more closely at how to assess a firm's current system before attending to the most difficult area: brand equity.

2 Brand equity is an elephant

Brand equity, for many companies, is far their biggest and most valuable asset. It lacks the attention it deserves because it is not on the balance sheet and it is hard to measure. Furthermore it is a relatively new, perhaps only 20 years old, part of the business scene.

The first step is to describe the beast from a number of points of view. Some commentators recognize the value of customers while others see brands and others again see competitive advantage. This gives the impression that we are looking at different things whereas in reality we are only looking at different aspects of the same thing.

Any complex asset, such as an industrial building, can be measured in all manner of ways. To make sense, we have to know the purpose of measurement. A glazier will want to measure windows when a tiler will want to measure the roof. Brand equity (the asset) is frequently confused with its value. Certainly the financial valuation is an important measure of a brand but it is only one measure and the number will differ according to the purpose of the valuation. A brand may not be worth the same to a seller as to a buyer.

The question arising, therefore, is how a firm should select the brand equity metrics in its particular situation. How it names this beast, e.g. 'reputation', in a professional services business is secondary to understanding it and measurement is part of that. Managing brand equity is a crucial role of marketing and thereby of transferring value from the market to the shareholder. It is the upstream reservoir of cash flow, earned but not yet released to revenue.

3 Financial fallacies

Chief executives, being busy people, are quite often appalled by all this marketing mumbo jumbo and demand a single number for performance or a single number for brand equity. The modern fashion is to bring everything down to shareholder value. That is what business is for and managing for value provides a universal framework.

That is a tempting road to take but this chapter explains why it is a dead end. Brand valuation is barely more helpful to brand management than putting a price on Mount Everest helps mountain climbing. Even those business issues that can be quantified cannot necessarily, still less usefully, be translated into financial numbers. The assumptions needed for the conversion go far beyond what the data can sustain. For example, we know that a psychological contract exists between a company and its employees. Maybe we can measure how strong that contract is on a five-point scale from very committed to very uncommitted, but few companies would care to assign a financial value to that commitment.

Modern management uses measurement to plan improvement and to learn from what is actually achieved. With learning, change can be predicted and then tracked from period to period in a controlled way. More importantly, sharing the business model can give direction to the whole firm. Financial proxies lose the reality of that process.

The second major difficulty is that we cannot measure the future. Management needs to predict the outcomes of their actions, or their options, but they cannot be sure of them. A number of modern techniques such as customer lifetime value (CLV) and brand valuation are based on taking the present value of future cash flows. These techniques are useful for choosing between various investment choices, but not for reporting on the progress made by marketing to date. In a sense they take the credit for future marketing activities and thereby deflect attention from the situation today.

A final, for now, danger of these techniques is tunnel vision. By projecting future income streams from current awareness, we do not allow for the wider world – sometimes known as 'white space'. The narrower our understanding of our brand and its customers and competitors, the narrower and more risky is the tunnel of vision. Innovation by our firm and others will reveal opportunities beyond anything now in the plan. Marketing eyes need to open wider to these peripheral developments, some of which may prove important new sources of cash flow. CLV, for example, is distorted by working from the current customer database rather than what it might be. Shareholder value is a useful technique for determining how best to spend cash flow but it makes little contribution to understanding where it comes from.

Important as financial metrics are, they distort reality and provide the illusion of control. Cannabis does much the same.

4 Metrics evolution: how did we get where we are?

Reporting on marketing to top management is, or should be, an intimate part of the way a firm does business. A new metrics system should not be bolted onto processes which otherwise continue unchanged. Since the metrics need to reflect business strategy, implicit or not, it follows that they should evolve along with the strategy. What is discarded is almost as important, and often more controversial, than what is added.

It is probably not very sensible to step straight to an ideal metrics solution. Culture and metrics need to evolve together over time but that can be accelerated. This chapter examines the experience of leading companies, shows how they reached their present situation and where they intend to go. The process is influenced by the size and type of business and its competitive sector. Know the metrics your competitors see but do not limit yourself to those numbers. Otherwise, the knock-on effect of metrics on strategy is likely to result in copycat marketing.

The general pattern of development begins with top management having little appreciation of the significance of marketing metrics. As the recognition of the need for control measures grows, they turn to the accountants for basic financial indicators such as sales, costs and profits. It then becomes clear that these are retrospective. Indicators need to be closer to customer and competitor and therefore have to be non-financial such as behavioural (e.g. loyalty, penetration) or what people have in their heads ('intermediate', e.g. awareness and attitudes). Very soon, top management is swamped by numbers. Marketers are asked to select a dozen or so key indicators. The final stage, to which many aspire but few achieve, uses the full database of metrics and performance to select those indicators which predict future performance.

5 A practical methodology for selecting the right external metrics

This chapter moves from how metrics evolved to how management can develop them. Changing even the external market metrics turns out to be a major problem.

Some of the troublesome areas include assembling a comprehensive database, gaining agreement that these are company-wide measures, not just private communication between the CEO and the marketing department, and the interaction between metrics and strategy. As noted above, to what extent should firms select the same measures as their competitors and where should they differ? Their source may dictate the choice: some research can only be gathered on a shared basis and other metrics are available only from the standard packages that market research agencies make available.

A single brand company operating in just one market has a much simpler problem than the multi-branded multinational. To what extent should metrics be standardized across all brands and territories? Different markets will want to use their own indicators, strategies will differ and consistent information may simply not be available from data suppliers.

Very large companies may, like Unilever, have scope for a department that specializes in marketing information, independent from their marketers. But for most companies the only function in a position to integrate financial and non-financial marketing metrics is the finance department. In other words, turning over market research responsibility to the chief financial officer (CFO) has much to commend it:

◆ Marketers are widely seen as selective and/or manipulative in the way they present information. Independence would add credibility.

◆ Metrics are not a high priority for marketers despite the increasing pressure for accountability. Most managers are tired of surveys and questions from business schools. Even so, we were surprised by the low interest shown by marketers. With honourable exceptions (notably those who contributed to this book), marketers are more interested in making runs than scoring. Perhaps this is as it should be.

◆ Marketing information is widely dispersed in large organizations. Only part of it exists in the marketing department, even if there is one. The finance function routinely penetrates all sections of the firm.

◆ Alignment, or consistency, is needed across functional and geographic boundaries as well as across hierarchical management levels. Ways to evaluate the marketing mix (advertising, promotions and pricing) need to be consistent with evaluating marketing as a whole. Again, the finance function is skilled in assembling consistent information.

◆ The costs of marketing information should be treated in the same way as other management information costs, such as the management accounts, and not deducted from the marketing effort.

◆ The finance function should be within the marketing tent in order to understand where the cash comes from. Thankfully, we found the old adversarial relationship between marketing and finance to be largely a thing of the past, but direct responsibility for the numbers will help cement the partnership.

In short, this is a minefield but at least knowing where some of the mines are and their nature improves the odds of getting through. Standing still is not an option for long.

6 Using metrics to improve
innovation performance

This chapter leads us from the external marketplace to the two main internal indicators of marketing performance: innovation and employees. The mantra 'innovate or die' is broadly accepted but implementation is tough and finding the right performance indicators is even more difficult. Top managements want to monitor 'innovativeness' and yet few believe that key performance indicators (KPIs) provide the solution. Boots the Chemist, the UK's major health and beauty care retailer, appointed a director of innovation, but carries out little measurement beyond the number of product launches and the proportion of sales from recent launches.

The quality, not the quantity, of innovation is the crux. Indeed, many large firms today suffer from an excess of innovation, or initiative overload. The three phases of innovation (creativity, development and implementation) require different skills. Culture (the way things are done) and process (what is done) are merely enablers, not drivers.

3M very successfully uses just a few simple metrics, such as the proportion of sales due to recent innovations. Many other firms have copied these metrics, but few have succeeded because their leadership styles and cultures are different. The moral is that firms should get away from the detail and first measure these bigger picture variables.

Thus it is mostly a question of leadership and then culture rather than process. In large companies, much of the process gets in the way and should be dismantled. These metrics prove to be very similar to those used for assessing employer brand equity, i.e. what the employees carry around in their heads about the firm they work for.

7 Employee-based brand equity

Some companies, and especially consumer service companies, see employees as their first customers. If management correctly markets to employees, then the front-line employees will take care of the external customers. In this perception, internal marketing becomes, for the top management, even more important than external marketing and therefore its own set of metrics is the more crucial. Whether 'marketing' includes employees is academic: synergizing human resource and marketing skills can bring rich rewards. The 'employer brand' concept helps these two functions to learn from each other. Tobacco company Gallaher, for example, sees marketing in pan-company terms and has marketing, sales and financial people working together in teams.

Which segment of 'customer' is the most important depends on when you ask the question. Employee issues will need to be addressed first and the end user will be satisfied last. Marketers will plan things the other way about, i.e. start with the consumer, but the motivation of all the segments needs to be measured whichever way the company goes.

Many firms now measure employee indicators but few cross-fertilize employee and customer survey techniques and measures. They should. The relationship between employee and customer satisfaction is commonplace.[10] BP found, unsurprisingly, a good correlation between the two. To some extent, employees can provide, far more cheaply and easily, proxies for external research though this needs careful quality control. In a service company especially, customers form their impressions, i.e. brand equity, from their interactions with the employees.

8 Brand transparency

Beyond customers, competitors and employees, the contribution of other stakeholders to cash flow is indirect but it can be influential. This chapter mainly concerns the interaction between the company and its shareholders, sometimes proxied by analysts. We researched the disclosure of market metrics to shareholders in annual reports.[11] Broadly, 85 per cent of company respondents agreed that shareholders are entitled to information about brand equity, often their most valuable asset. At the same time, few companies supply many metrics at all.

This chapter explores the reasons why they do not and, conversely, why it is in the interests of companies that they should.

9 Assessing the performance of the marketing mix

Returning to the nitty gritty of marketing expenditure, most CFOs want to know the particular contributions from advertising, promotions and other parts of the marketing mix. This is not the return on marketing as a whole, which is meaningless, but whether increasing or decreasing the elements of expenditure increased profits and/or brand equity. Better still, they would like to know this ahead of time when budgets are set.

Few companies have fully grasped just how fundamental marketing and brand equity are and the consequential unwisdom on focusing on efficiency ratios such as ROI but they are moving in this direction. We found increasing emphasis on effectiveness (achieving what matters) rather than doing the wrong things more cheaply. Of course companies want both effectiveness and efficiency and to measure the contribution of each element of the mix to those ends. A process for doing that is proposed.

While too many unknowns prevent this being a science, a few techniques, discussed in this chapter, will help and, importantly, at least achieve internal consensus on the optimal expenditures. Furthermore, the different elements of the mix, eg electronic media, have their specialist metrics which warrant separate consideration.

10 Getting the right metrics to the top table

Gaining this consensus requires both the top management and the specialist marketers to be looking at the same performance indicators. Shell calls it the 'line of sight'. Aligning metrics with strategy and aligning key measures both across functional silos and up and down the hierarchy sounds easy but it is not.

This chapter suggests practical steps to bringing it about. Managers are wedded to the metrics they have and this type of change takes more time than they can divert from daily priorities, or think they can divert. Ship-to-ship transfer in the open ocean only looks attractive when you know your ship is sinking. Wait that long to modernize your marketing metrics and it is too late.

11 The fuzzy future

The final chapter is cautionary. A business cannot be run just by numbers. Standardize everything and it will die. Shifting management bonuses to marketing metrics, as users of the Balanced Scorecard have discovered, may be unwise. Ignoring the indicators of cash flow and the reservoir called brand equity is terminal but so is ignoring everything else.

Top management should be wary of calls for oversimplification. We are not dealing with a hygiene matter where boxes can quickly be ticked before moving on. Indeed, using marketing metrics in a mechanistic way denies their very purpose. Even if the metrics are the same, the sources of cash flow – the reasons why consumers buy and might buy more – are the discussions which the metrics should trigger. The book offers a design process to decide the right marketing metrics for your company, taking both the tailored and general points of view into account.

A certain fuzziness helps the firm achieve a great future.

Action this day

Here are five top actions for the chief executive officer, and today is as good a time as any:

1 Appoint a team led by a top executive to develop the metrics reporting system.
2 Ensure it is cross-disciplinary with members from finance, human resources, sales and marketing (at least).
3 Give them a six-month deadline, with an interim top management report after three months.
4 Publicize the task and the reasons for it, and encourage firm-wide participation.
5 Set a date in the calendar for the CEO and top executive team to review the draft recommendations.

Just as gold prospectors celebrated when they departed for the hills, so any company should rejoice when it sets out to rediscover the sources of its cash flow. A healthy flow will provide the wealth for everything else.

Notes

1 Marketing Metrics project research with UK plcs, December 1999.

2 Operational matters, supplies and suppliers, corporate governance, employee issues, interest, taxes, dividends, and capital expenditure take far more time than the motivations of the ultimate customer. But these are all ways to spend, or at least count, the cash, not increase its flow.

3 We found a 0.25 correlation between customer orientation and performance. The precise figures vary but this result is similar to comparable studies noted in the book.

4 David Cowans's Marketing Forum Presentation, Oriana, September 1999.

5 See Acknowledgements.

6 Marketing Leadership Council (2001) *Stewarding the Brand for Profitable Growth*, Washington, DC:Corporate Executive Board, 20.

7 Marketing Leadership Council (2001) *Measuring Marketing Performance*, Washington, DC: Corporate Executive Board, 2.

8 Website: www.fitforthefuture.org.uk

9 Quoted in *The Role of Marketing*, research report by KPMG, 1999, 7.

10 This is developed in Chapter 7 with citations.

11 Ambler, T., Barwise, P. and Higson, C. (2001) *Market Metrics: What Should We Tell the Shareholders?*, London: Centre for Business Performance.

Metrics top tables

Standard profit and loss (P&L) account metrics (Chapter 5)

Actual metric	% compared with plan and/or prior year	% compared with competition
Sales	Volume/value	Market share
Marketing investment	Period costs	Share of voice
Bottom line	e.g. economic profit	Share of profit

1 The board will review the company's sales and bottom line, certainly monthly and maybe weekly, but this is the profit by marketing unit analysis.

2 First and second order derivatives (trends and rates of change in trends) are more important for board review than snapshot metrics.

3 The availability of diagnostics for analyzing variances in metrics is assumed.

General brand equity metrics (Chapter 5)

Consumer metric	Measured by
Familiarity	Salience, i.e. familiarity relative to the other brands in the consideration set
Penetration	Number of customers or the number of active customers as a per cent of the intended market
What they think about the brand	Brand preference as a per cent of preference of other brands within the consideration set or intention to buy or brand knowledge
What they feel	Customer satisfaction as per cent average for the consideration set about the brand
Loyalty	This may be behavioural (share of category requirements, repeat buying, retention, churn) and/or intermediate (commitment, engagement or bonding)
Availability	Distribution, e.g. weighted percentage of retail outlets carrying the brand

Innovation metrics shortlist (Chapter 6)

Strategy	Awareness of goals (vision)
	Commitment to goals (vision)
	Active innovation support
	Perceived resource adequacy
Culture	Appetite for learning
	Freedom to fail
Outcomes	No. of initiatives in process
	No. of innovations launched
	% revenue due to launches during last three years

Employee-based equity metrics (Chapter 7)

Awareness of corporate goals
Perceived calibre of employer
Relative employee satisfaction
Commitment to corporate goals
Employee retention
Perceived resource adequacy
Appetite for learning
Freedom to fail
Customer-brand empathy

Is your metrics system good enough?

ACCORDING TO RESEARCH by the Washington-based Marketing Leadership Council, 63 per cent of their blue chip members are dissatisfied with their marketing performance measurement systems.[1] They reckoned that, on average, they were wasting 26 per cent of their marketing budgets. While no two firms address the question in quite the same way, this chapter provides the basis for assessing your own system.

Our research found that most firms do not have a clear picture of their overall marketing performance which may be why they cannot assess it. They prefer to fumble around in the dark. It's easy to see why: fumbling has a lot going for it. More adventure, more creativity, more surprises and more fantasies are all possible. But you may not like what you see when the lights do go on. Clarity of goals and metrics separate the professional from the amateur. Professional marketers quantify results against intentions to keep raising the bar. Professional athletes do the same.

Before we get into the basic criteria, you may wish to check out your marketing assessment system against the ten questions in Table 1.1. Score it from the answers in the references for this chapter.[2] How fully marketing engages top management is really the key. Get that right and everything else is relatively straightforward. I will shorthand the top executive group, or committee, of any organization as the 'Exec'.

A key issue arising from this list is the alignment of metrics with strategy. Few businesses have explicit strategy with quantified milestones (metrics) to indicate progress. More often, as Professor Henry Mintzberg has shown,

Table 1.1 ◆ Ten questions to rate your firm's marketing assessment system

1	Does the Exec regularly and formally assess marketing performance?	(a) Yearly (b) Six-monthly (c) Quarterly (d) More often (e) Rarely (f) Never
2	What does it understand by 'customer value'?	(a) Don't know. We are not clear about this (b) Value of the customer to the business (as in 'customer lifetime value') (c) Value of what the company provides from the customer's point of view (d) Sometimes one, sometimes the other
3	How much time does the Exec give to marketing issues?	...............%
4	Does the business/marketing plan show the non-financial corporate goals and link them to market goals?	(a) No/no plan (b) Corporate no, market yes (c) Yes to both
5	Does the plan show the comparison of your marketing performance with competitors or the market as a whole?	(a) No/no plan (b) Yes, clearly (c) In between
6	What is your main marketing asset called?	(a) Brand equity (b) Reputation (c) Other term (d) We have no term
7	Does the Exec's performance review involve a quantified review of the main marketing asset and how it has changed?	(a) Yes to both (b) Yes but only financially (brand valuation) (c) Not really
8	Has the Exec quantified what 'success' would look like five or ten years from now?	(a) No (b) Yes (c) Don't know
9	Does your strategy have quantified milestones to indicate progress towards that success?	(a) No (b) Yes (c) What strategy?
10	Are the marketing performance indicators seen by the Exec aligned with these milestones?	(a) No (b) Yes, external (customers and competitors) (c) Yes, internal (employees and innovativeness) (d) Yes, both

strategy simply emerges and can only be seen after the event.[3] In this case, identifying the metrics that really matter also indicates what the implicit strategy must be. Explicit or implicit, strategy should be aligned with metrics to indicate the progress the firm is seeking. Simply rocking up to a metrics warehouse to buy the fashionable data is counter-productive and yet that is what managers mostly ask. 'Just give me the top metrics', they say 'and I can get back to work.' Brain surgeons are not likely to go out of business in the near future.

Accountants see strategically aligned metrics as part of control. The analysis of variances is indeed valuable but, as we will discuss later, the role of metrics in giving direction to the business is far more important. The rest of the company will take their cue from the indicators which top management regard as important. So alignment in another sense (up and down the hierarchy and across functions) is a key part of the value of metrics. Shell calls this the 'line of sight': the same measures being used from the top to the bottom of the organization so that everything can evaluate performance in the same terms.

Few companies find it easy to balance the long- with the short-term needs of the business. Their intangible, market-based assets provide the security for future profits. Brand equity will be defined in the next chapter but for now it can be seen as the reservoir of future cash flow. In other words, good marketing has built up that asset but the cash has yet to flow to the revenue line of the profit and loss account. Some top executives, including Lord Sheppard, then Chairman of the GrandMet alcoholic beverages, Pillsbury and Burger King company, used to dismiss the need for balancing short- and long-term priorities on the grounds that the long term is merely the sum of all the short terms. Optimizing the short term, in his view, took care of the long. That is only true if brand equity, the brand's health in its internal and external markets, is adjusted for. If the asset has grown, the short-term profits are enhanced, but if it has weakened, the short-term profits are misleadingly high. Any marketing assessment system needs to include the change in brand equity over the period.

> Marketing rarely enjoys the same disciplines as other forms of investment, partly because financial returns are more difficult if not impossible to determine

John Hooper, when Director General of the Incorporated Society of British Advertisers, put it this way: 'Everyone accepts that measuring the performance of marketing communications programs is vitally important, but the reality today is that this issue does not feature in most marketing directors' top ten priorities.'[4] Few firms today pay their advertising or promotions agencies by results. Why ever not? In future this will become common practice. Procter & Gamble set the lead in October 1999. More broadly, marketing rarely enjoys the same disciplines as other forms of investment, partly because financial returns are more difficult if not impossible to determine. At the same time, marketing can be far more accountable than it usually is. This book is dedicated to showing how.

This chapter covers the following topics:

◆ *How marketing generates cash flow*: understanding the role of marketing is a prerequisite for gauging performance.

◆ *Performance engages the question 'compared to what?'* We need three types of comparison: assessing performance against internal expectation and against the market or competitors; adjusting for any change in brand equity so that like is compared with like.

◆ *The challenge of more complex brand architectures*: large companies have many brands in many markets, so providing the Exec with details of all these would be excessive. Multinationals select those that matter most.

◆ *Sector issues*: metrics considerations across business sectors are more alike than different, but these differences need attention.

Figure 1.1 shows it graphically.

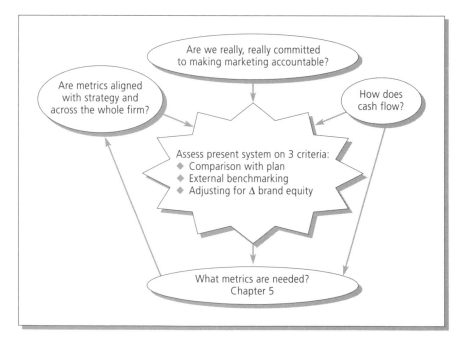

Figure 1.1 ◆ Assessing your marketing performance assessment system

How marketing generates cash flow

Marketing is the means whereby a firm achieves its key objectives. Even a not-for-profit organization has to bring in the cash to enable it to fulfil its mission. Seeing things entirely from the customer's side makes no more sense than taking a uniquely shareholder viewpoint: the art lies in using customer empathy to achieve wins for both sides.

The market-oriented firm consciously takes the consumer's viewpoint first. Other orientations regard customers, if they regard them at all, as somewhere between an important means of satisfying shareholders and a necessary nuisance. More likely, they have simply delegated customers to the sales force.

Professionalism means making market orientation explicit and putting numbers on what needs to be done. Professionals walk the customer talk. Where the immediate (trade) customers are not the end users, they consciously and consistently put end users first, in order to understand and meet their needs better – better than before and better than competitors. Research shows that market-oriented firms make more money than their otherwise-oriented cousins.[5] Yet these other orientations are deeply rooted. Ever since Ricardo vanquished Malthus in their supply versus demand debates of 200 years ago, supply-side thinking has dominated business thinking. The 'supply chain' accumulates value from the wrong end because value only arises from what customers are prepared to pay for. The 'demand chain' alternative view, which starts at the right end, analyzes how their needs can best be met.

> Marketing is the means whereby a firm achieves its key objectives

The Exec needs to begin with the wider perception of marketing and only then should it consider whether specialist marketers and budgets are needed. Few small companies need a specialist department. Advertising, promotions and other specialist marketing activities may just appear in the general budget. On the other hand, all firms need a consumer-first attitude. Different firms assign these responsibilities in different ways. While British Airways, for example, regards marketing as extremely important, the specialist marketers have only recently been given direct responsibility for most of the four Ps (product, price, promotion and place, i.e. distribution) of marketing (*see box*).

British Airways

British Airways was a nationalized industry privatized in the 1980s. Its success since then has been built around leadership in products and customer service, such as Club World in the 1980s and, recently, completely horizontal flat beds in that class.

The airline industry faces enormous challenges. It is not a profitable industry by its nature and with a few exceptions most companies tend to struggle to make reasonable profits on a global basis. Consolidation is not happening at the pace one might expect were the industry not so heavily regulated.

Shareholder value is now the overriding measure of success.

In 1998, marketing was brand development, product development and Masterbrand (BA's term for the corporate brand) communications. BA Marketing now consists of about 400 staff, and organization covers corporate communications, e-commerce, retail business (e.g. duty free sales, inflight entertainment, media business), as well as the fleet and network management, product development, brands, pricing and inventory management (4Ps). It also has responsibility for setting fares.

The first metrics stage took BA to nine measures reported every quarter but only to the marketing leadership team. There were two key learnings.

1 Going down to only a handful of metrics and discarding everything else limited the value unless one looked at what was really behind the metrics. A dashboard without back-up is useless.

2 Information tended to be scattered around the business with an individual having expertise in just one bit of it. This took a lot of the energy.

The second stage is just complete and reflects the wider interest of the marketing department across the business. In the past the marketing department focused on revenue and gave less thought to the assets and costs. The six new metrics give a more balanced view via the dashboard:

◆ premium market share

◆ customer satisfaction

◆ quality net revenue (QNR), taking account some elements of cost

◆ marketing and commercial costs

◆ marginal contribution for each of the main segments

◆ cost base – absolute cost

A key lesson has been gaining the commitment and upfront agreement about how the dashboard will be used. The management team commit to put time aside together to review the metrics and to drill down where the figures show a story. The dashboard only flags up the possibility that there might be something off track. It only takes a quarter of an hour to go through the dashboard but the subsequent discussion often takes a couple of hours at least. The ensuing actions and follow-up link the metrics, this process and the new culture. And the dashboard provides valuable learnings for the wider marketing group as well.

Source: Interview with Lynne Embleton, Manager Business Performance and Process for British Airways, 6 June 2002

Marketing has to satisfy three groups of people: immediate (trade) customers, end users (consumers) and, thereby, all the firm's stakeholders. The marketing function is not usually responsible for customers, employees, shareholders or any other stakeholders: its indirect responsibility is merely (!) to make sure the cash flow is large enough to cover these needs. Later chapters extend marketing to include employees as customers in the internal market but for the time being 'customers' just means those in the external marketplace. Figure 1.2 shows the key flows of cash:

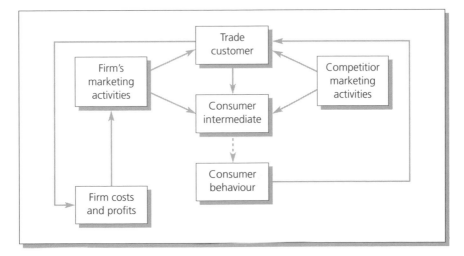

Figure 1.2 ◆ Simple marketing cash flow model

Here's how it works:

1 The firm must prime the pump with end users through advertising or
   sampling or other ways of raising demand. Competitors do that too, and
   Figure 1.2 shows this as cash to the end user. The demand may be raised
   via the immediate customer, but this is not shown.

2 Immediate customers buy the goods/services from the firm (and from
   competitors) for onward sale to end users. That brings cash from end
   users to the firm via the immediate customers.

3 Thus equipped, the firm can pay employees, shareholders and other
   stakeholders.

On the demand side, customers with different needs may need to be segmented. In other words, where customer needs and the competitive offerings
are too different to treat all customers alike, a separate marketing proposition
will be needed for each group. In any case, marketing manages the customers' demand to be pleased by, or at least satisfied with, the products
(goods and/or services) the firm supplies. On the supply side, marketing
manages the supplies of resources needed to meet the demand.
Conventionally these are termed the 'pull' and 'push' aspects of marketing.
Pull involves marketing communications of all types (including promotions)
whereas push involves the sales, product, packaging and service attributes.
Price facilitates the matching.

The market environment sets limits as to what can be achieved. At the
same time, the environment largely falls outside what management can control and is therefore excluded from performance assessment except in the
sense that a changing environment may explain performance variances. But
this is a matter of opinion. Some believe the size of the market to be a control metric; others believe that sales and market share are enough. And of
course, the total market can be calculated from the last two anyway. The
answer is empirical: what marketers can be expected to change should be
assessed within the context of what they cannot.

Pull and push activities together comprise 'the marketing mix', the
virtuous circle by which the ultimate users of the products are satisfied and
– simultaneously – provide the money to service the entire system.
Marketing pays for the rest of the business. Thus marketing process has
four specific characteristics:

1 The product must fit with end-user requirements, however hard they are
   to predict ahead of time.

2 Competing successfully requires the product to be differentiated from that of competitors. Being better sounds fine but a product cannot be better unless it is different. Most companies believe their products are better, but hard end-user evidence is needed both of actual relative quality and of perceptions.

3 Business relationships need to be enhanced transaction by transaction. Staying in business depends on building the marketing asset, i.e. brand equity.

4 Continuous learning should drive continuous innovation and product quality improvement to keep ahead of competitors who are doing the same.

Figure 1.2 hints at issues the Exec needs to understand. Whatever the business, be it goods or services, consumer or industrial, the Exec should develop a passionate and consuming curiosity about where the firm's money comes from:

◆ Are all customers alike or should they be clustered into separate segments?

◆ How do customers differ from non-customers?

◆ What customer problems are solved by the products? How can customers solve these problems more easily or better, perhaps with more gain for the firm? Nobody needs a spade; they just need to move the soil.

◆ What aspects of the products, and competitors' products, please and displease customers?

◆ How are our products perceived by customers? Are they different? Is quality better? What improvements do they want? Do perceptions of comparable products match realities?

◆ What are the purchasing frequency and amounts, and why?

◆ What is our strategy on pricing for the trade and for end users? Do we understand the impact of price changes?

◆ What unique customer insights do we have?

Answering these questions requires market research, but not necessarily specialist marketers. The Balanced Scorecard, for instance, was devised by two Harvard professors of accounting, Robert Kaplan and David Norton.[6] Their performance system aims to strike a balance between financial and non-financial measures and to recognize the diversity of all stakeholder interests. Unfortunately when they invited contributions from all business functions, marketers did not show up for the party. As a result, trade customers were not distinguished from end users and competition, market share apart, does not appear at all. They ask how 'customers want to see us?' but the reality is that customers do not want to see 'us' at all. Customers want their problems solved. The Balanced Scorecard is a good foundation but it needs to be supplemented by the market perspective. Figure 1.3 provides an example from the German steel giant ThyssenKrupp.[7]

For most large companies, 'marketing' means what the marketing department does – whatever that may be. Our research revealed little awareness of pan-company marketing or of linking explicit overall goals to the marketing process. Plans are instead adapted from previous plans in the light of experience. US research into budget allocations similarly confirms that the content of the previous budget dominates other factors such as competition or managerial rewards.[8]

Three basic criteria for assessment

How well marketing is performing depends on three types of comparison: what was expected, external benchmarking against the market or competitors, and adjusting for any change in brand equity in order to compare like with like. In other words, what were, or should have been, the goals? We found only a minority of firms (by number) to have some strategy process for setting non-financial goals explicitly. Most set financial targets. Nevertheless, management usually has some sense of what the company is trying to achieve beyond the financial.

These three types of comparison are criteria for assessing your own system. Let us look at each in turn.

Internal expectations

Any large firm has a cycle of analysis, planning, implementation and then reviewing their plans against results. In smaller firms, the process is informal. Formal plans are written for the bank manager but there is still an intuitive sense of the business model and that should predicate the metrics that matter.

Our research found marketing plans to be primarily financial documents in the sense that financial measures (sales, costs and profits) feature more often, and are given greater importance, than market measures such as consumer, customer or competitor. An exception is market share. Of course, sales

2. Customer retention	3. Customer acquisition	
◆ Customer share ◆ Customer satisfaction ◆ Customer loyalty ◆ Referral rate ◆ Price quality/ price premium ◆ Complaint behaviour ◆ Customer age ◆ Customer willingness to repurchase ◆ Share of consecutive orders and their structures ◆ Lost customer ratio	◆ Number of visits to new customers ◆ Cost per visit ◆ Share of new customers ◆ Sales per first purchase ◆ Number of contacts/visits before closure ◆ Costs of acquisition	**6. Internal fitness of sales organizations** ◆ Quality of interfaces to customer ◆ Customer orientation ◆ Order income and number ◆ Costs per order ◆ Hit ratio ◆ Costs of sales force vs sales ◆ On-time delivery ratio ◆ Sales force productivity ◆ Order processing time ◆ Customers per salesperson

1. Customer value

◆ Contribution margin per customer
◆ Shipments/net sales per customer
◆ Market share
◆ Customer lifetime value
◆ Customer classification (ABC)-analysis
◆ Cross-selling potential
◆ Degree of value added
◆ Average order volume
◆ Costs per customer
◆ Future repurchase rate
◆ Open claims per customer

4. Brand equity	5. Product innovation
◆ Brand knowledge ◆ Degree of familiarity ◆ Image/ reputation ◆ Advertising and communications ◆ Brand personality ◆ Market presence/Market share ◆ Audience perception	◆ Number of product development projects persued ◆ Share of projects realized ◆ Product improvements ◆ R&D investments ◆ R&D productivity ◆ Product quality and performance ◆ Translating customer needs in technical solution ◆ Innovation index

Figure 1.3 ◆ Sales metrics dashboard at ThyssenKrupp

volume and turnover are themselves market measures and many firms include some specific market goals such as customer gains, retention, distribution and consumer behaviour and intermediate measures, especially where these are key objectives for the plan. The overall balance, however, is financial.

Within that, the content of a marketing plan varies widely. To misquote Canadian humourist Stephen Leacock, a marketing plan is a device to arrest the intelligence of the chief financial officer long enough to take money off him. These plans are often little more than contracts between the finance and marketing functions. In this case, or so the reasoning seems to go, there is only a down side in including any targets that do not interest finance. The marketers have, perhaps, target numbers, e.g. for their advertising and promotional agencies, but they are not made explicit in plans. Features of good marketing planning practices are shown in Table 1.2.

Table 1.2 ◆ Non-financial targets expected in good plans

Category of measures	Examples and reasons
Environmental assumptions	Inflation, category or market size and growth. These are not actual performance measures, but wrong assumptions may explain variances
End-user behaviour	Consumers gained, retained and lost/loyalty
	Purchase frequency and quantities
	Per cent bought when on promotion
	Prices paid
End-user thoughts and feelings	Based on market research, these seek to explain why consumers behave as they do – from feelings of satisfaction and perceived quality, for example
Direct customer and trade targets	Distribution (how many outlets)
	Pipeline (how much stock is held)
	Delivery service satisfaction
Innovation	Achieving a pre-set share of turnover with recent introductions is a popular target. The number of new launches required can risk quality for quantity when managers launch what should not be launched to make the numbers
Competition	Measures can be compared as competitive ratios, e.g. price can be shown as the price relative to the market as a whole

In previous research we found that, in general, plans have a good track record: performance tends to match what is specifically planned,[9] in the sense that companies, by and large, achieve what they measure. The crucial question here, therefore, is whether the key corporate goals are connected all the way through the marketing plans. The building society (co-operative bank in US terms) Bradford and Bingley provides an example (*see box*).

Bradford and Bingley

Bradford and Bingley is in the process of reinventing itself following demutualization at the end of 2000. Its traditional lines of manufacturing mortgages and savings have been enhanced by the launch of The MarketPlace (the largest independent financial advisor in the UK).

For management, it is dealing with the tension of financial versus customer-centric measurement systems. Its traditional measurement approach was failing due to lack of customer framework, poor information quality and availability, poor focused development initiatives and excessive production costs.

Today, management is evolving a customer-focused framework that identifies value creation across customer acquisition and retention. They are building strategies to enrich consumer loyalty to the brand. Following the implementation of a data warehouse solution, which was rolled out for demutualization, the criticality of data quality, value-based activity and aligned behaviour have been further brought to focus. The key is to be selective in identifying the simplest and most valuable activities on the evolutionary path to balancing shareholder value and customer centricity.

Source: Interview with Mark Howe, Marketing Director, Distribution, 13 August 2002

Where plans do not include the key metrics for comparison, firms are forced back on the previous year's actual data. We found many firms preferred those anyway since they are more firmly grounded than the inevitably speculative plan. Pragmatic as that is, the previous year does not tell us what management was trying to achieve in this year.

Finally, comparing plan metrics with actual is essential for debriefing. Firms devote far more resources to planning, which may just reinforce behaviour, than they do to debriefing, which may change it. US fighter pilots, for example, are trained more in their debriefing than in the preparation or in the flying. Debriefing is frank and can be painful but it is where behaviour is changed. Interestingly, rank is no protection. A colonel is unlikely to fly missions very often. So when they do, they are treated as rookie pilots and debriefed accordingly. What matters is that the next mission learns from the one before.

External comparison

The second criterion for assessing your system is whether performance is compared with that of key competitors, or the market as a whole, or benchmark companies. If a non-athlete runs 100 metres in 20 seconds, this might be an outstanding personal performance – but it would not gain admission to the Olympics. Some firms have more audacious targets than others. Performance against the firm's own targets only gives half the picture: best practice requires external comparison.

There are two formal ways to do this: benchmarking and obtaining, through research or intelligence, comparable performance metrics of which market share is much the most common. Much of the market research industry is occupied with the supply of these comparable figures, sector by sector. More economically, but with a lot more hassle, all the market players can supply their own figures for pooling, consolidation and reissue by an independent and confidential third party.

Some firms have more audacious targets than others

Formal benchmarking, whether through direct or indirect data pooling, is rare in marketing, but common for supply and logistical functions. While our research did come across a few examples of leading companies that benchmark marketing performance measures against key competitors, for obvious commercial reasons they did not wish to publicize details. They are right: this form of market intelligence has competitive advantage. Furthermore, if firms start to measure alike they may begin to think alike and marketing is about differentiation.

A formal marketing audit compares the firm's marketing *process* against theoretical standards.[10] Consultants have been offering this service since the 1970s and the more experienced can bring practical improvement. Note, however, that these concern marketing processes, not performance and not the metrics. British building products company Caradon plc, for instance, recently conducted this type of marketing audit.[11] As a result the company says that it has begun to develop more of a measurement culture, customer focus, an appreciation of marketing and new processes and initiatives. It is a matter of taste but I am unconvinced that textbook marketing process produces textbook performance. Old fashioned as it may seem, I subscribe to the notion that an artist should be able to draw even if his pictures do not give that appearance. In the same way, brilliant marketers should get basic textbook training but their processes may evolve into something quite different. But the basic rule remains the same: performance should be judged against what it was supposed to achieve and against the competition.

In practice, large firms gain the experience of their recruits from other firms. For example, marketers trained by 'marketing universities' like Procter & Gamble, Unilever or Mars are valuable not only for their skills but for the training they bring with them. The top marketer at Shell has a Nestlé background, and the marketing supremo at UK supermarket giant Sainsbury was formerly at Abbey National, and with Mars. Our research revealed a high degree of consistency across companies, which we attributed mostly to this cross-fertilization of senior marketers. Payless ShoeSource provides a good US example of careful comparison of metrics (*see box*).

Payless ShoeSource

Payless ShoeSource is a $3 billion, US-based public corporation. With nearly 5000 retail stores, Payless is America's largest family footwear retailer. It operates in the USA, Canada, Central America, South America and the Caribbean and also sells its products over the internet at Payless.com.

As a publicly traded company, success is defined by increasing shareholder value driven by top line and same store sales growth. Apart from traditional financial indicators, they use industry measures, including store-for-store sales, market share, foot traffic, customer conversion, average retail price and market basket size. These measures are compared with internal growth goals, Wall Street expectations and benchmarked with ten top retailers.

Although Payless is a shoe retailing specialist, the direct competitive set includes organizations such as Wal Mart, K Mart, Target, Sears and JCPenneys. Payless ShoeSource must compete successfully against organizations 70 times its size.

Two types of marketing metrics are employed: spending efficiency and effectiveness, and business building.

▶

Spending metrics

◆ ROI by advertising medium

◆ Wear-out analysis of creative and spending

◆ Persuasion and clutter breakthrough of our communication

◆ Performance against theoretical spend modelling

◆ Promotional effectiveness analysis

◆ Ad effectiveness tracking

◆ Advertising to sales spending metrics

Business building metrics

◆ Market share – aggregate and by category

◆ Customer traffic

◆ Customer acquisition and cost of acquisition and lifetime value

◆ Ratio of loyal to new customers

◆ Share of requirements captured by customer segment

◆ Customer satisfaction measures including product, communication and shopping experience

◆ Attitude and usage quarterly tracking

Because of the importance of marketing to the success of the company, marketing is part of the CEO's executive committee and as such all of marketing's key performance metrics are under regular, ongoing scrutiny. The recently introduced 'Brand Health Scorecard' is a quantitative approach to measuring organization-wide performance. It includes sales, profit and expense as well as our customer satisfaction performance.

Source: John Haugh, Chief Marketing Officer and Senior Vice President of Business Development, 20 September 2002

Adjusting for change in brand equity

The third criterion of success is quite different from internal and external benchmarking. To compare like with like, we need to ensure that each time period under review is not sullied by the effects of other time periods. For

example, if a factory is comparing the sales of widgets with the cost of production, they adjust the quantity produced with the stock of widgets at the
beginning and at the end. If you finish up with more widgets at the end
than you started with, you have obviously made more than you have sold.
So it is with marketing. The short-term performance needs to be adjusted
by the increase or decrease in the market-based asset, i.e. brand equity. The
third criterion is whether the Exec formally reviews the marketing assets and
the amounts by which they have changed from period to period. Marketing
expenditure may initially appear excessive, but seem good value for money
later, when the increase in brand value is taken into account.

This adjustment for change in marketing assets is not just to ensure that
like performance is compared with like. It is the key to the long debate
about short- versus long-term performance.
Whether marketing expenditure is simply a
cost or an investment has been a dialogue of
the deaf for decades. If advertising is an
investment, where is the asset that arises from
the investment? Brand equity, a concept only
invented in the 1980s, supplies the answer.
The debate should now be over: either mar-
keting expenditure pays back in the short term, or if it is 'investment' then
the benefit should show up as an increase in brand equity. You cannot measure the future but you can measure assets today, which is why brand equity
measurement provides such solid ground. If the Exec is asked to believe in
future benefits that do not show up in asset growth today, they should consider whether their metrics system is subtle enough or whether it is just
snake oil. It is rarely an easy call. In the scotch whisky business in Thailand
in the late 1990s, the brand leader doubled its market share advantage without any apparent improvement in brand metrics.

> Marketing expenditure
> may initially appear
> excessive, but seem good
> value for money later

The challenge of more complex
brand architectures

So far this chapter has assumed a single trading entity with one brand, or
trading name, operating in one market. Firms trading across borders with
multiple brands need more sophisticated solutions. Readers who do not

have to deal with complex brand and organization architectures are advised to skip this section.

One solution is simply to treat the parent company/superstructure as a financial holding company, leaving marketing issues, including performance evaluation, to the trading units. However, this has shortcomings. The group fails to exploit its internal learning opportunities. Multiple brands in multiple markets give the advantage of intra-company comparisons. How Burger King is performing in one market is a valuable benchmark for performance in another.

Unless the group Exec gains, and maintains, a thorough understanding of the mainsprings of their group's wealth as a whole, they can expect unpleasant surprises. If a group is too diverse for the main Exec to empathize with the key consumers, it is time to split the group up.

Shareholders and analysts are seeking more information as to how their directors are marketing and stewarding the group's key assets, notably brands. Before they can inform shareholders, directors need to know the information themselves; 75 per cent of UK analysts, for example, thought companies in their sectors should publish more information on marketing expenditure, but only 25 per cent of the companies concerned agreed.[12] Informal research in Wall Street indicates similar attitudes.

The group may also find it hard to isolate business units. How much of the Disney brand equity in France, for example, is due to French marketing efforts and how much to those in the USA and globally? With the growth of digital and global media, marketing inputs and performance will be increasingly hard to match on a purely national basis.

The same is true of brand structures. Japanese corporate brands such as Sony, Matsushita or Mitsubishi span a variety of product categories and price/quality levels. Performance in one category will not match that in another although some effects will cross over.

These grey situations cannot be portrayed perfectly as either black or white. Drink multinational Diageo has defined the brand market unit (BMU) as the meaningful building block for both global brand and market planning and reporting. Mega- or umbrella brands, like BMW, can be divided into 'brands' for this purpose by product linkage, e.g. the BMW5 series is the brand unit. That broadly mirrors how consumers see brand/product combinations. Sony TV is one brand, Sony Walkman is another and Sony video-recorder is a third. However, while the consumer sees these entities as distinct, the brand equity of one will be affected by the experience the user has of another.[13] And while a 'market' would usually be a single country, it may also be a group of smaller ones, such as Benelux or Scandinavia, or part of a large one, such as the US West Coast.

A typical BMU structure in an international company implies three types of marketer: brand manager (BMU manager), country manager (managing the market for all the brands in the portfolio) and international brand manager (reciprocally, managing the brand across all markets). Clearly the BMUs in any group have to match the organizational structure and, as structure changes, metrics may struggle to keep up.

This problem is how to assess marketing performance in the pan-company sense since, as noted above, no one market or brand is insulated from all others. So the Exec of a complex organization needs to keep a close eye on the balance between international brand development and the needs of end users who are, ultimately, local. For the purpose of assessing your current metrics system, compare your approach with this one:

◆ Deconstruct the whole organization into brand market units (this implies brand, country and international managers, each of whose areas can be assessed).

◆ Assess marketing performance at BMU level, before and after the allocation of indirect, e.g. international, expenses back to BMUs.

◆ Take the small number of BMUs which, in all probability, represent the great bulk of shareholder value (80 per cent of shareholder value typically comes from 20 per cent of BMUs).

◆ Assess these directly at Exec level, and the other BMUs in aggregate.

Sector issues

The principal difference between sectors is between those who supply end users directly, e.g. retailers, and those who deal through channels, each customer supplying the next stage of the chain. Better communications, notably the internet, are reducing the length of these chains but many companies have at least one link between themselves and the consumer. The widespread use of the word 'customer' to embrace all these links is unhelpful. Satisfying Wal-Mart is a far cry from satisfying one of Wal-Mart's customers.

The distinction does not lie between industrial goods and services but between retail and trade buyers. The buyer of cars for the sales force has different interests and motivation from those of the drivers. The machine operative has a different perspective from the buyer of that machine. Thus the most important sector issue, so far as marketing performance measurement is concerned, is the number of customer levels that need to be considered, and the priorities of push versus pull marketing.

As shown in Figure 1.2, this book assumes two levels: the immediate trade customer and the ultimate consumer or end user. Even if the pipeline is far more extensive, this is a valid approximation. In the case of retail chains, each branch can be seen as a surrogate for the external customer. They need to be 'sold' and supplied in much the same way and, if they are franchisees, then they are customers by any definition. Here are four other sector issues to bear in mind for marketing performance measurement:

1 The line between goods and services is not absolute. Goods are increasingly bundled with services. Does McDonald's supply burgers or convenience? Even so, the suppliers of services are less concerned with product inventories and more concerned with the way front-line employees deal with their customers.

2 Managerial perceptions of sector differences are greater than this brief overview suggests. For example, the pharmaceutical industry typically considers itself to be very different from other markets. In other words, experience shows that the inhabitants of this sector often feel they have little to learn from other sectors. These perceptions are enhanced by the high failure rate of marketers who transfer from one sector to another.

3 Similarly, high-technology firms may think the new order has replaced smoke-stack business thinking, including brands and marketing. The reverse is the case: increased diversity and complexity reinforce the need for basic marketing disciplines and brand mnemonics. A recent Marketing Science Institute working paper suggested that, for high-tech companies, marketing is more important than research and development (R&D), and enhances the width and effectiveness of introducing innovation.[14]

4 Government regulations and safety considerations impose special measurement needs.

The engineering giant, Rolls-Royce, provides some insights into the subtlety of metrics in a complex business to business context (*see box*).

This chapter should have tested your market assessment system. If the system is below standard, here are some decisions to put in hand before going any further. The Marketing Leadership Council has provided a useful 'Give–Get' tool for achieving a unified market orientation.[15] Intended originally for reinforcing brand strength, the tool would work as well for

Rolls-Royce

With over 500 airline customers and a 30 per cent share in commercial jet engines, just over half of Rolls-Royce sales are in civil aerospace. The four other sectors are: defence 22 per cent; marine propulsion and hydrodynamics 13 per cent; energy, where gas turbines are used for gas compression, oil pumping and power generation, 10 per cent; financial services – engine and aircraft leasing, and electrical power project development.

Technical innovation is at the heart of what the company does and the unifying aim is for 'Rolls-Royce to be trusted to deliver excellence'. The long-term strategy is to:

◆ deliver shareholder value

◆ build leading profitable positions

◆ develop effective partnerships through a customer-focused organization to gain aftermarket and service opportunities

◆ leverage competence in technology

◆ satisfy other stakeholders – including employees, governments, joint venture partners and the communities where the company operates

Marketing is devolved to business units and these are at differing stages of development. It used to mean promotional expenditure, but is now understood to be what the marketing department does, i.e. analysis and forecasting, strategy and planning, marketing operations (positioning, communications, etc.) and performance measurement.

An example shared by Mark King, Executive Vice President Customer Business, Airlines, is illustrative: 'The obvious marketing metric in use in Airlines is market share versus General Electric and Pratt & Whitney which we look at by aircraft type and in total. There are a number of ways to look at this statistic – e.g. aircraft in service, deliveries in a particular year or orders taken in a particular year. Within the latter, there are also announced orders or firm contracts only plus a decision whether to include options. Finally there is a decision on how to allocate orders for joint ventures such as International Aero Engines, in which Rolls-Royce has around a third share, and CFM International, comprising GE and Snecma, to the bigger original equipment manufacturers (OEMs).

'We also measure such things as average price levels achieved and percentage of customers who have signed up to Total Care Packages.

▶

'We use the traffic light system (red, amber, green) extensively as a quick and visual way to review the state of the business. The most significant marketing example is our customer satisfaction monitor for which each customer scores us red, amber or green against a number of categories such as product quality, delivery performance, commercial responsiveness etc'.

Internal employee surveys are undertaken and RR benchmarks against key competitors, notably General Electric and Pratt & Whitney and other publicly quoted companies including BP and GSK.

Source: Interview with David Howie, Head of Brand Communication, and Martin Brodie, Head of Corporate Media Relations, Rolls-Royce plc, 27 June 2002. Additional material from Mark King, Executive Vice President Customer Business, Airlines, 5 August 2002

integrating marketing and its performance measures across the business. In essence the CEO invites each member of the Exec team to discuss the benefits that department gets from strong pan-company marketing and what, in turn, they should give, i.e. contribute. For example, the HR function, as will be later discussed, can use similar metrics for employee brand equity that the company uses for assessing customer brand equity, e.g. perceptions of quality and satisfaction.

Executive minutes

1 Exec to appoint a task force to conduct a more formal review and recommend changes.

2 Specialist marketing skills, whether internal or outsourced, to be reassessed in terms of added value to the firm's total marketing effort.

3 Each member of the Exec should report on the 'Give–Get' that they can achieve from unified marketing and metrics.

4 Task force to provide evaluation of the status quo within three months and improvement recommendations within six months. Their work plan required after one month.

5 Exec to establish timetable for new process, i.e. when metrics should be presented.

Notes

1 Marketing Leadership Council (2001) *Measuring Marketing Performance*, Washington DC, Corporate Executive Board: 6.

2 Scores for the evaluation test: Table 1.1

1	Does the Exec regularly and formally assess marketing performance?	(a) 10 (b) 10 (c) 5 (d) 0 (e) 0 (f) 0
2	What does it understand by 'customer value'?	(a) 0 (b) 5 (c) 10 (d) 10
3	How much time does the Exec give to marketing issues?	> 30% 10, 20–30% 6, 10–20% 4, <10% 0
4	Does the business/marketing plan show the non-financial corporate goals and link them to market goals?	(a) 0 (b) 5 (c) 10
5	Does the plan show the comparison of your marketing performance with competitors or the market as a whole?	(a) 0 (b) 10 (c) 5
6	What is your main marketing asset called?	(a) 10 (b) 10 (c) 5 (d) 0
7	Does the Exec's performance review involve a quantified review of the main marketing asset and how it has changed?	(a) 10 (b) 5 (c) 0
8	Has the Exec quantified what 'success' would look like five or ten years from now?	(a) 0 (b) 10 (c) 0
9	Does your strategy have quantified milestones to indicate progress towards that success?	(a) 0 (b) 10 (c) 0
10	Are the marketing performance indicators seen by the Exec aligned with these milestones?	(a) 0 (b) 7 (c) 5 (d) 10

If your total is greater than 90 per cent, ask the bookshop for your money back. If your total is 70–90 per cent, congratulations. More than 50 per cent is good. Less than 30 per cent means what you think it means.

3 Mintzberg, H. (1994) *The Rise and Fall of Strategic Planning*, Englewood Cliffs NJ: Prentice-Hall.

4 John Hooper, CBE, Director General, Incorporated Society of British Advertisers, 21 October 1999.

5 Kokkinaki, F. and Ambler, T. (1999) 'Marketing performance assessment: current practice and the role of firm orientation', Cambridge MA: Marketing Science Institute working paper, 99–114.

Meehan, S. A. (1997) 'Market orientation: values, behaviours and performance', unpublished PhD thesis, University of London.

Narver, J.C. and Slater, S.F. (1990) 'The effect of a market orientation on business profitability', *Journal of Marketing*, 54, 20–35.

Slater, S.F. and Narver, J.C. (1994) 'Market orientation, customer value, and superior performance', *Business Horizons*, March–April, 22–8.

For links between market orientation and business performance see also the special issue of the *Australian Journal of Management*, 25 (2), September 2000.

6 Kaplan, R. S. and Norton, D. P. (1992) 'The balanced scorecard', *Harvard Business Review*, January–February, 71–9.

7 Horstmann, R. and Josefiak, T. (2001) 'Forging an effective sales organization through sales metrics', draft 2. Rembert Horstmann and Thomas Josefiak are respectively Director and Manager of Marketing and Sales Coordination of ThyssenKrupp Stainless in Duisburg/Germany.

8 Low, G. S. and Mohr, J. J. (1998) 'Brand managers' perceptions of the marketing communications budget allocation process', Cambridge MA: Marketing Science Institute working paper, 98–105.

9 Swartz, G., Hardie, B., Grayson, K. and Ambler, T. (1996) 'Value for money? The relationships between marketing expenditure and business performance in the UK financial services industry', Chartered Institute of Marketing, April.

10 See Kotler, P., Gregor, W. and Rodgers, W. (1989) 'The marketing audit comes of age', *Sloan Management Review*, winter, 49–62. In the UK, the Chartered Institute of Marketing provides a number of frameworks for marketing audits.

11 Presentation by Nick Moss, Marketing and Product Development Director, Caradon plc, UK Industrial Division, at The Marketing Council's 'Marketing Metrics' seminar, London, December 1997.

12 *The Brand Finance Report* (1999) Kingston upon Thames: Brand Finance.

13 See, for toothbrushes and toothpaste: Erdem, T. (1998) 'An empirical analysis of umbrella branding', *Journal of Marketing Research*, 35, 339–51.

14 Dutta, S., Om, N. and Surendra, R. (1999) 'Success in high technology markets: is marketing capability critical?', Cambridge, MA: Marketing Science Institute working paper, 99–119.

15 Marketing Leadership Council (2001) *Stewarding the Brand for Profitable Growth*, Washington DC: Corporate Executive Board, 63.

2

Brand equity is an elephant

WE HAVE ALREADY SEEN WHAT IS MEANT BY BRAND EQUITY, so does it now need a whole chapter to itself? Indeed it does – we are still breaking new ground with a concept that only gained publicity in the 1990s. The Marketing Leadership Council research discovered that almost half their respondents gave their inability to quantify brand equity as a reason for dissatisfaction.[1] Auditors may concern themselves with company assets right down to the last paperclip but brand equity, by far the most valuable asset in most companies, still does not appear on their radar screens.

The elephant metaphor works at various levels described later but we can start with size: brand equity is such a big concept that people have difficulty describing it. The variety of its characteristics leads sceptics to suggest we are seeing different beasts. In fact, customer equity and company reputation are largely different aspects of the same animal. Once one has the whole picture, the pieces fall into place.

> Brand equity is such a big concept that people have difficulty describing it

Our metrics research showed that 'brand equity' is by far the most frequently used term to describe market-based assets, followed by 'reputation'. So, for simplicity, any market-based asset, be it reputation, goodwill or customer satisfaction, will be called 'brand equity' from now on, even though the term 'brand' is not generally used by some sectors.

The commonest business form is the single-identity company operating in one market. It is the basis for this chapter but the concepts can then be easily extended to multi-brand, multinational companies. In a multi-brand company, the corporate brand itself is just one of the brands. The chapter addresses these key questions:

◆ If brand equity is so big, why can't the CEO see it?

◆ Different perspectives of the beast, e.g. brand and customer equity. Is brand equity the distinction between sales and marketing?

◆ Why is brand valuation at best only part of the measurement issue?

◆ What is current practice in brand equity measurement?

◆ If this is so obvious, why is marketing not making its case at CEO level?

◆ So how should you measure the elephant?

Figure 2.1 provides a chapter overview:

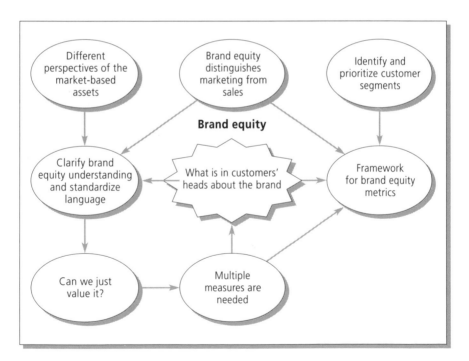

Figure 2.1 ◆ Measuring market-based assets

If brand equity is so big, why can't the CEO see it?

One has little perspective of an elephant if one is riding on it. Rather, it provides a platform for an elevated view of the surrounding countryside. In the search for new lands to conquer, the well-being of the elephant itself is easy to overlook. Elephants, like brands, are expensive to maintain. If the CEO cuts its rations, performance, in the short term, is undiminished and the return on investment (ROI) has gone up. So the rations may be cut again. If that continues,

> CEOs are not mahouts and all too few recognize that they should keep the beast in fine fettle

the elephant will one day have the best ROI in the jungle. The next day it will be dead. CEOs are not mahouts and all too few recognize that they should keep the beast in fine fettle.

Brand equity works the same way: Burger King seemed to be going well in the USA in the late 1980s even though prices were being raised and the size of the 'Whopper' reduced.[2] Suddenly, consumers cottoned on and brand equity crashed. After a period of intensive care (lower prices and a much larger 'Whopper'), the brand slowly recovered.

For middle managers too, the greyness of the elephant merges into the general fog of business as they go about their separate tasks. Yes, the BK managers were vaguely aware of what was happening but the CEO was not interested.

Brand equity supports the business because it stores what marketing has achieved but has not yet reached the profit and loss account. Of course, brand equity, like the elephant, can be maintained and enhanced without actually measuring it. Successful companies have long done that with the CEOs providing the necessary refreshment. Today's pressures to cut costs mean that the no-measurement culture is no longer enough. Brand managers bid for as much fodder as they can get from the chief financial officers, not least because they judge their status by the size of their budgets, but that may not indicate what they really need. The only way they, or the CEO, can judge the right balance is to measure the inputs, outputs (market performance) and state of brand equity. Strange as it may seem, elephants excrete

25 per cent more than the food they ingest[3] and, however unattractive the metaphor, brands also return more than you put in.

CEOs also tend to give too little attention to brand equity because they do not usually report their stewardship to shareholders. They certainly do

Table 2.1 ◆ Some major brand companies' values

Company	Market capitalization $bn	Brand valuation $bn	% of capitalization
Single brand companies			
Coca-Cola	329	69	21
Microsoft	354	65	18
IBM	184	53	29
General Electric	433	42	10
Nokia	102	35	34
Intel	195	35	18
Disney	56	33	59
Ford	46	30	66
McDonald's	37	25	68
AT&T	47	23	49
Multibrand companies			
Johnson & Johnson	161	68	42
Procter & Gamble	93	45	49
Nestlé	51	42	81
Unilever	75	38	51
Diageo	36	15	42
Colgate-Palmolive	30	14	48
Danone	18	14	74

Sources: Capitalizations: *http://finance.yahoo.com* (August 2001).

Brand valuations: *BusinessWeek*, 6 August 2001, 52–5

not have to. As intangible assets, especially brand equity, progressively dominate the tangible, the situation may change. Chapter 8 deals with this question but Table 2.1 shows its importance.

Different perspectives of brand equity

Sceptics, such as Professor Andrew Ehrenberg of South Bank Business School and Paul Feldwick of Omnicom, claim to doubt the existence of brand equity.[4] They say that measures such as market share already provide perfectly adequate descriptions of the market-based asset. In 1996, Feldwick wrote: 'We can also put a value on brands as assets when necessary, and buy and sell them, but we can do all this without assuming the existence of anything called brand equity. In fact we might find the whole area easier to understand if people stopped using those words altogether.' Six years on, he modified that position very slightly.[5] But their case founders partly on terminology: sometimes they are confusing the measures of those assets with the assets themselves and sometimes they use the word 'brand' in two ways. The brand the customer buys, e.g. Tide, is not the same as the asset the company, Procter & Gamble, retains. We need two terms for these two things: consumers buy brands and thereby increase the value of the brand owner's asset, brand equity.

Marketing assets exist and companies pay good money for them, as Coca-Cola did when it paid $2 billion for Schweppes in line with theoretical estimates of the brand equities involved. Intangibles like these are hard to measure, but they are both real and capable of dramatic reduction – as a brand like Perrier testified when contamination was discovered in the bottles.

Is a pile of coins an elephant? The question usually bemuses an audience and yet that is precisely the way some academics see brand equity. They confuse the asset, brand equity, with what the asset is worth, the brand's valuation. Keeping elephants in England is not a very profitable business so a small pile of coins correctly represents the discounted cash flow of net earnings from my elephant. But it is no more an elephant than it is brand equity.

So we have to distinguish the asset itself – brand equity – from measures that, like valuation and market share, merely quantify it. A car is an asset but its top speed, number of seats, fuel consumption and value are simply measures of it. As the confusion is so common, the emphasis on the distinction is necessary. Neither is 'brand health' a popular term for the condition of the asset, a synonym for the asset itself.

We need measures of brand performance that go beyond short-term sales, profit and market share because customer attitudes and behaviours become so entrenched. Past marketing efforts create a momentum of effects into the future. What actual and potential customers think, feel and buy today strongly influences what they will think, feel and therefore purchase tomorrow. Thus it is these present thoughts, feelings and behaviour that we seek to measure in quantifying brand equity.

There is, however, more to brand equity than connections in human memory alone. Our auxiliary brains – computers – now carry many of our memories. Systems are habituated to brands in similar ways. When a clerk enters 'order more vodka' and the computer translates that into an order for ten cases of Smirnoff, those bytes of computer program and database are part of Smirnoff's brand equity. Elevating the brand to that position with that customer is the result of past marketing efforts. Expressed another way, a brand's existing distribution is part of its brand equity. Qualifying statements about the relationship between our memories and these auxiliary brains becomes cumbersome so, from here on, this view of brand equity ('what is in people's heads about the brand') includes computers and business systems. Compare this with four other perspectives:

◆ Professor David Aaker first popularized the concept of brand equity in his 1991 bestseller,[6] which highlighted the role of senior management as brand custodians. He defined brand equity as 'a set of assets and liabilities linked to a brand, its name and symbol, that add to or subtract from the value provided by a product or service to a firm and/or that firm's customers' (p.15). His five components of brand equity were: brand loyalty; name awareness; perceived quality; brand associations in addition to perceived quality; and a bundle of intellectual properties such as patents, trademarks and channel relationships.

◆ In a contemporary Marketing Science Institute paper, Professors Srivastava and Shocker defined brand equity as 'a set of associations and behaviours on the part of a brand's customers, channel members and parent corporation that permits the brand to earn greater volume or greater margins than it could without the brand name and that gives a strong, sustainable and differential advantage'.[7]

◆ More recently, Dartmouth's Professor Kevin Lane Keller defined (customer-based) brand equity as 'the differential effect that brand knowledge has on consumer response to the marketing of that brand'.[8]

◆ To an accountant, brand equity is the accumulated intangible asset from past marketing that has not yet been taken into profit. The metaphor mostly used here is that of the reservoir behind a dam, which absorbs the benefits of marketing and may be drawn upon to a greater or lesser

The BBC: creating a brand culture

The BBC brand represents the values and reputation of the corporation. However, in the past the strengths of the BBC – integrity, truthfulness, pioneering creativity, innovation and entertainment – were at best implicit in much of the corporation's work, and sometimes poorly understood. The culture of the corporation was devolved and fragmented. Ideas drawn from the market, such as branding, were viewed with suspicion.

The insight was that, despite initial resistance, the brand could become the catalyst for uniting the whole company behind a new strategy for shaping the BBC's future competitiveness. The institution of common brand disciplines and brand health measurement has consolidated the new thinking.

Source: The Marketing Council booklet, 'The whole company ... designed for customers' (1999).

degree according to the demand for short-term profits. If it is allowed to dry out, however, it may become permanently dysfunctional.

The BBC brand represents the first three of those perspectives; it has to be stewarded by top management, it coincides with the culture of its community and it colours the way the BBC is seen.

Figure 2.2 shows how brand equity arises and influences future behaviour. In this model, the firm's marketing mix represents products (goods and services), packaging, pricing, advertising and promotions. Communications are filtered by our defence systems and modified by our perceptions of the environment, product category (sector) and the competition. Enough gets through to modify our memories and, maybe, what we do. What is in our heads, and what we do today, define what will be in our heads tomorrow. The right-hand box in Figure 2.2 has no marketing mix

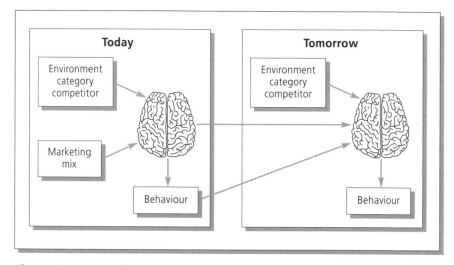

Figure 2.2 ◆ Brand equity

communications. Of course, the products are still available. We buy them because of the effects of earlier marketing efforts. This lies at the heart of the distinction between marketing and sales that we consider shortly.

The people whose heads carry this around may be direct trade customers, end users and consumers, employees, journalists, shareholders or suppliers. While 'consumer brand equity' is the segment that most interests professional marketers, every segment has some importance for the firm as a whole. Their relative importance is a matter deserving explicit Exec attention as goals are identified and resources allocated. Does the firm care about 'supplier brand equity', for example?

Customer equity

More recently, attention has shifted from the brand to the customer, meaning end user. 'Customer equity' has been defined as the net present value to the company of one or more of its customers.[9] This contrary use of equity, as valuation not asset, is confusing but the more important question is whether we are talking about a different beast or another view of the same beast.[10] The valuation procedures supply the answer: the financial worth in both cases is estimated by taking the present values of the same cash flows. They cannot be added together when valuing the company as a whole. Therefore we are largely seeing different perspectives of the same asset.

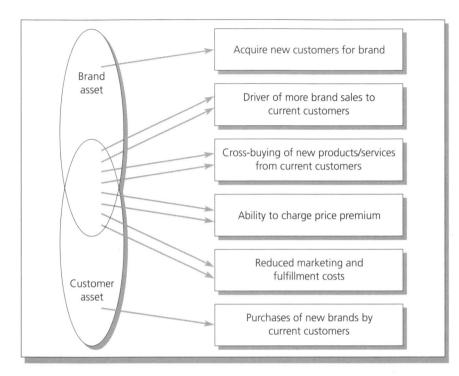

Figure 2.3 ◆ The relationship between brand and customer equity

But it is not quite as simple as that. Figure 2.3 is derived from a similar analysis in a paper constructed by six academics following some heated debate of these matters.[11] To avoid the confusion with the word 'equity', 'asset' is used for both brand and customer.

In essence the difference lies in the acquisition of new brands and customers. For the existing brand and customer, the brand asset and the customer asset are one and the same. In looking forward, however, each neglects the new brands or customers that can be gained. The customer asset perspective, for example, tends to put the emphasis on retention rather than seeking new customers. In the short term this may be right but in the long term all customers die. Brands, however, can be refreshed with new products and be, near enough, immortal. Neither perspective is right or wrong; we need to see the elephant in the round.

Total equity

Perhaps the total market-based asset, including brand and customer perspectives, should be called total equity, but that is too pedantic so we will stick with brand equity.

Table 2.2 ◆ Allocation of brand equity responsibilities

Brand equity segment	Responsibility
Consumer	Marketing
Direct trade customer	Trade marketing/sales
Employee	Human resources
Journalists and non-channel influencers	Public relations
Shareholder	Investor relations
Supplier	Procurement

A brand's total equity is therefore the sum of the equities in each stakeholder segment. Table 2.2 lists the principal segments for which brand equity can be measured separately and the related departmental responsibilities. In practice the need for separate measures is driven by the organizational structure. If a firm has, for example, a Vice President for investor relations, then it should measure shareholder brand equity as part of assessing investor relations performance.

In practice few companies explicitly assess performance across departments in this way. However, the growing interest in corporate branding and the 'employer brand' suggests that best practice is moving in the direction of a more active overseeing of the brand equity across departments. (The latter is discussed in Chapter 7 on internal marketing metrics.) The shared interest in the corporate brand equity is becoming the glue that should unite a company.

Table 2.2 should be used by companies to decide which segments should be measured formally, which informally and which not at all. The answers should depend on the level of investment. If public relations are the firm's major marketing investment, then the resulting brand equity in that segment should be measured.

Brand equity as the distinction between marketing and selling

A final perspective on brand equity is the distinction it makes between marketing and selling. In essence, selling seeks an immediate order for the product: it aims to increase the revenue line of the profit and loss account right away. Marketing, however, invests resources at some point of time before it expects to reap the rewards in sales. Sales people who expect instant gratification make lousy marketers. The main problem of assessing marketing performance lies in measuring the latent benefit of that investment before the sales emerge.

Advertising provides an example of the interval of time between creating, or sustaining, the demand for the product and actually making the sale. We may see a TV advertisement for a car weeks before we actually purchase one. Advertising should be judged by its effect on brand equity rather than its effect on sales because, direct response advertising aside, the sales impact

Coca-Cola

Coca-Cola may be one of the best known global brands, loved by its drinkers, 130 years old and ubiquitous, but Julia Goldin, Brands Director for Coca-Cola and Diet Coke at the Coca-Cola Company in the UK, is in no doubt that without marketing the franchise would erode. In such a competitive environment the brand can never be complacent, she says, because it needs to build new connections with each generation of consumers. With the estimated 80 million soft drinks being consumed in Great Britain daily and more choices available than ever before, each consumption opportunity matters. Key to the process is to understand and tap into core attitudes, behaviours and drinking occasions.

The company sets specific targets for volume, profit and brand health that are tracked on a monthly basis. The most challenging of these to establish is the correct measures for 'brand health' or 'brand equity'.

Over the years the Coca-Cola company has investigated a variety of techniques to best understand and measure brand health. This has ranged from cognitive mapping, the 'conversion model', and other brand dynamics frameworks, all with the key objective to link marketing activities to brand equity to volume.

They now believe there are five core measures that help them best measure brand equity, which can be directly correlated to volume.

The primary performance measure for brand health is claimed daily drinking. Daily drinking is seen to reflect how consumers feel, their top of mind awareness and the connections or role the brand plays in their lives. Continuous tracking allows this to be tracked against different consumer groups on an ongoing monthly, three-monthly and annual basis.

▶

In addition, the other four measures used are: advertising awareness; an affinity measure 'brand for me'; an experiential measure 'great tasting'; and a value measure 'worth paying more for'. These measures are evaluated on longer term horizons as key indicators of brand equity.

More traditional measures such as household penetration also provide strong indicators of short-term volume, particularly within the grocery channel. Given the ubiquity of Coca-Cola in all channels, grocery alone is insufficient. Daily drinking is important because it is not a survey of what is actually going into homes so much as what people feel about the brand and their perceptions of the brand.

In addition, given the focus on forging enduring brand relationship with each generation of consumers, the brand 'bond' with the consumer is also evaluated through a variety of other ad hoc research projects.

Source: Interview with Julia Goldin, July 2002

is, at most, indirect. More often advertising effects the price the consumer is prepared to pay, but this too is indirect. The only direct effect of advertising is changing what we have in our heads about the brand, i.e. brand equity. Coca-Cola is a highly advanced marketing company owning, perhaps, the most valuable brand in the world. Even so, it is still working on the measurement of brand equity (*see box*).

The marketing time-lag is a fundamental challenge to management: either they have some mental model of how brand equity works or they are simply throwing bread on the water. If they have spare bread and there are plenty of fish, this may well be a successful strategy, albeit wasteful. Small and start-up companies, in particular, may find it more efficient to adopt this policy because sophisticated data gathering and analysis is relatively expensive. But they should still be thoughtful about it. Marketing is almost always a better strategy than merely selling because it builds for the future as distinct from existing hand to mouth.

Large companies, however, need a more formal understanding of how marketing investment grows brand equity and that in turn grows future profitability. An explicit model is better than implicit and quantified is better than intuitive because the learning can be shared between the current managers and from year to year. Marketers come and go more frequently than other specialists. To paraphrase Saki, 'she was a good marketer as marketers go, but as marketers go, she left'. So the formalization of the business model is important for company-wide learning and for explaining to other stake-

Bacardi Martini

Bacardi was founded in Cuba in 1862 and after Mars it is the second largest family owned consumer goods business in the world.

Freedom from reporting earnings to financial analysts allows time for brand building and this is the priority followed by developing distribution for the company brands and those of third parties it distributes. Internally the business is measured by a company index – called the Margin Improvement Index.

The intangible measure for brands is termed brand essence. There is no intention to sell the brands so a financial valuation of the brand asset is not undertaken. Each brand has a scorecard and the number of dimensions measured varies by brand. For Bacardi Rum the eleven measures are:

◆ market share

◆ relative consumer price versus competitors

◆ consumption in the last month

◆ perceived quality and esteem

◆ consideration – a measure determined by the frequency of selection as first preference – a top of mind rating

◆ salience

◆ sales volume

◆ promoted sales volume

◆ image on a number of dimensions

◆ ad. spend and share of voice

◆ brand building

◆ marketing initiatives

The company uses Millward Brown brand equity models, need state studies, retail audits, and brand U and A studies (every two years).

Internal attitudes are measured through an employee audit and the company has actively sought to change its business culture through involvement groups – an example is setting up an internet café at their offices.

Chris Searle sees the functional marketing model giving way to pan-company marketing. There is increasing commitment to a scientific approach to metrics and evidence-based analysis.

Source: Interview with Chris Searle, Executive Director Bacardi Martini UK, June 2002

holders, such as the shareholders, why marketing investment is important and why it has best been spent the way it was. The global drinks giant, Bacardi Martini, shows how they have recently formalized brand equity measurement (*see box*).

Brand valuation is at best only part
of the measurement issue

Many large firms seek to deal with brand equity in purely financial terms. In theory, brand valuation quantifies the state of the marketing asset and the net change in the valuation from the beginning to the end of the financial period is used to then adjust the short-term results. Life would be much simplified if non-financial market measures could be avoided altogether. Expenditure, brand valuation and the increase in the bottom line would be the only variables. Unfortunately brand valuation turns out not to be the solution but merely one of the many metrics needed. If you already know that, skip to the next section.

A number of methods are used to value brands but as the principal ones involve discounting future cash flows, we can focus on that. According to Raymond Perrier of the world's largest brand valuation firm, Interbrand Newell Sorrell, valuations are a rich source of learning that help firms to become more explicit about brand strategy and the priorities for resource allocation. In our research, we found an increasing number of firms routinely using brand valuation as a part of brand equity assessment. Cranfield Professor Bob Shaw confirms that the use of brand valuation is growing fast, but also dropping away as practitioners do not find it as helpful as they had hoped.[12] Some of the flaws are:

◆ It is subjective. Brands are rarely sold, and purposes change valuations anyway.[13] Value for insurance is not the same as value for sale, for example. The choice of methodology is subjective.

◆ It is coarse-grained. Value methodologies are too crude to detect the fine tuning resulting from yearly marketing activity. Changes in a well-managed brand's equity are not only slow in themselves but are often slow to show up on the bottom line.

◆ Assumptions change. The primary methodology, discounted cash flow (DCF) calculation, is critically dependent on assumptions of future interest rates and inflation. Future brand earnings are calculated and then discounted back to their value today. Obviously, if all forecasts are being made at the same time, e.g. to compare alternative investments, then these assumptions are neutral. In performance assessment, however, we are using two sets of assumptions, one year apart, so the change in brand valuation may owe far more to changed environmental perceptions than to the quality of brand management. If, to avoid this, assumptions are held steady, then at least one set will be unrealistic.

◆ It lacks theoretical underpinning. Brand valuation methodologies employ some non-financial measures to assess brand strength, e.g. market rank and how international the brand is. While these seem superficially to be valid, they have not been empirically or even theoretically justified.

◆ Brand valuation is inadequate as a single measure of brand equity. We would not accept a single indicator – pulse or temperature, say – of our own health. The relationship of a brand to its consumers is similarly complex. Unsurprisingly, the International Accounting Standards Committee has found it difficult to harmonize intangible asset accounting standards. Its Secretary-General, Sir Bryan Carsberg, put it thus: 'We do not account for intangibles very well and perhaps cannot do so under traditional accounting.'[14]

◆ It anticipates the future. DCF methods take future marketing efforts into today's valuation. This is not an issue of discounting inflation and the cost of money but of separating marketing efforts to date, for which we can take credit, from those beyond the period under review, for which we cannot. Theoretically these could be split, but it would be difficult and is not done in existing methodologies.

This last problem is the most serious: estimating the state of an asset today from the way it may look in the future is guesswork, not science. That is why accountants with integrity have long avoided improving today's profits by anticipating tomorrow's. It is especially illogical to judge the performance of today's brand managers on the basis of what their successors may achieve.

The alternative is to use current indicators of e.g. brand commitment, perceived quality and customer preference to describe the brand equity today. The correct way to judge contemporary performance is how much the short-term results and the brand equity have improved from the start of the period until now.

The flaws in brand valuation might make a long list but should not be overstressed. In aggregate they only warn us to be cautious. Successive brand valuations can provide useful indications as to the direction and amount of change. More importantly, brand valuation brings key marketing considerations to the Exec in familiar financial language. It brings finance and marketing together to analyze brands and positions them, often the most valuable, alongside all other assets.

The reason why no single indicator will suffice is illustrated by Richard Chay's aeroplane metaphor: the pilot (brand manager) uses a variety of guidance indicators to reach the desired destination. The different gauges provide different information on the health and position of the plane.

Extending the metaphor, the modern aeroplane (brand) now has far more indicators than did its predecessors. At the same time, cost pressures are cutting the number of people in the cockpit. Top management is less interested in what is going on in the plane than in how soon the objective will be reached. This distracts the pilots and may do little to change the performance of the plane. The system does not distinguish between on-time arrival in good conditions and outstanding flying through turbulence. So performance enhancement requires a thorough understanding of the full instrumentation. The plane operators, or owners, may be preoccupied by its arrival time, but they should also be concerned with its condition and profitability.

There can thus be no such magic metric, any more than a single number can describe a car. That is not how it works. To revert to the medical metaphor, human health is revealed by double negatives: a whole list of numbers need not to be wrong. In a medical examination, the doctor is making sure our blood sugar is not too high, cancer cells are low, the weight to height ratio is not excessive and so on. Health means not failing any of these tests.

So it is with brands. Certain ratios need to be in balance, relative price with price strategy, and relative consumer satisfaction. Trends need to be non-negative. And we need traditional metrics as well as new technology, just as doctors will continue to check the patient's pulse as well as using functional magnetic resonance imaging (MRI). Technology has opened a whole new e-world of measures that monitor who our consumers are along with their interest in our brands, e.g. 'cookies', but traditional metrics matter too.

This multiple double-negative concept is true of all marketing, not just metrics. Great marketers never know what to do; they just know what to avoid. Differentiation lies at the heart of marketing and the consequence is that great marketers are constantly trying new things. Those that work they continue, those that do not they avoid. Poor marketing does what others do, too little and too late.

So metrics should be many and balanced. We are looking for unhealthy trends in a wide range of brand health indicators. Some of these depend on brand maturity. A new brand needs awareness first but for a well-established brand, awareness is just a yawn. Differentiation may not matter to a new brand but a mature brand with a host of imitators needs to keep fresh and separate.

Current approaches to brand equity measurement

Some advertising agencies and groups have packaged measures of brand equity that are empirically based on worldwide market research. Young and Rubicam, for example, have BrandAsset Valuator (BAV), which is made up of two pairs of metrics.

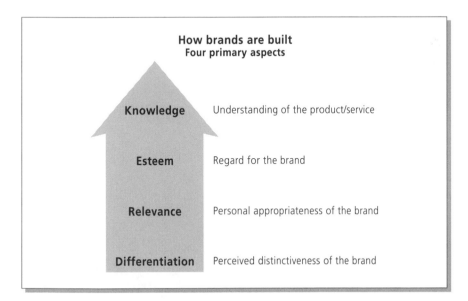

Figure 2.4 ◆ Y&R's BrandAsset Valuator

Source: Y&R presentation, 1997

Figure 2.4 shows that differentiation is the first driver of brand equity. As the brand develops, the next aspect (metric) is relevance. Relevance and differentiation, taken together, form brand strength. While these will provide initial growth, long-term repeat business requires esteem, i.e. perceived quality, which, with greater product experience, will be supplemented by brand knowledge. These, taken together, are termed 'brand stature'. But while the higher order aspects are being built the original differentiation may be allowed to decay. In that event, no matter how highly regarded it is, the brand will lose its identity and be prey to private label or other brands.

The WPP BrandDynamics Pyramid model is comparable. Both models, unlike many others that are not securely built, were based on extensive global consumer research across dozens of product categories and cost millions of dollars. Here the brand–consumer relationship is linked with brand share of the consumer's wallet. Figure 2.5 shows the lowest level of relationship and share as 'presence', where the consumer is vaguely aware of the brand but has little to do with it. Those at the top of the pyramid have such a loyal relationship with the brand that WPP describes it as bonding. The idea of a ladder of relationships is not new and has intuitive appeal.

The size of each layer of the pyramid is determined by the number of consumers in that category. While there will normally be fewer bonders than those merely aware of the brand, the more the diagram forms a vertical column, rather than a flattish pyramid, the better for the brand.

This book is not endorsing these models. Those of many other advertising

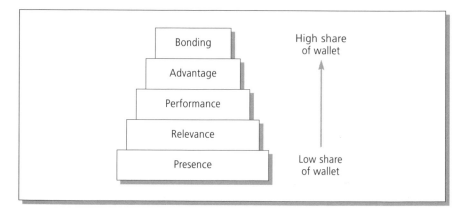

Figure 2.5 ◆ WPP BrandDynamics Pyramid

Source: Farr, A. (1999) 'Does your brand have the energy to compete?', *Admap*, 35, Exhibit 1, April

and research agencies may be just as valid. Research International has a similar brand equity model and the research agency Hall and Partners uses what it calls 'brand chemistry' to analyze the different factors that make up a brand:

◆ The core elements: personality, product, positioning.

◆ The motivational element: inner needs and outer needs.

◆ The performance element: what does it do and what do people do with it?

◆ The personality element: emotional values.

◆ The geography element: where does it fit in?

◆ The people element: who uses it and what are they like?[15]

The Ipsos-ASI market research agency makes the bold claim:

Brand Evolution is a model of Brand Health or Brand Equity, primarily intended for use in Market Evolution and in full Usage and Attitude studies, although it could also be used in many other types of studies. Brand Evolution uses a highly streamlined, standard module of questions, requiring less than 5 minutes to administer. It can be used with any data collection method. It encompasses all the main issues that are considered relevant to brand equity or brand health by most commentators on the subject.[16]

Quite apart from confusing the health of the asset with the asset itself, the width of commentator opinion in this area makes it unlikely that a five-

---

3M

Tim Hewtson Le Roux sees 3M as a very personal place to work, rather like an extended family. The company is clearly committed to innovation and development with a strong sense of employee loyalty and a continuing culture centred around diversified technology and helping customers succeed. 3M prides itself on being first-to-market with new products and services. Recently, the company embraced performance management and business planning (using GE derived models) to increase its focus on customers.

The ultimate measure of success for the company remains financial (currently 11 per cent sales turnover growth, 12 per cent profit growth and 13 per cent earnings per share growth). Other drivers are happy employees and shareholders. One measure of success is seen as the customer's success.

▶

Key metrics are reputation (value of 3M brand), sales and profit, price premium and efficiency (employees/sales profit). The marketing asset is measured using intent to purchase, familiarity, differentiation and loyalty. The brand's equity is seen as being a value in a customer's mind rather than the value of a transaction.

Hewtson Le Roux considers the company to be moving from the 'market focus' towards the 'pan-company' stage of metrics evolution, described in Chapter 4.

Source: Metrics interviews with Tim Hewtson Le Roux, Brand Strategy and Market Intelligence Manager – Europe, Middle East and North Africa, 1999 and 18 June 2002

minute questioning using any collection method could summarize the brand equity for any type of brand. Ipsos-ASI is a major world market research company with thousands of happy customers. I single out this example from many purely as a caveat to marketers employing standard agency solutions in an area so fundamental to their business.

The 3M case study takes us from agency models to reviewing the extent and the frequency with which companies measure brand equity now (*see box*).

Brand equity measurement is becoming common practice. Of US companies, 43 per cent were measuring brand equity according to a 1994 survey.[17] Of the blue chip marketing company members of the Washington-based Marketing Leadership Council, 48 per cent were measuring brand equity in 2001 and 43 per cent valued their brands.[18] The proportions were higher in business-to-consumer companies that sold indirectly, e.g. via retailers. About two-thirds of these companies measured brand equity and, apart from packaged goods, valued their brands. These figures probably underestimate the numbers attempting to measure brand equity since, as noted at the beginning of this chapter, 49 per cent say they are unable to do so. One way and another, the appetite for measuring brand equity is certainly there.

The UK (1999) figures were slightly lower. About 40 per cent regularly measure brand equity non-financially, 25 per cent value their brands and about 20 per cent do both. These figures may be exaggerated due to non-response bias or overclaiming. Our in-depth research with leading companies has indicated caution since many large companies have the measures but do not routinely provide brand equity overviews for their top executive committee.[19]

Once we accept that brand equity should be reported to the Exec, the question is 'how often?' For example, UK supermarket chain Tesco meas-

Table 2.3 ◆ Regularity of tracking the marketing asset

	Never	Rarely/ad hoc	Regularly yearly/quarterly	Monthly or more
	%	%	%	%
Financial valuation	51.4	23.6	16.9	8.0
Other measures	36.8	22.2	28.7	12.3

ures customer perceptions of Quality, Value, Service and Trust quarterly. Customer perceptions of performance on 41 attributes are measured twice a year together with ad hoc research seeking customer insight.[20] Table 2.3 summarizes the responses to the UK research.[21] Given the confusion over terminology noted earlier, it seems likely that the marketing specialists track the key data monthly, but report full brand equity overviews to top management less often.

Why marketing is not making its case

at CEO level

Drawing attention to such an enormous beast as brand equity tends to provoke annoyance or bewilderment rather than gratitude. Yes, it is obvious that marketing provides inward cash flow and the firm's store of goodwill will provide future revenue. Nine times out of ten, the reaction of senior managers is to dismiss the subject or to relegate it for action at a future date. But if brand equity is so obvious and so important, why is it not tracked at each executive meeting? Why do marketers have to beg and plead for money to invest in their brands? Why is brand equity ignored when marketing ROI calculations are prepared?

Suggesting that senior executives need psychiatrists more than they need accountants tends to curtail the conversation. Successful managers in successful companies reckon they must be getting it right already. If the business is in trouble, it may be too late to fix brand equity. Part of the problem is converting what firms know into what they do and this, as Professors Pfeffer and Sutton have demonstrated, is surprisingly rarely done.[22] Most firms operate most of the time as they habitually do. Meetings follow a set cycle and the agendas for executive meetings follow their customary patterns.

The same research noted at the outset of this book which showed that, for large UK companies only 10 per cent of executive meeting time went on marketing, separated out the firms with and without the senior marketer as a full member of the executive committee. The expectation, naturally, was that the presence of a marketer would increase the time given to marketing. Not so; it went down. One possible explanation for this is social: new members do not seek to change the rules of the club they have just joined.

> Gaining agreement to a major change in the top management information takes time

Another cause is the short term driving out the long. Gaining agreement to a major change in the top management information takes time and, in a large company, setting up a brand equity tracking system takes even longer. Faced by a choice of fighting for that disruption or for a larger marketing budget for next year or protecting the budget for this year, most chief marketing officers will opt for the budget. Furthermore, most CMOs change jobs faster than their peers in any other discipline.

A third cause is self-protection. Marketers know better than anyone that marketing performance is hard to measure. However good a job they may be doing, the metrics may not come out right. So long as they can secure decent budgets, why rock the boat? This is short-term thinking. So long as marketing is not accountable, the discipline will not gain the respect of its peers, still less the CEO, unless the CEO is also a marketer.

Those CMOs who decide or are coerced to accept the accountability challenge typically adopt the managing for value, or shareholder value, methodology. Current best practice it may be, but it is also the wrong answer as will be discussed in the next chapter. The challenge is tougher than that but we can make a start by examining how brand equity can be assessed.

How should you measure the elephant?

The difficulty is that brand equity cannot be measured directly. We cannot look inside people's heads and count the brand synapses (memories), nor can we quantify brand bytes in computer programs and business systems.

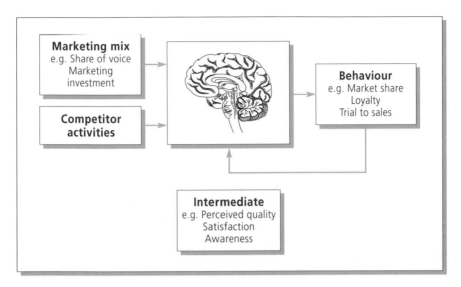

Figure 2.6 ◆ Measures of consumer brand equity

So we have to use proxies of three kinds: inputs, intermediate measures and behaviour. Figure 2.6 gives an overview of consumer brand equity.

◆ Inputs include the amount of advertising and communications (the prime driver of brand equity).

◆ Intermediate measures seek to estimate what is in people's heads. Awareness and attitudes such as how relevant they perceive the brand to be to them, its perceived quality and customer satisfaction provide fuzzy data needing care in interpretation, even if collected to the highest standards. Such responses are unreliable, especially emotions and feelings. We are good at answering questions about what we have done and what we know, but neuroscience indicates caution about reported feelings and intentions.

◆ Behaviour is widely considered to be the most reliable indicator of what we really think and feel. Sales are the most popular metric. Perhaps the next most useful are market share and relative price (share of market by value divided by share of market by volume), provided that it is sustainable in terms of quality and reputation. Customer gains, retention, loyalty, penetration and whether the brand appeals to frequent or occasional users are also popular.

Competitor effects may be monitored directly. More typically, marketing metrics are shown in absolute (e.g. customer satisfaction) and relative terms (e.g. customer satisfaction as a percentage of the same numbers for the key competitors or total market). The score relative to competition is generally a better indicator than any score for the brand in isolation. For example, the absolute level of customer satisfaction has been shown to be an unreliable indicator whereas satisfaction relative to the target competitor is a better predictor of performance. That makes sense: however good you may be, you still have to be better than your competitors.

Michigan's Professor Gene Anderson and colleagues found that a composite measure of absolute and relative satisfaction was closely linked with companies' market value.[23] The American Customer Satisfaction Index (ACSI) uses a screened sample of 50,000 recent users of brands and reduces the 15 questions each to a single index score for each brand. For an average Business Week 1000 company, a one unit improvement in the ACSI index adds $287 million to market valuation.

Marketing, then, is first and foremost the building of brand equity. Do that right and profits will take care of themselves. Brand equity is not something apart from but central to business decision-making.

Measurement has two primary roles: control and direction. Marketers recognize the importance of control but dislike the inhibition. This colours all assessment metrics, which is a pity. Audacious targets, well presented, can be motivational and even inspirational. Metrics, as is worth repeating, flag the route from today to those targets. They also flag the business model. Nothing better demonstrates the market orientation of a business than the Exec requiring regular measures of brand equity. And that is a flag that marketers can salute.

So the way to measure brand equity is to decide how the business model can best be described and then quantified. Does customer retention matter more than acquisition? Do you want customers to buy more of the same or broaden their range? What motivates them to buy? And to buy more?

The metrics that matter should unite the company. As such, 'market' metrics may be a better term than 'marketing' metrics. They give marketing, finance, human relations, operations and buying a shared language to understand strategy, performance and the drivers of success in the market.

In larger firms with formal systems, brand equity measurement frequency is set by the planning and reporting cycle. Brand equity should be an intrinsic component of performance review and decision making. Major decisions to cut or increase marketing functions and/or expenditure are often taken mid-year in response to changing circumstances. The basic principle is that marketing decisions should be based on brand equity as well as profit considerations.

Large companies tend to have too many planning cycles and spend too much time on planning in general. The quarterly reporting cycles in the USA can be a particular problem in this regard. Brand equity is a tender plant. It is unhelpful to pull it up every week to see how the roots are doing. Most firms with regular brand equity systems measure on somewhere between a yearly and quarterly basis, but some as often as monthly. This is too much: six monthly is the optimal brand equity measurement frequency for most firms.

Small and medium-sized firms, however, may not have formal planning systems at all. In this case, an annual review of marketing performance and brand equity may well be enough. No firm is too small for the questions 'What are we trying to do?', 'Compared to that, how are we doing?' and 'In the light of that, what should we be doing?'

Executive minutes

1 Exec to determine clear use of marketing language, including brand equity and valuation, metrics and diagnostics. Consider defining brand equity as 'what is in people's heads about the brand'.

2 Exec to make business model explicit and to invite the market metrics task force to deduce the best metrics from that in the light of data availability.

3 Finance director to report on relative importance of brand equity/equities compared to other company assets and brand equity measurement strategy.

4 Exec to be provided six-monthly with key brand equity metrics for each 'customer' segment (consumers/end users, direct trade customers, employees, shareholders, etc.) by the relevant functional director (marketing, sales, human resources, investor relations, etc.).

5 Finance director to provide annual valuations of the (leading) brand(s) within the total brand equity measurement system.

6 Brand equity to be considered alongside profitability for all major business decisions.

Marketing performance, in essence, is given by short-term results adjusted by the gain or decrease in the marketing asset. No one can measure the future. Brand equity – or whatever term is used for the marketing asset – stands for the present value of future performance insofar as it has already been earned. We should not take into account the future results from future activities. This concept of an asset as a store of future value is nothing new. 'Receivables', in the balance sheet, stands for money that will be paid and 'inventory' for goods that will be sold. Brand equity may not feature on the balance sheet but it is an asset in exactly that sense: it is the storehouse of future profits that resulted from past marketing activities.

Notes

1   Marketing Leadership Council (2001) *Measuring Marketing Performance*, Washington DC, Corporate Executive Board: 7: 49 per cent, followed by 'reporting cycle too long', 42 per cent, and 'unable to validate measurement tools' 35 per cent.

2   Internal case study, October 1992.

3   The explanation for this zoological quirk is that they drink a great deal to digest their mostly dry food.

4   Ehrenberg, A. S. C. (1994) 'The case against brand equity: if you're strong why aren't you bigger?', *Admap*, October, 13–14.

5   Feldwick, P. (2002) *What is Brand Equity, Anyway?*, Henley on Thames: WARC. He cites his earlier paper on p.57 and comments in an Afterword on p.60.

6   Aaker, D. A. (1991) *Managing Brand Equity*, New York: Free Press. See also Aaker, D. A. (1996) *Building Strong Brands*, New York: Free Press.

7   Srivastava, R. K. and Shocker, A. D. (1991) 'Brand equity: a perspective on its meaning and measurement', Cambridge, MA: Marketing Science Institute, working paper no. 91–124.

8   Keller, K. L. (1998) *Strategic Brand Management*, Upper Saddle River NJ: Prentice-Hall.

9   Rust, R. T., Valarie, A. Z. and Lemon, K. N. (2000) *Driving Customer Equity: How Customer Lifetime Value is Reshaping Corporate Strategy*, New York: Free Press.

10   For a full discussion of this issue see: Ambler, T., Bhattacharya, C. B., Edell, J., Keller, K. L., Lemon, K. N. and Mittal, V. (2002) 'Relating brand and customer perspectives on marketing management,' *Journal of Service Research*, 5, 13–25.

11   Ambler, T., Bhattacharya, C. B., Edell, J., Keller, K. L., Lemon, K. N. and Mittal, V. (2002) 'Relating brand and customer perspectives on marketing

management', *Journal of Service Research*, 5, 13–25.

12 Shaw, R. (1998) *Improving Marketing Effectiveness*, London: Economist Books.

13 Barwise, P. (1993) 'Brand equity: snark or boojum?', *International Journal of Marketing Research*, 10, 93–104.

14 Carsberg, B. (1998) 'Future directions of financial reporting', in Carey, A. and Sancto, J. (eds.) *Performance Measurement in the Digital Age*, London: Institute of Chartered Accountants of England and Wales, 36–40.

15 Hall and Partners (1999) *A Brief Word About Us*, London: Hall and Partners.

16 www.ipsos.com/prod/Evolution/home/index.htm 20 October 2002.

17 Davis, S. and Douglass, D. (1995) 'Holistic approach to brand equity management', *Marketing News*, 16 January, 4–5.

18 Marketing Leadership Council (2001) *Measuring Marketing Performance*, (supporting data) Washington DC, Corporate Executive Board.

19 Kokkinaki, F. and Ambler, T. (1999) 'Marketing performance assessment: current practice and the role of firm orientation', Marketing Science Institute working paper, 99–114.

20 Marketing Council booklet (1999) 'The whole company … designed for customers'.

21 Kokkinaki, F. and Ambler, T. (1999) 'Marketing performance assessment: current practice and the role of firm orientation', Marketing Science Institute working paper, 99–114, 531 responses.

22 Pfeffer, J. and Sutton, R. I. (1999) 'Knowing what to do is not enough: turning knowledge into action', *California Management Review*, 42 (1), 83–108.

23 Anderson, E. W., Mazvancheryl, S. and Fornell, C. G. (2002) 'Customer satisfaction and shareholder value', MSI Conference on Measuring Marketing Productivity, Dallas, 3 October.

3

Financial fallacies

JUST AS IN AGES PAST knights errant sought the philosopher's stone, so twenty-first century executives errant try to express important concepts in single financial numbers. 'That's a great idea,' they say, 'but what will be the effect on shareholder value?' In the research for this book, we routinely found top-flight managers who were unable to understand brand equity as being anything but its valuation. If this made sense, management would be simplified. Dennis Malamatinas, then CEO of Burger King, used to ask his executives to put a value on red roses he bought for his wife. They could cost them but not financially value them. Or to make his point more strongly, what would have been the value of the red roses, if they had been delivered erroneously at home enclosing a card addressed to a mistress?

This chapter addresses the dangers of misusing financial figures in assessing marketing performance or in marketing generally. If finance is not a dominant aspect of your corporate culture, skip to the next chapter. The chapter looks at two kinds of reservation, conceptual and behavioural. In the first, the difficulty is fundamental, such as comparing brand valuations with market capitalization. In the second, the theory may be adequate, or innocuous, but the way the ideas are applied lead to suboptimal practice. The two cannot be neatly separated: shareholder value analysis, for example, may be fine if management had all possible scenarios to test but this is not conceptually possible, still less behaviourally.

Managing for value has become a dominant philosophy in many modern companies. Strategic options are analyzed to provide their forecast shareholder value and determined accordingly. Costs are reduced and assets are squeezed effectively, but the question here is whether this approach assists or damages the generation of inward cash flow, i.e. marketing. We should not be surprised if any new managerial panacea such as this turns out to have hidden dangers.

Four centuries intervened between Sir Walter Raleigh's promotion of tobacco in Europe and our recognition of its damage to health. In moderation, the mind-altering effects of alcohol are benign; damage results only from excess. Financial analysis is both essential for modern business and, in moderation, beneficial but addiction may cost your company dearly.

Although Boots, the UK retail health and beauty care chain, emphasizes financial metrics, and especially Total Shareholder Return, non-financial metrics are an important part of their perspective (*see box*).

The organization of this chapter is as follows:

◆ Maximizing the ROI on marketing.

◆ The dangers of brand valuation.

The Boots Company PLC

Boots has been a leading figure in the value-based management (VBM) movement for ten years and accordingly some might see Boots as a financially driven business, though the company itself would see VBM as more broadly defining the way to manage a business and taking market perspectives into account when shaping strategy.

Today in the UK, Boots is a chemist, optician and 'well-being' retailer. Outside the UK retailing is concentrated in Thailand and Taiwan. The company has moved from managing through strategic business units to a 'one-company concept' with greater focus on retaining and creating value for customers. Nevertheless our orientation questions placed the owners, i.e. shareholders, ahead of customers in terms of primacy.

Overall there is perhaps a 60–40 emphasis on efficiency, e.g. return on marketing investment, over effectiveness, e.g. achieving strategic goals. This dichotomy may be false as both are crucial. Innovation remains a priority for the Boots group to deliver new content in its stores.

Competitive measures are also important both at corporate level, where total shareholder returns are compared with both UK and global peers. Boots the Chemists key competitors are the food superstore operators (such as Sainsbury, Tesco and Asda) and Superdrug plus Watson's in the Far East.

Source: Interview with Mike Dutton, Corporate Development Manager, 15 July 2002

◆ Customer lifetime value (CLV) in theory and practice.

◆ Managing for value or the application of shareholder value to marketing.

◆ Using financial techniques in evaluating marketing performance.

Maximizing the ROI on marketing

Calls for marketers to achieve more but with less money have been growing. Other executives harbour the suspicion that marketing is extravagance and should be put through the same financial ringer as other functions. The call goes up to maximize the ROI on marketing. They do not, of course, mean marketing in the broad sense. That would be like asking the ROI on eating: if you do not do it, you die. A firm that suspended marketing in the broad sense would be bankrupted soon enough. No, the challenge is to advertising and promotional expenditure and especially advertising.

In principle, ROI is a useful way to choose the preferred options for the marketing mix when the total budget is fixed. This is further discussed in Chapter 9 but the concept is seriously misleading when it is used more broadly. In the first place, those using it do not usually mean an investment in one year that earns money in future years, but an expenditure that attracts revenue in the same year. If the net profit, i.e. the return, is positive the firm should do more of it until the returns turn south. Figure 3.1 illustrates the point: the high point of the profit line maximizes the return. On the other

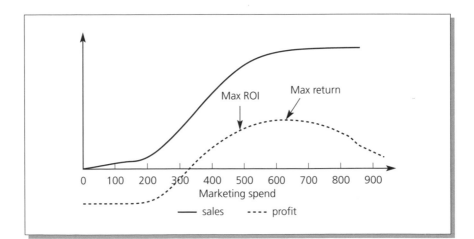

Figure 3.1 ◆ Marketing returns

hand, the maximum ROI, which divides the profit by the 'investment', is well short of that, i.e. a suboptimal choice.

The graphical point is more obvious from Table 3.1. If the objective is to maximize ROI, the firm would spend $500 but that would be suboptimal. ROI in this context ascribes too much importance to the cost relative to the profit. One can argue that revenue is doubtful and expenditure is certain but there are other statistical techniques to deal with that. The point is that the firm is seeking to maximize the net return.

Table 3.1 ◆ Maximizing ROI

	Max ROI	Max return
Revenue $	3550	4200
Profit before marketing $	710	840
Marketing spend $	500	600
Net profit $	210	240
ROI %	42	40

ROI makes more sense when, as may be the case for advertising or a new brand launch, it is truly an investment, i.e. the payback comes in later years, but here too it fails. Accountants have long since, and rightly, moved to the concept of present value, i.e. the discounted cash flow (DCF) less the cost of the investment. 'Payback', i.e. how long it will take to recover the cost of the investment, is the crude alternative and often a useful rule of thumb.

When people talk of the ROI from marketing, they usually mean the profit return after deducting the cost of the campaign: it is return *minus* investment, not return *divided by* investment. And of course we are considering discretionary marketing activities (the budget) not marketing as a whole. In making this point, one response has been that the ratio is still useful for comparing alternative uses, in marketing or in other areas, of the same budget. In fact, if the I is constant, then R–I peaks at the same point R/I does, so the ratio is still redundant at best and possibly misleading because the immediate reaction to a high ratio is the supposition that more investment would produce the same ratio again.

Thus DCF is a sound way to compare alternative ways to spend the firm's discretionary cash, but ROI is not. A more reliable process is to establish what levels of expenditure seem to be needed to achieve the firm's goals and then fine-tune the plan to achieve the same, or at least acceptable, goals for less cost.

In short, ROI is rarely if ever a useful ratio in marketing because it misplaces division where there should be subtraction. DCF and payback are, however, valid methodologies. If the comparison is just within a single year, then the net profit returns are enough. In all cases, allowance should be made for any significant change in brand equity.

The dangers of brand valuation

Some of the flaws in brand valuation were reviewed in the last chapter but we need to keep a balance. As an example of best practice, Figure 3.2 was developed by Adrian Joseph of A T Kearney using neural networks and shows a strong (0.7) relationship between the Millward Brown index of brand strength (Brandz Voltage) and the two subsequent years' profits for selected US and UK retailers. The vertical axis is 'Earnings Before Interest,

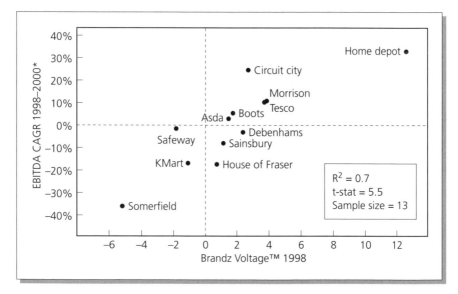

Figure 3.2 ◆ Brand equity drives future profits

Source: A T Kearney, 2002, Brandz Voltage™ from Millward Brown
*Compound annual growth rate of earnings before interest, taxes, depreciation and amortization
(June 1998–June 2000)

Tax, Depreciation and Amortization Compound Annual Growth Rate (EBITDA). The selection of retailers in this analysis was based purely on the availability of data and it is possible that some bias may have been inadvertently created thereby. Nevertheless, such technicalities do not detract from the successful use of brand equity as a predictor of future profits.

Figure 3.2 differs from the oft-made comparison of brand valuation and market capitalization.[1] One usually finds a decent correlation and the claim is then made that brand equity drives the share price. This is bogus. Most brand valuations are based on the forecasts of future cash flow less the hypothetical cash flows from an equivalent but unbranded product. Since the cash flow from a non-existent product are even more difficult to estimate, some judgement is made of the branding effect in year 1 and the cash flows thereafter follow similar trajectories.

Now the market capitalization is, at least in perfect markets theory, also a projection of cash flows from the same firm. Accordingly, all three cash flows are broadly the same. One would not expect them to be identical, since the markets are not perfect and the projections are made by different people, but correlation should be strong. This has nothing to do with brands driving anything, they are just projections of the same artificial data. If I chose to call the present value of this cash flow a turnip, then a turnip would be an excellent predictor of market value. Indeed, turnips may even be driving market cap. Amazing.

> **Brand valuation gets the marketing foot in the Exec's door if it is not already there**

Brand valuation is being used internally and its great attraction is the first impact made by its financial size. Brand valuation gets the marketing foot in the Exec's door if it is not already there. Thereafter the benefits prove elusive and companies either widen the market metrics they review or give up brand valuation. Some are more determined. A senior manager at a leading UK bank told us:

> *What we couldn't do was take that [brand valuation] and turn it into any kind of tangible measure and equate it to business decisions. There would be strange things, like we sell more product and make more money for shareholders, but the brand value would go down. There was a lot of peculiar things you just couldn't make sense of. The only thing we could equate it to was just the fact that it didn't take account of some of the financial management tools that we have to use in this market. And when other people's businesses shrank their brand value went up.[2]*

Abbey National is a company that has struggled to incorporate brand valuation into their management systems (*see box*).

Abbey National

There has been steady progress towards value-based measurement. Abbey National is looking at customer value rather than product valuations and maximizing the value of existing customers as a business strategy. On the other hand, it has moved away from doing a brand equity value measurement because it seemed financially flawed. Nevertheless it believes that brand valuation is the right route to take, as there is an intangible value to the business.

At the same time, marketing is very much driven by the profit and loss account and now by total shareholder returns. Within that, measures are volume or value: market share, units sold or cross-sold, new business level acquired, i.e. the number of new accounts, and two value measures, the net present value of the book of business and amount of premium held in the life market.

Abbey National defines marketing broadly – somewhere between pan-company and departmental – and considers itself at the 'market focus' level of evolution but is looking to drive on to 'scientific' soon (see Chapter 4). Since 1998, Abbey National has retained the same five brand values for the organization: more flexible, fairer, better value, easier to use, and more emotionally rewarding. The aim is to deliver business growth by differentiating. Customers think supermarkets are different whereas banks are all the same. That is the fundamental problem facing financial services companies.

In 2002, Abbey National introduced a new way of measuring the customer–brand relationship based on cognitive tracking. Microsoft and VW have also used it. Carat Insight creates maps of association with the brand. Similar to brand mapping but quantitative, it shows the relative importance of different attributes and their positive and negative associations with the brand. A monthly mystery shopper plus a customer panel make up a three-pronged approach to tracking the brand.

The marketing function has grown from 150 staff in 1998 to 200. Above- and below-the-line communications (advertising and promotion), customer value management and branch network communication continue but the increase has been in retail, such as design and the franchise network, and the customer database. Most people are in process-driven work around product and campaign development.

> An all-employee survey measures attitudes towards Abbey National as a place to work. It is quarterly and based on the Sears model which linked employee with customer satisfaction and thence an upturn in profit.
>
> *Source*: Keith Moor, Head of Marketing Communications, 5 June 2002

The companies using brand valuation as part of marketing performance assessment may well be right to do so if it is one of a range of metrics. For the reasons set out in the last chapter, it should not be used as a sole indicator of brand equity.[3] The specialist brand valuation companies themselves agree that the process of marketing analysis that leads to the valuation is important, not the number itself.

In all of this, the question of brands on the balance sheet has been a distraction. No country allows the value of brands to be placed on balance sheets although the UK allows the *cost* of certain acquired brands to be included. The cost has to be shown to exceed current [internal] valuations but unless the value has fallen seriously, it is the original purchase price that appears, not the current value. Internally, the financial value of the brand is unlikely to provide useful information beyond an appreciation of scale.

The next two sections address the other main uses of valuation. A common stream runs through all these sections, namely that valuation based on projections of cash flow is flawed both behaviourally (forecasting is inherently unreliable) and conceptually (because those forecasts include the results of future marketing).

Customer lifetime value in theory and practice

Faced by these difficulties, attention has moved from the brand to the customer with the recognition that customer retention typically provides a better financial return than seeking new customers. Within that, firms are recommended to analyze their customer base according to the profitability of each segment and allocate resources accordingly.[4]

The theory is based on customer loyalty. Professor Peter Doyle, for example, suggests: 'For most companies, customer loyalty is the single most important determinant of long-term growth and profit margins.'[5] Fredrick Reichheld instigated the movement and asserted that a customer loyal over, say, seven years contributes six or seven times more than a customer in his first year.[6] This arises from:

- increasing expenditure over time as loyalty breeds increased demand
- reduced operating costs as the company and customer become familiar with each other
- referrals as loyal customers increasingly recommend the company to others
- price premium as longstanding customers become progressively less price sensitive.

Plausible as they may seem, and each is true sometimes, all four claims are dubious. None have been supported empirically. Professor Robert East and colleagues have challenged the increasing gain from referrals.[7] They looked at recommendation rates in four types of services compared with the length of time that the respondents had been customers (tenure). In three out of four cases, recommendation declined over time. They concluded that the relationship between referrals and tenure was context, i.e. sector dependent. In most cases, initial enthusiasm can be something of a honeymoon effect. The exception was car servicing which is both complex and experience extends over several years. In these circumstances, compared with their other three services (current account banking, credit cards and car insurance) the views of long-term users would be increasingly sought and given credence. East and colleagues had previously found decreasing recommendations with tenure for hairdressing and supermarkets.[8]

Very similar conclusions were drawn in a larger US study by Professors Werner Reinartz and V. Kumar who do not pull their punches: 'Much of the common wisdom about customer retention is bunk.'[9] Like East and colleagues, they found that longer term customers were not 'necessarily cheaper to serve, less price sensitive, or particularly effective at bringing in new business'.[10] They also cast doubt on Reichheld's second and fourth points (cost to serve and price sensitivity). My colleague, Professor Kathy Hammond, is working on the first claim and her evidence so far does not support the Reichheld hypothesis.

Nevertheless the prevailing advice remains to analyze customers into segments but not to assume that they will automatically become more profitable with time. They will become more or less profitable according to their future needs and how you tailor your marketing to meet them.

This inverse relationship between referrals and tenure is not explained by age which proved not significant in East's research. The idealized form considers the return to a company from a single customer. Even Reichheld could not have imagined that the relationship between the value of the customer and tenure was linear because, sooner or later, all customers die. This is not as trite a point as it may seem because it is the key distinction between working at the individual and segment levels. Even where the customers are companies, they will sooner or later disappear. So let us assume it looks something like Figure 3.3.

In the first year, due to acquisition costs, the company makes a loss. Business expands quite fast up to year 5 and then more slowly until decline sets in and, ultimately, death brings down the curtain. Customer lifetime value (CLV) is defined to be the net present value of the customer, but here is where the fudge comes in. In practice, very few firms do or could do this calculation for each customer. In their place, customer segments are used. It could be a cohort that would march through time like a customer and ultimately die, but far more often segments are defined in fixed socio-economic or behavioural ways so individuals move through segments. For example, the segment pregnant mothers is forever pregnant.

If you plot the customer [segment] value over time, it will be fairly flat in a stable business. It will look nothing like Figure 3.3. The number of customers in that segment may also be constant because acquisitions are offsetting customer losses. In other words, the whole logic of the single customer life cycle is lost when customers are replaced by segments.

Of course, it is good practice to allocate marketing budgets to segments according to the probable cash flow consequences, as will be discussed later in the chapter, but this is not to say, as CLV enthusiasts often do in practice, that most resources should be allocated to the most valuable customers.

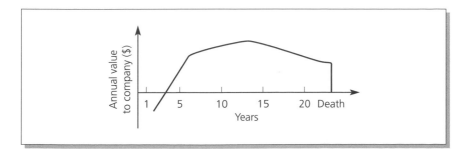

Figure 3.3 ◆ Customer lifetime value (CLV)

Retail banks in the UK all adopted this idea around the year 2000. They identified a 'wealth' segment whose members each had about $750,000 or more spare cash. This segment was age linked as they were mostly heirs to recently dead parents who had left them the family home in addition to the one they already had. We are talking about people in their fifties who have little or no mortgage commitment or money problems. Now, this is quite a good piece of segmentation as it is age related and one can empathize with the needs of these customers as a group. Unfortunately most of these people had also been around the block and could see their bank's computer brain thinking 'the easiest geese to pluck are those with most feathers'.

They discovered, as many have before, that the wealthy are often still wealthy because they are reluctant to part with their money. The banks were gently let down as this segment was also reluctant to move their accounts. Lower down the age scale, banks have long targeted college students, unprofitable as they are in the short term. They increase usage as they develop their careers and retention rates are high.

The moral, of course, is that it is not necessarily sound policy to allocate marketing resources to those that are now the most valuable customers, nor to those who have the most money. Retention may not be increasingly more profitable than acquisition and it may not be best to prioritize the most valuable segment that may already be spending as much as it ever will.

CLV, like most financial analysis, does have its place but we should note that the fallacies lie in giving cash flow forecasts more credence than they deserve and in regarding customers as assets. Customers are not owned by their suppliers and they are not there to be milked. The idea that the objective of marketing has changed from creating value for the customer to creating shareholder value, as suggested by Doyle,[11] goes too far. Of course he is simplifying in order to get the shareholder into the mind of the marketer, but we need to remember which comes first.

In summary, the retention literature that is one of the supports for CLV is unreliable. CLV relies on speciously precise cash flow forecasts that are mostly projections of the present day; in practice, forecasting cash flow from little understood customers when known competitors behave in known ways, i.e. as they do today. CLV in practice gives little attention to the unknowns of future competitors and customers behaving in different ways. The 'customer equity' approach discussed in the last chapter defines it as including all cash flows from existing customers and any that might exist in the future.[12] Conceptually, is it right to include potential customers who will be gained from future marketing activity or to omit those existing customers who will drop out due to inadequate future retention?

For both conceptual and behavioural reasons, anticipating the future in assessing the marketing performance to date brings huge problems. So let us now turn to shareholder value.

Shareholder value analysis

Shareholder value is the leading business principle of the early twenty-first century as it was of the late twentieth. Its roots lie in the perception that the main objective of any company is to maximize the shareholders' return on their equity. This is not a new idea but the formalization was developed in the 1980s thanks to Alfred Rappaport and various firms of consultants.[13]

In essence we are dealing with DCF just as we were with brand valuation and customer lifetime value. The technical adjustments for debt, risk and the costs of capital are important but not relevant here. See Professor Peter Doyle's thorough exposition of shareholder value analysis in the marketing context.[14]

Shareholder value analysis has been over-promoted from a useful tool for resource allocation to a universal framework for decision making.[15] Some dangers and fallacies below are conceptual and others arise from the way shareholder value analysis works in practice.

Conceptual

◆ In theory this tool gives a long-term view by forecasting the future but look more closely and you will find the future looks remarkably like today. By projecting the present into the future, without adequate allowance for external changes, management is condemned to relive Groundhog Day. (If you missed the movie, the plot is that the hero is awakened by his alarm every morning to discover it is the same day over again.) The long term is an illusion: we are just looking at today repeated with minor variations.

◆ The focus is internal, and on concepts that can be expressed in money terms. More important, but non-financial, drivers are excluded.

◆ Excessive emphasis on shareholder value leads to seeing customers and employees as merely means to the achievement of what the CEO really cares about: profits and share prices. It will not take long for customers and employees to get the feeling they are being used.

◆ The allocation of costs may give top management a false picture. Applying shareholder value analysis to business units, for example, requires central costs to be spread on some arbitrary basis that is probably false to the extent that the units do not directly give rise to these costs.

Behavioural

◆ Value analysis is a means to compare existing alternatives. In practice, the eyes-down nature of this analysis prevents managers looking for better alternatives; they just battle for the one they want against whatever alternative has been put up by their counterparts.

◆ Similarly, the complications enable marketers, who soon develop the technical skills, to apply their creativity to manipulating the numbers as distinct from implementing the best marketing programme.

◆ Conversely, marketing investments with outcomes that are hard to express in financial terms are more likely to be put on the back burner. Radical innovation leads to performance, by its nature, well nigh impossible to forecast and yet many firms owe their continuing existence to these leaps of faith. Using a higher discount rate to allow for increased risk is no solution: subtracting an arbitrary number from a wrong number can only make it right by chance. So the things that might transform the business are abandoned in favour of more cuts to the status quo: Groundhog Day again.

All the financial systems discussed in this chapter rely on projecting the present into the future and then believing that future to be realistic. If nothing much changes, not customers, not competitors, not the environment, then the future will indeed look much like the present but, with a more rapidly changing world, it is unlikely. Shareholder value analysis is a valuable technique for identifying the assets and costs, including marketing costs, that can be squeezed. It is a useful internal discipline but it tells us nothing about the marketplace, even though it may incorporate some market data; nor about the sources of cash flow, nor how they can be increased.

Although models of shareholder value do recognize, just about, that cash comes from customers, they are limited to what they can measure in financial terms. So while the company's capabilities, for example, are recognized as drivers of shareholder value, when it gets to the model presented to management, capabilities have dropped out because the accountants cannot put a dollar price on them.

A major problem with long-term planning systems, including share-holder value analysis, is tunnel vision. Jack Welch closed down the central planning system when he became CEO at General Electric because he recognized that it closed out the search for what he called 'white space'. Whatever instructions were given in practice, managers projected the businesses from the status quo. As a result, smaller more lively firms beat them to the draw in new countries and new product categories that they had not really thought about. In an empirical study with the Boston Consulting Group, we found that new product development, or at least radical new products, only entered the planning process after they had already been launched.[16] If success requires circumventing the system, then the system is flawed.

The research was exploratory and sample was 11 cases from 9 packaged goods multinationals. BCG consultants familiar with the cases and respondents gathered the data through in-depth interviews. Although only one respondent used the term 'brand equity' that appeared to be the key driver along with a generic need to enhance net cash flow. Considerations included rejuvenating the brand, protecting its image and leveraging the brand. Concerns were not to dilute the brand and the extent to which the new product fitted the brand. Profits were more of a hygiene factor: in all cases the extensions had to clear a predetermined financial hurdle. Where management was keen on the project, this did not prove a problem.

When a large drinks multinational introduced value based management in the early 1990s, the marketers were aghast but they soon learned to live with it. After a crash course in the methodology and language, Excel sheets became a key feature in marketing plans. The technicalities of value management, and especially the residual values for the cash flows ten years out, were used to justify the budget approvals they would have sought in any case. As anyone versed in large corporate life will appreciate, budget approval owes more to politics than to mathematics. Securing the appropriate budgets is good for the business but value analysis was contributing little to the process; it was simply a means to the preordained solution.

Perhaps the most surprising source for the observation that big new revenue-generating ideas flow from vision and drive, not DCF, is the economist, John Maynard Keynes. Keynes saw animal spirits as the 'spontaneous urge to action rather than inaction, and not as the outcome of a weighted average of quantitative benefits multiplied by quantitative probabilities'.[17] The term 'animal spirits' was adopted from Descartes and brings together the emotional, ideological and determination characteristics of human nature.[18] Descartes had positioned cognition as the driving force in human endeavour, leading to the Age of Enlightenment, with animal spirits being our pre-human inheritance that inhibited progress. Keynes, however, flipped the polarity and positioned animal spirits as the driver of progress, or at least wealth, *despite* reasoned analysis. They are not the antithesis of reason: if they were, Keynes, that most rational of men, would hardly have endorsed them. Animal spirits differentiate humans, and especially entrepreneurial humans, from computers.

Animal spirits may seem an archaic, albeit graphic, term but Stanford researchers Professors James Collins and Jerry Porras reached much the same conclusion in their study of 200 large companies. Their bottom line was that success was not driven by shareholder value but through 'let's try a lot of stuff and keep what works'.[19] Successful companies had vision and a core ideology that differentiated them from others. Maximizing shareholder value was only one objective among many.

Marketing is the means of achieving shareholder satisfaction through first achieving the goals of customers and employees. None of these groups is necessarily more important than the others any more than salt is more important than pepper. The point is the logic of the sequence: employees have to get cash from customers before the shareholders can have some. This is precisely why market metrics should be considered before shareholder value.

> Marketing is the means of achieving shareholder satisfaction through first achieving the goals of customers and employees

The last problem area may seem trivial in comparison but is a regular feature of executive committee debate. In a large company, shareholder value is used to evaluate the performance of the various brands or business units. Those that provide above average returns are presented as drivers and those below average as destroyers of value. No one would quarrel with the need to get low performers to do better but the discussion usually turns to selling them off or closing them down.

It may be obvious to you and me that doing so will result in the overheads being reallocated over a smaller number and brands or business units, thereby presenting a new list of value destroyers. In the heat of the discussion, executives tend to forget that they are actually reducing the sources of cash flow when the discussion should be about reducing overheads. As in so much of the practical application of value-based management, the pseudo-science diverts attention from the marketplace.

In summary, shareholder value analysis, or managing for value, is a useful discipline for squeezing assets and costs and reviewing investment choices: it is only dangerous in excess. As a dominant philosophy it damages innovation, customer and employee relationships, crimps imagination, and leads to downward spirals of cost cutting. It tells the company nothing about the sources of cash flow nor how those can be enhanced and still less about new sources of cash flow. Exaggeration? Maybe. The lawyers will not allow me to name the companies so you will have to take this test for yourself. How many companies that adopted this approach as their dominant philosophy ten years ago are still doing so? And what has happened to those who stayed with it?

No doubt you can add to this list of dangers and fallacies but we should now turn to the positive: how financial analysis should be best used to assist marketing performance.

Using financial techniques in marketing

The basic issue in this section is balance. Non-financial metrics will give a better picture of the market than the financial, but the financial tools should be used in moderation to explore the likely impacts of alternative marketing strategies and actions. The second balance requires more attention to be given to a scientific analysis of the facts today, rather than hypothetical lifetime values. However, historical data, bought-in data (eg for simulated test markets) and proven tools can improve the predictive qualities of those forecasts.

Today's reality can be measured but the future can only be guessed or estimated. I am not suggesting the elimination of forecasting nor of financial tools but only the importance of focusing on measurable facts (metrics). Get the decisions and actions right today and the future will be as good as it can be. In other words, we need to look more closely for the present signs of future consequences and spend less time with our Excel sheets.

This now versus the future issue can use more attention. The paradox of Groundhog Day is that the future is merely a repetition of today unless changes are made today. Looking to the future does not drive future cash flow but the actions we take today do. The competitive edge arises from applying different imagination to the same market facts.

Integrating information

The following chapters in this book discuss how to sift market metrics from the mass of data with which the modern company is assailed. For now, I will simply assume that some database of marketing information has been or can be assembled. This is a non-trivial first step. Large companies have pockets (ghettos) of market data all over the organization. They are commissioned by different people for different reasons and cover different time periods. The commissioners believe they 'own' the data and do not necessarily want to share it with colleagues. This is part of the argument for market metrics being consolidated under the CFO but only a minority of large firms agrees with that.

Francis Bacon mentioned four hundred years ago that knowledge, or perhaps information, is power, and it would not have been a new idea then.[20] Part of the strength of the financial perspective, and consequentially value analysis, flows from accounting information and responsibilities being closely integrated. That is not usually true for market information.

In one way or another, most if not all of the potentially important indicators need to be brought together. The UK leading supermarket chain, Tesco, recognized this in 1994 and appointed a small specialist company to manage their customer database. The objectives were to achieve better understanding of the customers and strengthen loyalty by making customers feel that their needs were receiving more personalized attention. Today dunnhumby takes care of 14 million customer records for Tesco, and offers similar services to large retail organizations in the UK and US (*see box*).

Tesco and dunnhumby

Tesco is the largest UK supermarket group. In 1995 they launched their loyalty Clubcard partly in order to gain better understanding of their customers and shopping behaviour. By then dunnhumby had already been appointed to manage the database and extract customer insights. Until 2000, analysis was based on 10 per cent sample of customers for whom all items where recorded. This allowed key marker products to be spotted and these were the tracked for all customers. This allowed dunnhumby to deliver insight without major investments in IT hardware and communications infrastructure. In particular they could distinguish the behaviours of specialist customer groups, such as the affluent and those living on tight budgets.

The decision was made in 2000 to take advantage of new technology in order to tackle the analysis of the mass market. Huge amounts of data were involved: 10 million Clubcard transactions per week, collected from 570 stores with over 40,000 products being sold each week; 9.5 million Tesco customers now have Clubcards in regular use.

dunnhumby started to look for products that predicted lifestyles. For example, people who buy Weight Watchers are likely to be counting calories. Those buying single portion products are likely to be cooking for one. Using this approach they identified 25 dimensions that started to explain how customers shopped. The challenge was to classify 40,000+ products against those dimensions. Starting with products that were indicative of a dimension, dunnhumby then identified other highly correlated products bought in the same basket or by the same customer at another time.

As traditional statistics could not help, they devised a new 'rolling ball' technique to classify all products against these dimensions. After two man years of analytic effort, they were ready to use this database to segment customers into 'Tesco Lifestyles'. These are used to finetune store ranges and offers as the profile of each store changes.

After the segmentation was completed in June 2001, it was tested in two ways. After just one shopping basket, the segment allocation of new customers proved accurate in 50 per cent of cases. Second, research with customer panels verified the segments adopted and provided insights into motivation. Lifestyles now provides a common language across the Tesco business. Major suppliers such as Procter & Gamble, Mars and Walkers use Lifestyles data to plan their strategy with Tesco and develop more relevant products.

The Lifestyles segments, overlaid with life stage and a recency/frequency segmentation, form the basis for tailoring the communications and coupons. Research shows that 90 per cent of Clubcard holders do not regard the magazines as junk mail and a 2001 segment-targeted offering of coupons had over 4 million variations but achieved a sales uplift of over £30 million.

Source: Clive Humby, Chairman, dunnhumby, 2 August 2002

Of course, databases of this type are driven by transactions, usually at point of sale and personal information provided by the customer when they sign up for their loyalty card. There are large blocks of important market information they exclude, competitive data for example.

Segmentation

A principle attraction of databases of this type is segmentation. Groups of customers with similar characteristics can be deduced from what they buy. The next step is to lead them to what, on the evidence from other members of their group, they might buy. These should be called 'affinity groups' rather than segments because even large corporations cannot have separate marketing programmes for each group. But what they can and do achieve is effective development of their business with each customer through merchandising and direct mail individualized to fit each affinity group.

Now we can estimate the value of each customer and affinity group. More importantly, we can realistically estimate their unfulfilled profit potential. Notice how this analysis is rooted in market data before it gets to financial valuation. Relatively few companies outside financial services and chain retailing have the resource, or the need, to conduct sophisticated segmentation in this way. Indeed, Professor Andrew Ehrenberg has challenged the whole concept of segmentation.[21] When he analyzed packaged goods purchases by the usual demographic classifications, he found no significant differences. Clearly the issue is category specific: poor people rarely buy premium cars.

For us here, whether segmentation is worthwhile is a side issue; the key is to use all available market information to establish a firm base for any forecasts. This is not just the base for year 1 but the likely out years too. Quite often, year 1 is simply projected without any specific attention to changes in the environment, competition and the company itself. Yet it is possible to draw inferences about these matters from current and historical information and these inferences should be used.

Using prediction to decide the best courses of marketing action

Finally we come to the main use for CLV and shareholder value analysis, evaluating alternative strategies. As Wharton's Professor George Day points out,[22] it is crucial to avoid rushing into financial evaluation before *all* the feasible strategies have been assembled and the less attractive eliminated through competitive assessment. Understanding how the marketplace will, or could, react to each strategy needs to precede value analysis.

The attraction of comparative assessment is that many of the future estimates, eg for interest rates, are less critical than for single assessments, eg brand valuation, because they are the same for both. In other words, they may be wrong but they net out. The extent to which the comparisons are affected to future estimates can be determined by sensitivity analysis. Once the Excel sheet is prepared, it can be copied to other pages and run with higher and lower future interest rates, for example. The future does not matter, only the comparison that is being made now.

In a perfect world, shareholder value analysis and monitoring brand equity would provide the same financial numbers. The future cash flows from today's brand equity would equal the forecasts in the value analysis. Either concept would inspire the same decision. In practice, both are needed in decisions such as line extensions (a new but similar product under the same brand name). A quick way to gain new sales and distribution in the market, line extensions may come at the expense of later sales of the original products and of brand equity, i.e. they are short-termist. Too often, a line extension is merely the shortest distance between two profit forecasts.

> Avoid rushing into financial evaluation before *all* the feasible strategies have been assembled

On the other hand, leveraging the existing brand (extension) is between five and ten times cheaper than launching a new brand. An analysis of 130 US consumer companies between 1993 and 1997 showed that the more leveraged brands generated, on average, 5 per cent more return than less leveraged counterparts.[23] One sophisticated approach to brand extension is described for DuPont (*see box*).

DuPont

DuPont, the inventors of numerous ingredient technologies such as Teflon®, Lycra®, StainMaster®, Corian®, Kevlar® and CoolMax®, was interested in entering a number of new product markets. They had identified four of their brands as the ones most suitable for use in these new markets. In order to inform the final strategy decision, DuPont engaged BrandEconomics to provide an assessment of the potential for each of the four brands to compete in the six markets, and to evaluate the economic potential for each brand/market combination.

The BrandEconomics approach involved answering two important questions about each brand/market combination: 'Does this brand have what it takes to compete – and stand out – in this market?' and 'How much value can be realized?'

▶

Based on research with 5000 consumers, the image profile of each of the four DuPont brands was analyzed for 48 image attributes and compared with the profile required to succeed in the six product markets. The image attributes were drawn from already successful players in those markets. Each of the DuPont brands was assessed in terms of its 'ability to play' (does the brand have the threshold attributes necessary to compete?) and its 'ability to stand out' (does the brand have the ability to achieve a differentiated position?) in each market. These dimensions were then combined into a success probability for each brand within the competitive context of each market.

In parallel, a financial analysis of the six product markets provided operating margins, capital intensity and growth prospects. This profile was based on in-depth analysis of the financial statements of companies operating in each of the product markets.

Combining the brand and financial analyses identified which of the four DuPont brands was best able to exploit the opportunity in each of the six product markets. The brand with the highest probability of success in a given market was not always the brand that was likely to generate the highest financial return. This combination of understanding the closeness of the 'fit' of each brand within each of the product markets and the level of market value added (MVA) per dollar of sales allowed DuPont to make an informed choice about which markets to target and with which brand.

The previous evaluation process relied on consumer perceptions (derived from a limited number of focus groups) and sales growth opportunity. Equipping brand managers with the quantitative information and framework for assessing the likely value impact of a particular brand extension has enhanced the dialogue between the strategic planning, finance and marketing functions at DuPont, and considerably simplified the strategic review process.

Source: Jonathan Knowles, BrandEconomics, 27 September 2002

Paradoxical as it may seem, shareholder value is best served by not giving it too much attention. In essence, marketing maximizes shareholder value through first attending to the aspirations and needs of customers and employees. This difficult three-way balancing act is not helped by worrying, at least at this stage, about other stakeholders such as suppliers and the wider community so we will defer their consideration until Chapter 8.

So the advice is regularly to compare brand equity metrics with shareholder value analysis and to see the extent to which previous brand equity metrics predict current changes in shareholder value, and the extent to which shareholder value predictions were accurate. Once a year is enough for this type of comparison. Where both forms of prediction are accurate, then obviously it does not much matter which is used. Differences are more interesting. If shareholder value predictions are proving more reliable, the finance enthusiasts will claim victory but they would be wrong. We are looking at something more serious: the firm's business model is false. Their own selection of market metrics is giving them misleading readings. Where shareholder value differs from brand equity analysis, then either the brand equity is right or the metrics need to be changed. In neither case should shareholder value analysis be preferred; it is merely a check on the firm's most valuable asset.

Executive minutes

1 Exec to develop shared understanding of the dangers and best practice in applying financial analysis to marketing.

2 Exec to determine the extent to which segmentation will improve effectiveness and efficiency of marketing programmes.

3 Brand valuations and CLVs to be tested to establish whether they provide reliable market metrics. If not, is the analysis process useful?

4 If the company is relying on loyalty or retention programmes based on the Reichheld claims, take a closer look at the real data.

5 If CLV thinking has been applied to the CRM system, then the Exec should review metrics covering customer satisfaction and whether it adds value for them.

6 Shareholder value analysis to be used for comparing the best strategic alternatives.

7 Shareholder value analysis and brand equity metrics to be recorded annually and then compared in the light of later cash flow. Selection of brand equity metrics to be revised if they perform poorly.

Notes

1 See, for example, Barth, M.E., Clement, M., Foster, G. and Kaszkik, R. (1998) 'Brand values and capital market valuation', *Review of Accounting Studies*, 3, 41–68, although in this case the brand valuation was short-term profit times a multiple.

2 Interview with Ian Hannah, June 2002.

3 Ambler, T. and Barwise, P. (1998) 'The trouble with brand valuation', *Journal of Brand Management*, 5, 367–77.

4 Reichheld, F. (1996) *The Loyalty Effect: The Hidden Force behind Growth, Profits, and Lasting Value*, Boston MA: Harvard Business School Press.

5 Doyle, P. (2000) *Value-Based Marketing*, New York: Wiley, p. 80.

6 Reichheld, F. (1996) *The Loyalty Effect: The Hidden Force behind Growth, Profits, and Lasting Value*, Boston MA: Harvard Business School Press.

7 East, R. Lomax, W. and Freeman, E. (2002) 'Lip service: variables associated with recommendation', *Proceedings of the Academy of Marketing*, Nottingham, UK, July.

8 East, R., Lomax, W. and Narain, R. (2001) 'Customer tenure, recommendation and switching', *Journal of Consumer Satisfaction, Dissatisfaction and Complaining Behavior*, 14, 46–54.

9 Reinartz, W. and Kumar, V. (2002) 'The mismanagement of customer loyalty', *Harvard Business Review*, July, 86–94. The quote is from p.86.

10 Reinartz, W. and Kumar, V. (2002) 'The mismanagement of customer loyalty', *Harvard Business Review*, July, 86–94. The quote is from p.86.

11 Doyle, P. (2000) *Value-Based Marketing*, New York: Wiley, p. 80.

12 Rust, R. T., Zeithaml, V. A. and Lemon, K. N. (2000) *Driving Customer Equity: How Customer Lifetime Value is Reshaping Corporate Strategy*, New York: Free Press.

13 Rappaport, A. (1998) *Creating Shareholder Value*, New York: Free Press.

14 Doyle, P. (2000) *Value-Based Marketing*, New York: Wiley, p. 80.

15 See Day, G. S. (1990) *Market Driven Strategy*, New York: Free Press, Chapter 13, for a similar analysis.

16 Ambler, T. (1996) 'Brand development versus new product development: towards a process model of extension decisions', *Marketing Intelligence and Planning*, 14(7), 10–19 (republished in *Journal of Product and Brand Management*, 6 (1) 1997, 13–26).

17 Keynes, J. M. (1936) *The General Theory of Employment, Interest and Money*, London: Macmillan, 161.

18 Matthews, R. (1991) 'Animal spirits', in J. G. Tulip Meeks, (ed.), *Thoughtful Economic Man*, Cambridge: Cambridge University Press, 103–25.

19 Collins, J. C. and Porras, J. I. (1994) *Built to Last*, London: Century, Myth 8, 9.

20 Nam et ipsa scientia potestas est. *Religious Meditations*. Of Heresies.

21 Ehrenberg, A. and Kennedy, R. (2001) 'There is no brand segmentation', *Marketing Research*, 13, 4–7.

22 Day, G. S. (1990) *Market Driven Strategy*, New York: Free Press.

23 Court, David C. *et al* (1999) 'Brand Leverage', The *Mckinsey Quarterly*, 2, 110–10.

4

Metrics evolution
How did we get where we are?

SO FAR WE HAVE LOOKED AT WHY firms should assess their marketing performance at the highest level. We have assessed the central role of brand equity, some financial fallacies and have considered how to go about selecting the right metrics. Now we take a more detailed look at the process of performance assessment itself. As with other company processes, it does not spring, ready formed, from some consultant's drawing board, but evolves slowly, often painfully. This chapter should help position your company on the evolutionary scale, and how best to move along it.

Darwin never claimed the 'survival of the fittest',[1] only that a species progressively adapts to its environment. While firms that fail to adapt also die out, or are eaten by more successful competitors,[2] companies can choose their own destiny. We call the conscious study of market signals and their response to them 'market orientation'. Some, such as the producers of Doc Marten boots, can be very successful without any market orientation; the public discovers them and likes what they find. But generally it pays to be market oriented because adaptation can then be managed. Lucky lightning rarely strikes twice.

In particular, firms can choose to develop what they already have (exploitation) or to develop new products and skills (exploration) or do both. Exploration may seem to compete with exploitation for scarce resources. If your company is doing well enough with what you have, why risk that by gambling on new opportunities? Professors Kyriakopoulos and Moorman found that companies with strong market orientation can do both; the strategies turn out to be complementary for those strongly focused on the customer.[3] Companies with weak market orientation, however, tend to fail if they attempt both. So there is an argument for ensuring that metrics are used as part of developing stronger market orientation. This chapter covers the following key points (see also Figure 4.1):

◆ The five stages of marketing performance assessment.

◆ Selecting the business units for marketing performance assessment.

◆ Frequency of assessment.

◆ Alignment of goals, brand market segments and metrics.

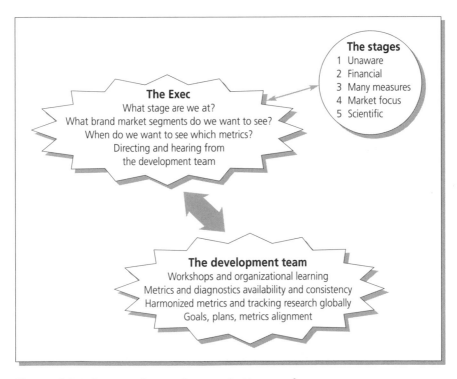

Figure 4.1 ◆ Stages of assessing marketing performance

The five stages of marketing performance assessment

We found that most companies develop their thinking about overall marketing assessment, and specifically the marketing asset, in five stages:[4]

1   The company is unaware of the issue. Marketing is not seen as something requiring the formal attention of the Exec.

2   Assessment is seen in terms of financial evaluation. Commercial matters for Exec attention need to be expressed as money. The Exec will review marketing, but only in terms of profit and loss account and cash flow, and perhaps brand valuation.

3   Financial measures are recognized as inadequate and a multitude of non-financial measures come into use. A diversity of measures exists in different departments. This is not the Tower of Babel but confusion muddles through.

4   The company develops market focus. Management streamlines the variety of financial and non-financial metrics to give a single coherent view of the market using the metrics it regards as most important. Standardization and improved clarity help communication but whether these are the 'right' metrics remains uncertain.

5   A scientific method of assessment is adopted. The database of past and current metrics, derivatives and diagnostics is mathematically analyzed to provide the shortest list of sensitive and predictive metrics.

This quest is not easy as a leading marketer, Duracell, can testify (*see box*).

Duracell

The company was acquired by Gillette in 1996, which led to centralized marketing activities for Europe. The Gillette brands encompass Oral B, Braun, Duracell and Gillette itself. Duracell is the leader in the UK battery market with over half of the value share of the UK alkaline market.

Marketing activities by the business unit (i.e. the brand) are geared fundamentally to develop and market the best products in each category. The assessment of the success of marketing activity is difficult to measure as many activities are undertaken in unison e.g. advertising, PR, promo-

▶

tional activity and display initiatives, all of which contribute to building an 'equity' associated with the brand.

Innovation is a key word in determining and indeed driving long-term brand stability and equity. Through innovation, long-term financial success will be generated whilst meeting the needs of both the consumer and the trade partners.

Source: George Allan, Business Unit Director, 20 August 2002

While short-cuts are tempting, leaping evolutionary stages compromises organizational learning. Pan-company marketing, by definition, concerns everyone and therefore everyone, not just the Exec, should understand what marketing is supposed to be achieving and whether it is doing so. When the UK building society Bradford and Bingley moved from the financial stage to making the customer central, it set up a series of workshops for each business unit to define functional mission and goals, and associated critical success factors and performance measures. Managing this evolution has a number of benefits: it promotes market orientation throughout the company and signals the priorities from the very top about what will or should be measured.

Of course, in practice, this evolution is not a neat and steady progression through the five stages. Some companies, following a change of management perhaps, move back from the 'many measures' stage to that of 'financial evaluation'. Dell is a case in point (*see box*).

Dell

In 1998, Dell decided to focus on its brand equity and align brand architecture and communications. Scott Helbing, an experienced marketing executive, became VP of Global Brand Strategy. By usual standards, these new marketing disciplines were remarkably successful. Brand equity, awareness, brand knowledge and desktop purchase consideration all improved substantially and their analysis was able to show how they in turn improved the ease of sales calls and helped drive increased market share.

Even so, Dell continues to use measurable financial returns as the basic hurdle for campaign approval. Their strong direct marketing database enables this level of precision and the validation of internal measures such as intent to purchase as an indication of subsequent sales.

▶

> The alignment of messages and media has been retained in their 'New Advertising Principles' which include requirements that every ad has a 'call to action' and no ad should depend solely on a price benefit.
>
> *Source*: Marketing Leadership Council (2001) *Stewarding the Brand for Profitable Growth*, Washington DC: Corporate Executive Board, August, 20–23

Stage one: unaware of the issue

In the first stage, the idea of assessing marketing performance has simply not arisen. For most British companies, the revelation that they are marketers is like Molière's M. Jourdain discovering that he had been speaking prose for 40 years. For many others, the annual cycle of plans may be so ritualized as to attract no critical marketing review. A profitable company doing well in the market may wish to leave well alone, ignoring the possibility that their market may be changing without their noticing. This fate all but overcame the UK retailer, Marks & Spencer, in the late 1990s. 'Marketing' was not a word permitted in their top management circles until the crisis all but destroyed the company.

Among leading US and international marketers, perhaps surprisingly, 25 per cent did not routinely report marketing performance information to their Exec and 4 per cent did not know if they did.[5]

When production was the problem, companies were rightly preoccupied with supply-side issues. Today supply is far less important than securing demand. Production is mechanized and can be sourced from any part of the globe. Doc Martens moved production from the classic English footwear area in the East Midlands to China.[6] Men released from factories and agriculture and women released from their homes have increased the numbers available for service-sector employment. Certain skills are ever short but employees, as a whole, are not, and nor is supply.

Thus while costs are always important, the focus should have shifted to creating demand. Companies of all kinds are becoming more concerned with revenue growth and, more importantly, growth in profitable sectors and segments. You might think that the importance of marketing is increasingly recognized? In the UK at least, the indifference to marketing is too ingrained. Hermes, one of the largest fund managers, published its ten 'Principles' by which it would assess public companies.[7] None of these mention brands, brand equity, marketing, where cash flow comes from nor how it might be enhanced. There are some references to 'strategies' (in Principle 7) and also to markets but these deal with competitors and competitive advantage, as distinct from motivating customers. Hugh Davidson, author of *Even More Offensive Marketing*, recognizing the reluctance of firms to embrace the term 'marketing', has suggested replacing it by 'demand management'.[8]

While a number of our respondents described how their companies had emerged from this unaware stage, other reports have shown that marketing is either ignored or deplored in many companies. Marketing tops the list of expenditure most likely to be cut when times are hard.[9] In 2002, 70 per cent of US CFOs reported advertising budget cuts, compared with 51, 47 and 44 per cent for human resources, IT and general counsel.[10] In 1999, UK CFOs considered that marketing budgets were at least twice as likely to be cut as human resources, training, research and development, with IT being ten times less likely. Worryingly, the disregard for marketing had increased since the previous survey in 1996. In both surveys the sample was 100 chief finance and 100 chief marketing officers drawn from *The Times* top 1000 companies. From the same KPMG survey, only just over half the CFOs saw marketing as a necessary investment for long-term growth (see Table 4.1). Perhaps of greater concern was that only 82 per cent of marketing directors saw marketing investment as necessary.

Table 4.1 ◆ Long-term investment priorities for CFOs

'To what degree do you see the following as a necessary investment for long-term growth?'	1999 %	1996 %
Information technology	92	91
Training	86	94
Human resources	79	79
Research and development	59	73
Marketing	57	58

Our UK research with CMOs and CFOs revealed that the main market metrics were seen by only one-third of their top executive meetings – and our sample was biased to the larger, more marketing aware companies. We can say without equivocation that the great majority of British companies are at this 'unaware' stage. For a lucky few, demand and the market take care of themselves. For everyone else, market performance is the crucial determinant of success, and yet most ignore it. The similar research in Spain showed a higher level of market orientation. On the positive side, Centrica is one of the many companies that have developed rapidly from the unaware to the later stages (*see box*).

Centrica

Simon Waugh is Group Director of Marketing at Centrica, which began life as the customer-facing part of British Gas. It trades and supplies gas and electricity for both consumers and businesses, has created a financial services business, e.g. Goldfish credit cards, and has retail stores. It was engineering led and, perhaps as a result, measures 90 per cent of what it does, including marketing. It now includes the Automobile Association and has expanded internationally.

At the Centrica group level, performance is assessed using five key indicators:

1 customer satisfaction levels

2 customer retention and growth targets (market share)

3 employee satisfaction targets

4 cash flow targets

5 shareholder value (bottom line)

While many of the measures overlap, marketing uses a wider and more detailed range of measures including brand equity, brand awareness, advertising share of voice, marketing ROI and customer switching rates.

More detailed measures cover average product holding per customer, market share and competitor share, brand and individual product awareness, individual brand attribute tracking vs competitor performance, customer satisfaction over a wide range of indices vs historical and targeted performance, complaint levels vs industry levels, campaign ROI including cost per lead/sale, price differentials vs competitors, sales performance, customer call volumes, employee sales performance, customer attrition and customer gains, customer value by segment, share of advertising voice vs competitors, and marketing employee satisfaction vs group levels.

Metrics have evolved as the group has developed from retailing gas supply and a nationalized, engineering perspective. Today it is more externally focused as the company developed its competitive offering in

▶

different market sectors (energy, financial services, telco, motoring). This trend has also been driven by use of a comprehensive customer database (customer hub) which allows us to identify and target customer by value rather than volume. Measures are expected to become more detailed by customer segment as the sophistication of the database increases and analysis skills develop.

The intangible market asset is called brand equity and measured by relative customer satisfaction levels vs our competitors, customer attrition and switching levels vs our competitors, spontaneous and prompted brand awareness across a range of key indices vs our competitors, overall perceived and actual price differentials, overall brand preference/quality vs our competitors, product/service availability through our various distribution channels, market share by volume and value where available.

Source: Simon Waugh, July 2002

Stage two: financial evaluation

Difficulties in affording and setting marketing budgets typically lead to questions of return on marketing investment and/or expenditure. As well as financial returns within the period as shown by the profit and loss account, marketers and accountants may look to financial valuation of brand equity. In the Marketing Leadership Council research in the USA, cited earlier, 15 per cent of their respondents considered that they were in this financial evaluation stage.

Most large companies assessing marketing are seeking financial solutions. Their many market measures are mostly to manage the mix within the marketing budget. They are not taken together for the purpose of overall marketing assessment. A few of our senior marketing respondents expressed surprise that they should share such measures with the top executive team as a whole. In their culture, non-marketing executives were not concerned with such details.

This 'black box' approach to marketing has much to commend it on the surface. The Exec remains concerned with the financial inputs, the costs and investment, and the outputs, i.e. the bottom line, and is not concerned with what happens in between. Some respondents even went so far as to attribute their success to keeping their senior colleagues out of marketing matters.

Similarly, some group level executives told us that they see marketing as an operational matter that should be reviewed only by subsidiary company management. The top holding company should deal with strategy, including mergers and acquisitions, shareholders and overall financial issues. They should not, they believe, be concerned with customers and other local matters. This is especially true for those companies operating worldwide in many sectors with a wide range of brands. In their view, if they even began to consider individual brand market segment issues, they would never be done.

These views, while worthy, are naive. For the reasons discussed in the Executive Summary, the CEOs and their immediate colleagues should make it their business to understand the sources of revenue. That is the only reason their organization, however big, survives; marketing pays the bills for everything else. Such understanding requires more than noticing that money turns up from customers from time to time.

Multi-brand, multi-market firms do indeed face complexity in determining the market measures that matter. But one of the largest and most byzantine groups, Nestlé, provides an example of how these difficulties can be overcome (*see box*). Note that it has allowed more divisional flexibility over measurement than others, such as IBM, permit. Sector, corporate culture and product diversity all play their parts in these decisions.

Nestlé

Much of the change to Nestlé's corporate structure over the last 15 years has been driven by acquisitions such as Carnation, Buitoni, Perrier and Rowntree Mackintosh. The business now has four sector divisions – confectionery, beverages, food and ice cream. As a very successful marketer over many years, marketing is left to sector division management although the main strategic brands operate within frameworks established by the head office in Switzerland. The group has 8500 brands worldwide and the main strategic ones are reported to headquarters in Vevey in a set format. The management committee has access to these reports but otherwise metrics are not completely standardized. The main measures of business success are real internal growth and earnings before interest, tax, depreciation and amortization (EBITDA). In addition, the key marketing metrics are brand share and image.

While some see it more or less broadly, 'marketing' means what the marketing departments do. Advertising has migrated toward major strategic brands to spread the cost. Metrics have been evolving toward more consistency across divisions and increasing emphasis on the more emotional aspects of brand image, whilst keeping a critical eye on product performance in competition.

▶

The intangible market asset is called brand equity or brand health and measured by image studies and campaign tracking. Similarly, Nestlé's corporate image is also monitored on an ongoing basis.

Source: Metrics interview with David Hudson, Communications and Corporate Affairs Director, 27 November 1998, revised July 2002

The three main approaches to reducing complexity and enabling top management to come to terms with their marketing assets and how to assess them are:

◆ Reducing the sheer number of brands. Note how Procter & Gamble and Unilever have been selling off their less important brands.

◆ Putting more products under mega-brand names such as Nestlé and Pillsbury.

◆ Selecting the key brand market units that make up the bulk of shareholder value. Rationalizing down to core businesses and brands. Profits may be reduced but shareholder value is enhanced by disposal of peripheral activities.

Despite the imperative to understand markets and the dangers in taking a wholly financial perspective, the financial evaluation stage is better than being unaware and the top management now considers marketing. Senior executives are comfortable with financial measures and there is a good case for putting marketing investment on a par with capital expenditure, especially if brand equity is treated as an asset.

Of course, one can operate financial and market metrics systems in parallel, as two examples now show. Cadbury, long a top marketing and brands business, has instituted state-of-the-art financial disciplines alongside marketing measures (*see box*).

Cadbury

Working together to create brands people love is the core purpose of Cadbury Schweppes globally and Cadbury Trebor Bassett in the UK. There is nothing more important to the long-term health of Cadbury Schweppes than looking after its brands and its consumers and the group's recently reissued Purpose and Values includes for the first time

▶

express commitments to its consumers – to maintain quality standards and strive to 'delight the consumer' with product delivery; to invest consistently in building the reputation of the brands they love; and to be leaders in innovation. The group has backed these commitments by creating a Sales and Marketing Academy.

The group's governing objective is to grow shareowner value over the long term and it does this by managing for value – setting stretching objectives, making value-based decisions, creating outstanding leadership capability, sharpening the culture and aligning management rewards with the interests of shareowners. Both the objective and the methodology have been consistent whilst John Sunderland has been CEO.

The commercial strategy of Cadbury Trebor Bassett in the UK is based on the rejuvenation of existing brands and the creation of new ones. The business has invested a lot of time and effort in working out its overall brand architecture (how everything fits together) and then establishing the essence, positioning and benefits of each brand using brand pyramids. Supported by a consumer planning and research department, the consumer marketing team has been refocused on brands and consumers. Consumer insight is now at the heart of commercial decision making and consumer measures are as important as traditional financial measures when tracking the performance of the business. Market growth and market share are as important as sales and profit. IRI track rate of sale and distribution of key brands and Taylor Nelson track their penetration, frequency of purchase and average weight of purchase. Barsby Rowe track share of voice.

Source: Nick Fell, Marketing Director, Cadbury Trebor Bassett, 1 October 2002

Gallaher also treats market expenditure similarly to capital expenditure (*see box*).

Gallaher

Yann Tardif is Group Marketing Director for one of the world's leading tobacco businesses, the Gallaher Group. His remit is to oversee all brand strategies in all markets. From a strong UK and Ireland base, Gallaher has grown over the recent years through 'organic' and 'external' growth (acquisitions of Liggett Ducat in Russia and Austria Tabak in Austria). The group now operates in more than 25 countries in Europe, CIS and Asia.

▶

Success is seen as being 'sustainable profitable growth' (SPG). Top and bottom line growth are important but what matters is the long-term view of brand performance. Beyond this is a commitment to stakeholders in terms of business continuity and personal development.

All marketing decisions, i.e. pricing, investments, new products, are made within the financial discipline of a five-year brand P&L projection and the SPG model. Whilst there is always a possibility to play a 'wild card' and bet, as success can never be guaranteed, this discipline is used both absolutely and also versus other projects. The marketing function therefore undergoes the same discipline as for capital expenditure.

Brand equity or brand goodwill are seen as difficult to measure and no terminology has been developed for these concepts. However, Gallaher tracks consumer and trade through ad hoc or ongoing research programmes.

As a large international marketer, the global interactions are interesting. A small group in the centre operates only a brand development budget but with veto powers on the programmes developed by the countries. This team is tasked with developing brand essence: positioning, thematic advertising, packaging and product. It works across all geographies seeking economies of scale and consistency.

National teams manage their own budgets as part of their countries' P&L. They are tasked with brand activation: media, advertising and promotion executions, pricing, etc. Although this type of matrix could create some tensions, it promotes alignment. The general business planning cycle allows for projects and initiatives to be reviewed and agreed within the marketing function prior to being validated by top management.

Source: Yann Tardif, 9 August 2002

However, as the top management committee gains confidence in marketing assessment, it becomes time to move on. Financial metrics reveal little about the marketplace or about the source of cash flow. A black box exists between the marketing expenditure and the sales revenue. Management needs to understand what is happening in that box.

Stage three: many measures

Metrics project respondents at this stage have recognized that financial (mostly internal) measures need to be balanced by non-financial measures, including those from the marketplace. They have a plethora of marketing indicators, which are used for many different purposes. Their information systems have improved, and new market research has been added as new services have become available. In the Marketing Leadership Council research, cited earlier13 per cent of respondents fell into this many measures stage. Marketers always have a great appetite for knowledge about their markets. Brown-Forman provides an example of a large company in this many measures stage but looking to progress to a more focused approach (*see box*).

Brown-Forman

Brown-Forman is a leading producer and marketer of premium wines and spirits such as Jack Daniel's, Southern Comfort, Finlandia vodka, Fetzer Wines and many other brands. It also owns Lenox china and crystal and associated brands. Brown-Forman is most closely aligned with the consumer packaged goods business. With sales of $2.4 billion, Brown-Forman ranks among the top six global drinks companies. Jack Kennard, Senior Vice President, directs Brown-Forman's global marketing services but this case study concerns global wines and spirits.

Success is measured financially by growth in operating income and return on invested capital. Depletions growth (movement of cases from wholesale to retail) and margin trends are closely monitored on a global basis and reported as key measures of success for all brands. Notable marketplace leadership successes or rankings related to brand building such as 'leading whiskey in the world in retail value' or 'leading premium American table wine' get attention. Shares of market trends are tracked and assessed internally but share trends are not viewed as the most critical business success measures. Other indicators of business success include new product introductions, distribution partnerships and brand affiliations or partnerships.

Marketing performance assessments are focused individual brands and, where appropriate, brand families, such as the Jack Daniel's family of brands. Financial metrics very similar to those reported for operating groups and the larger business entity are maintained and closely followed for individual brands. One could say 'Each brand at Brown-Forman must stand alone as a profitable business on a fully burdened basis'. In addition, Brown-Forman monitors and assesses a range of measures of marketing performance, primarily related to consumer brand building

▶

progress. Brown-Forman has strengthened its strategic focus, expressed with four initiatives:

1 Pre-disposing consumers to purchase our brands
2 Winning at the point of purchase
3 Superb resource allocation
4 Deeply embedding a brand building culture.

Metrics which are examples of the first and second initiatives include brand awareness, brand usage, growth in consumer user base, brand attitudes and brand image as perceived by consumers both among the brand's core user group and its broader target audience. Tracking studies of consumer awareness, usage and attitudes are maintained in key countries around the world to support monitoring of brand health. Many brands, both Brown-Forman brands and competitors, are included in continuous consumer tracking. Own brands are benchmarked against competitors. Pricing trends, distribution trends, events, sponsorships and co-brand promotions are monitored.

Brown-Forman at present has too many metrics to give adequate focus. The search is underway for each brand to identify those critical few metrics which reflect both the overall health of the brand franchise and the progress of the brand against a specific five-point plan in place in any given year. The company is evolving toward identifying those metrics and then embedding into company process and culture the commitment and practice to measure and act upon the insights they provide.

Woodford Reserve bourbon is a small super-premium brand in its early development stage and seeking to increase on-premise distribution. A much larger, better established brand might be seeking to increase top of mind awareness.

Brand equity is seen as very difficult to measure simply. Currently, there is no consensus in Brown-Forman but getting to a collective leadership view is a high priority and the topic of healthy debate. Jack Kennard's view is that brand equity is increasing when three conditions are present: (a) more adults are drinking the brand; (b) those who do drink the brand are increasing their loyalty to that brand; (c) the company is making more money on the brand. In the aggregate across the corporation increases in brand equity drive increases in the company's market capitalization.

Source: Jack Kennard, email, 11 October 2002

The problem is that the copious availability of data can be overwhelming. It has been likened to sipping from a fire hydrant with its massive force of water; nor is it unknown for managers to commission new research because it would take too long to find the same information somewhere in-house. And that in-house data is not always dependable. Steve Willis, then with AXA Sun Life, recounts that, in the course of auditing IT systems for a manufacturing company, he found a monthly report used by the finance director for key decisions where the grand totals missed out the leading digit. In other words, the £ million figure was missing but the lower numbers were correct. The report had been happily used (or not used) for quite a long time. No doubt we all have similar tales.

So, as new demands and questions are raised, market research and internal measures increase faster than they are culled. Moreover, those charged with collecting information like to keep data coming, as they never know what questions will be asked next and because historical comparisons will be needed.

The variety of possible measures is almost endless. Wharton's Professor Marshall Meyer cites 117 measures in use by Skandia, the Swedish financial services firm.[11] The more the marketing effort is segmented by customer type and the more that other audiences are recognized (e.g. employees), the more measures there are likely to be. For each audience or segment one should consider both their expressed behaviours – what they do – and intermediate measures – what they know, think and feel about the brand. These can all be provided as absolute measures, or relative to the market and/or specific competitors. Then they can be supplied as graphs or charts to show comparisons over time.

In understandable reaction to surfeit, pressure grows for one single measure to summarize the many. Brand valuation is the most frequent candidate but, as we considered earlier, no single indicator or index will serve. We need to look for signs of ill health and there are many possible. Whether in reaction to an attempt to use a single measure or just because it makes sense, marketers, at this stage, assemble a variety of financial and non-financial market and internal indicators for the Exec.

A major difference between large companies and small and medium-sized enterprises (SMEs) should be noted here: as a general rule, large companies have too much data and SMEs have too little. An excessive variety of measures obscures any overview of marketing performance and the state of brand equity. Nevertheless, a top team conditioned to a multitude of measures at different times and in different contexts may well continue in that mode. Enough detailed control may give the impression that an overview is simplistic or redundant. At some point they will recognize the need for rationalization and move to a more focused assessment using the measures that truly matter.

Stage four: market focus

The drinks giant, Diageo, for example, uses only about two dozen measures in its 'Brand Health Monitor'. Traditional profit and loss indicators, such as sales and profitability, balance consumer and competitive metrics. Consumer behaviour indicators include loyalty and penetration; consumer intermediate indicators include awareness and attitudes; input measures such as advertising's share of the marketing budget and competitive measures include share of market and voice and relative price. Its main innovation in the early 1990s was the use of 'traffic lights' to indicate improving, steady and worsening performance. Thus a complex chart covering these twenty-odd indicators for many countries (columns) instantly communicated overall performance to busy top management, which reviews one page for each of their top global brands. The colour dominance of red, green or amber says it all.

Unilever has a similar system. Both companies, after some internal difficulties, have standardized the measures across brands and countries. Diageo allows some differences between its beer, spirits and wine brands but they are minor. When their monitor was first introduced, it also covered Pillsbury and Burger King. Insiders were surprised to learn that their very different businesses could be assessed with the same metrics, even if the methods of data collection were different. While 'perceived quality' is important for almost all sectors, the questions asked to determine quality would vary, e.g. across car services, hairdressing and fast food outlets.

The presentation of this refined set of metrics is often known as the 'dashboard' to help drive the business. In the Marketing Leadership Council research 35 per cent of their respondents claimed to be at this stage and another 14 per cent intended to introduce them. Interestingly they reported relatively few metrics, an average of just over eight, although they considered they should have 25 per cent more. That still looks low as, in my experience, large companies need closer to 20.

Companies adopt both formal and informal processes to get from 'many' to market-focused metrics. Some gather senior marketers from different sectors and countries to trade their experiences of the various indicators and discuss how useful they are. This debate can be a marketing education in itself. Some form of external moderation is usually required. In practice, rationalizing metrics is more difficult than it may appear; marketers hold tightly to familiar indicators for reasons good and bad. A good reason, perhaps the best, is to maintain comparable trend data.

For multinational companies, the decision to move from many measures to a more focused approach may be driven by corporate style. Multi-locals like Nestlé accept diversity, while those seeking globalization, like Diageo and Unilever, push for consistency. They are more likely to have strong central market research (information) departments and encouraging the learning that comes from country-to-country comparisons. These are difficult without harmonized metrics.

This, however, is limited by whether data can be purchased. Sophisticated measures are available in the US but not everywhere. Even where available, data on small brands in small countries may be too expensive. Flexibility has to be left for change and development. And determining the 'brand', or unit of measurement, see below, can be troublesome where there are complicated brand architectures.

This debate reflects a fundamental tension between those who regard each management unit as needing the freedom to develop its own marketing solution and those who regard learning across internal borders, i.e. synergies, as the main justification of being part of the larger organization. After all, if the larger formation brings no benefits, why remain part of it? The next chapter delves into just how metrics should be selected both for single unit businesses and more complex organizations. Meanwhile we only need to recognize that firms do progress, somehow, from the disorder of a multitude of metrics to a focused and deliberately chosen smaller set.

All these pragmatic factors will determine the number of metrics suitable for each company. As a rule, larger companies can handle more, say 20, metrics because they have more to draw on, whereas SMEs may need only five or six. Progressive though this stage is, the metrics may not provide accurate market understanding.

Stage five: scientific

Top marketing companies aspire to being able to measure each part of their business model. In an ideal world, one should be able to track the competitive effects of marketing on consumer mindsets, and those in turn on consumer behaviour and then shareholder value. The metrics would form a database with subsidiary diagnostics to examine variances. Past history would allow projections to alternative scenarios so the long-term shareholder value optimizing plan could be determined and form the basis for subsequent performance assessment. If only.

In the US Marketing Leadership Council research, 8 per cent claimed to have reached this ultimate 'scientific' stage. Looking more closely at the data, they may be optimistic. Kraft, part of General Foods, has come close in the USA, but not internationally, and brand equity, or the marketing asset concept, had not yet entered their framework by 2001. Problems include ever-changing organizational structures, the diversity of markets, or managers' perceptions of those markets, and technical: few companies have a comprehensive database for all types of metrics, product groups and countries with comparable data over many years. The vast General Motors only began to harmonize its market metrics around the globe in the new millennium.

Where a comprehensive metrics and diagnostics comparable database is available, the candidate measures can be subjected to quantitative analysis, to determine which were best for predicting current performance. The fact that certain past metrics predicted today's performance is not, of course, a guarantee that today's metrics will predict tomorrow's – but it helps. The resulting pool of metrics should be widened to allow for this uncertainty. From this widened pool, the best-performing metrics can be presented to top management. In other words, the database needs to hold a broader selection of measures than are used at any single point of time to allow evolution.

Continuous modelling can also be seen as developing an expert system. Results are compared with predictions and the model parameters adapted progressively. No computer system can predict discontinuous changes and those are precisely the ones that matter most. On the other hand they can identify discontinuous change more quickly (as unexplained variance) and they can systematize marketing performance assessment to improve managerial learning.

None of our UK respondents claimed to have reached this final stage. The modelling tools exist and specialist services, such as Novaction,[12] provide both databases and techniques for forecasting. Perhaps those using these techniques for overall Exec-level reporting are keeping quiet for competitive commercial reasons. What does, of course, routinely exist is the use of such models for testing variations of marketing mix (communications, packaging, pricing, product enhancement and promotion). A small amount of empirical data can be enhanced to provide reliable estimates of national demand. These, however, are different applications from overall marketing performance assessment. Perhaps, for the wider remit, organizations just do not stay still long enough for the scientific calipers to be applied.

Nevertheless, if the Exec wishes to maximize marketing learning and control, it would be right to strive for the ideal and it should apply pressure to move the evolution of metrics to the scientific stage.

Selecting the business units for marketing performance assessment

Skip this section if your concern is with a small business where the unit of analysis is the company itself. The issue here is how large companies, and especially multinationals, should select marketing units for performance review. Adding everything together gives top management an overview but loses too much information. The resulting picture is simple but also misleading.

Where one brand name spans many product types, the unit will usually be the brand–product combination, e.g. Boeing 777, but this can vary by country. In large organizations, the business unit for assessing marketing performance is usually a single brand in a single market (country). For example, Sony video recorders in Brazil would be a single brand market unit. The Sony Walkman in Brazil and Sony video recorders in Mexico are two further units.

Lloyds TSB

Lloyds TSB is one of the leading UK retail banks. The dominant measure of success is shareholder value, but market share, customer satisfaction and pricing information by business unit are also reported to top management. Market share is mostly volume based as value is difficult to measure in this sector but efforts are going in that direction. Customer satisfaction is reported as a composite index established in early 2000 that is the sum of all customers' dealings with all parts of the organization. The diagnostics also help Lloyds TSB to identify separate areas of service satisfaction from a customer-centric view. Customer satisfaction is also compared with close competitors such as Barclays and NatWest as well as Halifax, Abbey National and niche players like First Direct.

Following the Sears lead, the company has linked staff satisfaction with profitability. Connecting all the metrics together gives a holistic picture and allows the company to understand knock-on effects.

▶

Econometric modelling is now assisting in this understanding.

'Marketing' means what the specialist function does and other departments, e.g. service quality report some of the market metrics to top management. Although the variety of metrics is small, the provision of marketing information to top management is extensive since they are reported for each of the product markets. Marketing assessment is at the 'financial' stage of evolution but parts of the organization are moving to the next stage.

Brand equity, called reputation, is tracked with four weekly brand image perceptions but it is not regularly valued.

Source: Interview with Chris Strange, Senior Manager Market Research, Lloyds TSB, 30 October 2002

The difficulty is exemplified by Nestlé with its 8500 brands in 200 world markets. Clearly these 1.7 million brand market units could not be monitored at the highest level. In practice multinationals manage by identifying the relatively few brand market units that make up most of the profit. By and large, 20 per cent of the brand market units do make up 80 per cent of shareholder value. In the case of Unilever in 1999, 50 brands, 3 per cent of its then portfolio, accounted for 63 per cent of its revenues.[13] By tracking top brand market units as well as group totals, large multinationals can stay close to their sources of cash flow.

Sometimes even the brand market unit is too much of an aggregation. A company which formally segments its consumer base may also require that information to be presented at Exec level. For example, Maybelline is a beauty product sold by L'Oréal which markets many beauty brands globally. Maybelline in Taiwan would be a single brand market unit if all its end users were in the same segment (young females). However, if Maybelline were marketed separately to younger and older female users, perhaps with different products under the same brand, each would be a separate unit.

In practice, reporting separate segment metrics is very rare for multinationals but is much more likely for large single country companies such as Lloyds TSB (*box above*). The UK mail-order firm Argos takes all customers together but publisher EMAP segments customers by 'attitude (streetwise, into cars, anti-establishment, inward/outward focused, attitude to subject matter) and (less importantly) age and social class'.[14]

Royal Mail has a database with 1.2 million business customer records. For their direct mail activities they can segment their markets by revenue and type of revenue, customer loyalty, sector, seniority of customer contact and many other dimensions. But what they can do, what they should do for mid-level marketing and what should be presented to top management are three different issues.

Can we get some general rules here? I think we can. The logic flows from the simple fact that pieces of paper and electronic screens are two-dimensional. A list of metrics takes up one dimension and that leaves another for brands, or countries, or consumer segments, or time – but not all four. A single brand company does not need the brand dimension, nor does a single market business need countries. If top management wants to see trend lines, then they will need as many pages as segments if segments are important. We will consider tricks of the presentation trade later, i.e. ways to show both time and another dimension on the same page, but the rule emerging is that top management should determine the key dimensions for their business model and then use that to specify the main units for marketing performance assessment, aggregating the lesser units.

This does not mean that the organization should be structured in this way, nor that mid-level marketers should restrict themselves to these metrics. Clearly, they will have a similar issue to resolve at the next level down. Indeed, structural issues tend to make the selection of metrics for top management review more difficult. Executives understandably want to identify metrics with responsibility but organizational structures tend to change more quickly than metrics can. Furthermore, metrics are most useful when trends can be determined, or modelled, from years of comparable data. Thus the units for assessment need to be relatively independent of management structure, i.e. they will remain valid after the next restructure so that trends can be tracked.

Frequency of assessment

The frequency of assessment is similarly a pragmatic matter. One can argue that any executive meeting that makes marketing decisions, such as rebudgeting, should see the market metrics alongside the financials. We saw earlier how Bradford and Bingley track customer defection and retention rates monthly. Supermarket firms track market metrics weekly.

The danger with that is that brand equity can be tracked too frequently. Brand equity is a delicate plant which grows slowly; tearing it up regularly to examine its roots may not give any impression of change and may even damage the plant. Those concerned with measuring advertising effects, for example, have long argued about whether there can be long-term effects if there are no short-term effects. It is obvious that if the brain has not registered the effect then there is no effect, but the issue is more subtle. Omnicom's chief guru, Paul Feldwick, has made a neat analogy.[15] After each visit to the gym, he was conscious of some negative effects (pain and cost) but no benefits. The benefits only emerged from repetition over time. So it can be with advertising: repetition is crucial and even though the effects are too small to be measurable in the short term, they can be radical if the advertising is given time to develop.

The main review of marketing metrics should probably be twice a year. Too much routine destroys fresh insight and half-yearly can fit with beginning and finalizing the annual planning round. Year-to-year consistency, in terms of both which indicators are used and how they are compared, is important since it is the change, not the snapshot, that is important. For the same reason, indicators should not reflect only the current strategy, which changes periodically, but

> The strength of metrics usage flows from their alignment with strategy and goals across the whole firm

rather a representative range of strategies for all seasons. Because metrics need trends, they adjust to new strategy more slowly than a supertanker changes course.

Alignment of goals, brand market segments and metrics

In theory, metrics should emerge from the company's business model: they identify progress towards corporate goals. Metrics should flow from strategy. In practice, business models and strategies are rarely that explicit. You probably stand a better chance of identifying strategy from the measures that the CEO considers important than from the last strategy document. Orientation can certainly be determined from the questions asked on a visit to a new business unit.

The strength of metrics usage flows from their alignment with strategy and goals across the whole firm. Accordingly, the same metrics should operate across what Shell call the 'line of sight' up, down and across the organization. I am not suggesting that market metrics, whether financial or non-financial, are the only measures that matter; only that consistency is crucial to their effectiveness. And so is simplicity. I have suggested earlier that any organization so big that the top management do not understand where the money is coming from, is too big. It should be broken up or the tail chopped off. When Unilever discovered in 1999, as noted above, that 63 per cent of its revenue came from 3 per cent of its brands, it reduced its brand portfolio and focused on the core brands.

Following a similar line of thought, strategic performance measurement (SPM), as a route to improved business results, is a key issue for chief executives, according to a 1999 study carried out by the Conference Board, the global business research organization.[16] It is based on advice and feedback from A T Kearney, chief financial officers, corporate strategists, a survey of 113 companies and a review of current business literature. Companies in the study include Siemens, Caterpillar, Dow Chemical and National Power (*see box*).

The Conference Board findings

◆ Of the companies responding 77 per cent said that strategic performance management (SPM) is very important to the chief executive officer (CEO) and in half the companies the CEO leads the process.

◆ Companies whose share price outperforms that of their competitors are likely to have a formal SPM system. While the SPM system may be characterized primarily as either value-based management or Balanced Scorecard in origin, there is no statistically significant difference between them. Many companies attempt to integrate these two systems.

◆ Companies whose share price outperforms that of their competitors are likely to use an SPM system to communicate feedback about SPM targets to division and senior managers as well as to the Exec. SPM systems can gauge progress on strategic goals, which is a major advantage to management, and can also assist the Exec in making difficult divestment or restructuring decisions.

◆ In addition, companies whose share price outperforms that of their competitors are discussing SPM targets with investors and analysts; thereby opening a new channel of communication with those professionals who value strategic information highly.

▶

◆ Over the next three years, the majority of companies expects to publish SPM targets and results in their annual reports. Additionally, over the next three years, the most frequently cited financial SPMs will be cash flow, return on capital employed and economic profit. The most frequently cited non-financial SPMs are customer satisfaction, market share and new product development.

◆ An overwhelming majority of companies will link their SPM system to business unit strategy plans and incentive compensation over the next three years. The majority of companies are aligning performance measurements down to the business unit level and linking them with incentive compensation targets.

However, the study finds some major challenges facing companies trying to implement these systems. First, the systems are not viewed as 'strategic' enough and are focused on internal goals, such as tracking financial or operating activities, rather than on strategic goals.

Second, translating the vision and strategic objectives down to performance measures relevant to activities at the business unit level is proving difficult, as is getting 'buy-in' from business unit managers and employees.

Third, information technology capabilities are often deficient to support what the SPM systems demand. Finally, the cultural and political resistance can be strong, although only 9 per cent of responding companies consider identifying key stakeholder reasons for resisting the SPM effort.

One major problem identified by the study is the fact that although chief financial officers and corporate strategists have to rely on the skills of other professionals to develop new measures for human resources activities like employee development and performance, or marketing measures for brands and customer satisfaction, not one respondent mentioned HR or marketing professionals as participants in the development or maintenance of SPMs.

In large companies the alignment of strategy and measurement needs sustained task force activity. The whole firm needs to evolve through the stages. The task force needs to assess the workshops, costs and timetables that will be needed. Metrics need to be fully integrated with the rest of the data warehouse: they are simply the part of the iceberg visible to the board. A separate stand-alone metrics system may provide a quick fix but will surely fail as the dislocation from the main stream cuts off routine data supply.

Organizations can be profoundly affected by this process, not structurally but culturally. The adoption of a shared market orientation should change the way functions work together, the data they buy and the data they share.

The challenge to the task force is to design a programme that will move smoothly from the present stage toward the scientific, without disruption, while taking the rest of the team with them. They have asked not to be named but one of the best known and most successful consumer packaged goods companies in the world embarked on this path only in 1999. They represent best practice, but best practice is not out of reach.

Executive minutes

1 Assess the current stage of metrics evolution and the pace required to move to the next stage.

2 If immediate progress is expected, appoint a task force with clear responsibilities, objectives and timetable.

3 Exec to decide primary units of analysis across brands (products), markets (countries) and customer segments.

4 Reporting units to be selected on basis of share of shareholder value. Primary units to be reported individually; secondary units to be reported in aggregate.

5 Exec to determine frequency of full metrics assessment, e.g. half-yearly, and whether brand equity is included in other market decision making.

6 Align goals, plans and measurement as closely as possible. Where they change from year to year, double-run the metrics to preserve comparative figures.

Notes

1 It was Herbert Spencer in *Principles of Biology* (1865).

2 See de Geus, A.P. (1997) *The Living Company: Growth, Learning and Longevity in Business*, London: Nicholas Brealey.

3 Kyriakopoulos, K. and Moorman, C. (2002) '*The paradox of marketing exploitation and exploration strategies: the overlooked role of market orientation*', unpublished working paper, Fuqua School of Business, Duke University, Durham NC.

4 See for example: Clark, B. and Ambler, T. (2000) 'Marketing performance measurement: evolution of research and practice', in A. Neely (ed.) *Performance Measurement – Past, Present and Future*, Cambridge, 19–21 July, 104–111.

5 Marketing Leadership Council (2001) *Measuring Marketing Performance*, Washington DC: Corporate Executive Board, August, 13.

6 Press statement, 25 October 2002.

7 Watson, T. and Pitt-Watson, D. (2000) *The Hermes Principles*, London: Hermes Pensions Management, October.

8 Davidson, H. (1997) *Even More Offensive Marketing: An Exhilarating Action Guide to Winning in Business*, Harmondsworth: Penguin.

9 *CIA MediaLab Finance Directors Survey 2000*. Research conducted by NOP Corporate and Financial. Published by IPA in association with KPMG and the Financial Times, 14 February 2000.

10 Marketing Leadership Council (2001) *Stewarding the Brand for Profitable Growth*, Washington DC: Corporate Executive Board, December, 25.

11 Meyer, M. W. (1998) 'Measuring and managing performance: the new discipline in management', in A. D. Neely and D. B. Waggoner, (eds.) *Performance Measurement: Theory and Practice*, vol. 1, Cambridge: Judge Institute, xiv–xxi.

12 Acquired by the global market research agency, Ipsos-ASI, in 2001.

13 Marketing Leadership Council (2001) *Stewarding the Brand for Profitable Growth*, Washington DC: Corporate Executive Board, December, 179.

14 KPMG (1999) *The Role of Marketing*, KPMG Research Report, 6.

15 Feldwick, P. (2002) 'Building brand muscle', *Admap*, 37, 47–49.

16 The Conference Board (1999) *Aligning Strategic Performance Measures and Results*, no. 1261–99–RR, The Conference Board.

5

A practical methodology for choosing the right external metrics

NO MARKET RESEARCH AGENCY can provide its client with a complete, ready-packaged set of metrics and few companies design a set of metrics from scratch: they begin with what they already have and proceed incrementally. The CEO may request an ideal solution but this chapter shows why no such answer is possible off the shelf. It provides the route to selecting the right metrics for your company. Two pieces of advice from senior executives in leading companies contrasted the general approach with the tailored:

> *Keep your metrics down to the few which can be applied in every company. Don't complicate it with long lists or advise every company to choose a different set. The metrics message will not get across unless it is simple and, to make comparisons, everyone needs to use the same. Companies should be required to report these few universal metrics externally as well as using them internally.*

> *No two companies are alike. Each has its own strategy and positioning which should determine the relevant metrics. Just as positioning requires differentiation, so their metrics should differ too. Only when they know exactly what they are trying to achieve can they choose the measures that matter.*

Figure 5.1 provides an overview of this chapter. First we need to define the brand, the market and the customer segments for which we are determining the metrics. Then we explore both paths. The general approach leads us to three profit and loss accounts and six brand equity metrics. The tailored approach derives the metrics from the firm's strategy and business model. Then the two solutions can be merged and tested to decide the shortlist or dashboard, which will allow the Exec to drive the business.

The process essentially involves two stages. First we assemble all possible metrics into a long list from the general and tailored approaches. Then we find ways to reduce the variety to a shortlist of about 20 that provides the Exec of a large company with a broad enough picture of market performance. A medium-sized company probably needs about a dozen and a small business may have to settle for half of that due to the financial and administrative cost of managing the data.

Note that we are still considering overall marketing performance. Chapter 9 deals with assessing the performance of elements of the marketing mix such as advertising and promotional campaigns.

Part of the problem for a large company is excess: so many measures are used by different parts of the organization, each with its own advocates, that reducing them to the few most important is far from easy. The problem in a small company is the reverse: they are likely to have too few market metrics and will be reluctant to pay for more.

Before we get to the main framework, it is worth considering two other international surveys of metrics usage.

Insead's Professor Larréché has been developing measures of the competitive fitness of global firms. The idea is to assess the overall fundamental

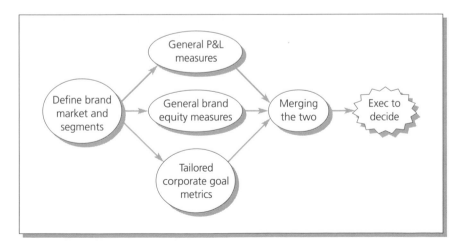

Figure 5.1 ◆ Choosing the metrics

operational capabilities in all departments: 'It is a measure of how fit a firm is to compete in the marketplace.' For the 2002 survey, 134 metrics were reduced to 12 capabilities, but for our purposes here it is interesting to review the external and internal market metrics themselves. The *box below* lists the external measures and their ranking, out of 134, in terms of the average score for the firms assessed. The implication, although the connections have not yet been statistically made, is that these metrics, in declining order of importance are the milestones on the road to success for global companies. The key internal metrics are shown in Chapter 7 and, in both cases, I have only listed the top 20 or so. The other metrics, naturally, cover other aspects of the business but it is interesting to note that 75 per cent of the top measures proved to be external and internal *marketing* metrics.

Indicators of corporate competitive fitness

Ranking	External market metric
1	Quality of products and services
4	Market effectiveness as priority
6	Delivering high quality products
8	Market segmentation strategies
18	Rationalizing product portfolio
18	Quality of company image
21	Focus on key countries
21	Present competitive position
25	Market share information available
35	Price competitiveness
35	Firm's market influence
35	Admired by others
35	Customers' needs as priority
39	Segment growth information available
39	Customer orientation by competitors
44	Customer satisfaction top priority
44	Collecting customer information
44	Complaints system
44	Balanced product portfolio
44	Past performance relative to competitors

Source: Larréché, J.-C. (2002) *The Competitive Fitness of Global Firms 2002*, London: Pearson Education; also *www.corvaltec.com/2002report/Appendices.htm*

In the second, Havas survey, nearly 700 respondents were asked about six metrics and whether they were regularly reported to the Board (or equivalent).[1]

Table 5.1 ◆ Current metrics regularly reported to the board
(per cent of those mentioning any now or planned)

Metric	Total (n=697)	USA (n=224)	Japan (n=117)	Germany (n=120)	UK (n= 120)	France (n=116)
Market share	**79**	73	57	97	80	90
Perceived product quality	**77**	77	68	84	71	75
Customer loyalty/ retention	**64**	67	56	69	58	65
Customer/segment profitability	**64**	73	40	74	65	59
Relative price	**63**	65	48	84	53	63
Actual/potential LTV[(1)]	**40**	32	35	51	32	58
Average	**64**	**64**	**51**	**77**	**60**	**68**

(1) Customer or segment lifetime value

There is significant variation by country. The results for Germany are above average for all six metrics, and especially for market share (97 per cent) and relative price (84 per cent). Those for Japan are all below the average, especially market share (57 per cent) and customer/segment profitability (40 per cent). The USA and UK are fairly close to the average – the UK a bit lower – while France is a bit high on market share (90 per cent) and customer/segment lifetime value (58 per cent).

Reporting of all six metrics was expected to increase in the near future, especially customer loyalty/retention (from 64 per cent to 72 per cent) and customer/segment lifetime value (40 per cent up to 48 per cent).

Performance, as we have seen, is the sum of the short term, as given by the profit and loss account, and the change in brand equity. For simplicity, most of this chapter assumes a single brand business in a single country (market) but then we look at multi-brand and multinational businesses.

In practice, the difficulty lies in measuring customer-based brand equity or, in other words, how the brand stands in its marketplace. Perhaps the best way to express this is how well the distributive channels and end users 'love' the brand. Love, as we all know, is a many splendoured thing but tough to pin down. When neuroscientists showed photographs of acquaintances to young people newly in love, brain scans showed little differences in the cognitive or emotional parts of their brains as between photographs of friends and loved ones. The differences appeared in quite a primitive area of the brain associated with addiction. By inference, what we think and feel about brands is not as important as our addiction to them, or lack of it. This may explain our rage when we sense that we have been spurned by a brand we have supported.

Defining the brand and customer segments

The first step in selecting metrics is to be clear about context and direction. What is the marketing aiming to achieve? This should be given by the brand positioning statement.[2] What are the distinctive or important characteristics of your brands and who are the intended audiences? Curious as it may seem, too many companies carefully define their target market and then, because the market research is packaged that way, they measure awareness

> **What matters is consistency**

and attitudes for other groups. A niche brand may be targeted to a small audience such as married women, aged 25–30, in which case the opinions of older men are little guide to marketing performance. On the other hand, the Exec may consider that performance should be judged against the whole market. Neither view is necessarily right: what matters is consistency.

Figure 5.2 shows the flows of cash in a simple marketing model. The firm invests in marketing activities with the trade customer and the consumer. Despite competitive activity, the consumer transfers cash to the trade customer who in turn pays the firm. If measuring marketing performance was just a matter of sales, we could stop there. Note that this model continues to omit environmental factors for the reasons described in Chapter 1, because they are outside the marketers' control.

Figure 5.2, reprises the model from Chapter 1 and defines what is special about the brand, its trade channels and the intended end users. This may be straightforward enough, but defining the competition and the 'market' is usually not. J&B Rare Scotch Whisky had annually increasing market shares in the USA in the 1980s despite falling sales of J&B in a static Scotch

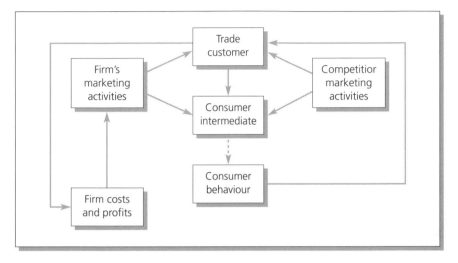

Figure 5.2 ◆ Simple marketing model

market. How was that possible? The explanation was that the local marketing team had redefined their market, first to Scotch imported in bottle, and then to premium Scotch imported in bottle.

Good arguments are always available for redefining a market. We have found some variations and lack of clarity in the way most firms defined their markets, with different departments seeing things in different ways. Some start with the competition. The main competitor to Amtrak is not other railways but the bus, the car and the airplane. But the market may not be all forms of transport on those routes if, say, car drivers and passengers are simply not prepared to switch. Research will be needed to determine the realistic alternatives to Amtrak and, together with Amtrak itself, they form Amtrak's market. In other words, the competition and the market are defined by the firms you might lose business to or get business from.

These discussions are needed before metrics are defined. The whole process loses meaning if the goalposts are moved. Accordingly, the metrics should always be accompanied by a description of what 'market' means and confirmation that it has not changed. From time to time, market definition will need to change, but then both versions should run in parallel so that comparisons are maintained until the transition is over.

Market share calculations also need care to ensure that the numerator and denominator (company's sales and total market sales) are at the same stage of distribution. In a Christmas seasonal business, for example, the peak sales into retailers will be in November but sales out to consumers will peak in December. Dividing the manufacturer's monthly sales turnover by total retail sales will therefore distort market share unless the pipeline effects are adjusted.

Many industries share data, via some neutral service, so that all firms have like-for-like comparisons. When it works well, it is cheap and effective. But not always: after 40 years of practice, the joint data collection system for the UK brewing sector still fell down.

The general approach

The idea of identifying just a few standard metrics that could be used by all companies has arisen frequently during discussions with marketers. 'It is easy,' they say. 'I could list the five key metrics now.' We invited them to do that and, you guessed it, merging their shortlists produced quite a long one.

In reality, large companies such as IBM have an almost continuous debate about the appropriateness of the various metrics (*see box*). Nevertheless, we found consistent themes. Firms look first to profit and loss account financial metrics such as sales, profit and the amount they spend on advertising and promotion. Apart from market share, most of their metrics are absolute (their own figures) and not expressed relative to the competition, e.g. relative price. Depending on their stage of metrics evolution, these financials are balanced by market measures of which one of the most popular is now customer satisfaction.

IBM's marketing transformation

As the world's largest information technology company (with global revenues in 2001 of $85.9 billion), IBM creates, develops and manufactures advanced information technologies, including computer systems, software, networking systems, storage devices and microelectronics. IBM translates these technologies into value for customers through their professional solutions and services businesses worldwide.

Rated as the ninth largest company in the Fortune 500, IBM is the world's largest vendor of computer hardware and is the number one IT services company. About 70 per cent of all the corporate data in the

▶

world is managed by IBM software, and IBM is the world leader in the provision and own use of internet technology and services. In 2001, IBM generated $27 billion revenue through ibm.com and saved $400 million in paperwork associated with procurement alone.

Having been the undisputed leader of the IT industry for several decades up to the 1980s, IBM lost that position in the early 1990s when business and technology analysts forecast the imminent demise of the company before a host of new, agile competitors. But the astonishing transformation of IBM and its re-establishment of leadership in the mid-late 1990s has become a case study in corporate reinvention. A major reason for this 'reinvention' has been the cultural shift of IBM from a product- and sales-oriented company to a market-oriented company.

While IBM's entire business, from organizational and management systems to internal business processes and external 'routes to market', has been reconstructed from a multinational model to a global model, no part of IBM has been more dramatically changed than marketing. Today, marketing in IBM is core and Abby Kohnstamm, Senior Vice-President of Marketing, is a powerful member of the corporate executive team. Under her leadership, the IBM brand has been re-established as one of the world's most recognized and valuable brands. From being a collection of largely autonomous and disparate units, marketing is now a centrally managed global operation, utilizing computer-based techniques covering all elements of the marketing management process, from market analysis and market segmentation, right through to execution and control of integrated marketing communications. Market information, campaign measurement and marketing effectiveness are tracked against standardized metrics and shared instantaneously over the internet.

IBM is a leader in the application of technology to marketing and use of electronic customer relationship management (eCRM), business intelligence and database analytics. It is from these pivotal marketing information sources that IBM can evaluate marketing effectiveness. Taking the IBM brand as a case in point, IBM is able to quantify brand equity – often the most difficult of business measures – highlighting the awareness, reputation and preference of the IBM brand. IBM also uses widely accepted studies, such as those by Interbrand, to measure progress. eCRM helps IBM continually to manage customer relationships and monitor issues, enabling IBM effectively to eradicate these issues and reduce the potential gap of expectation versus customer experience.

Source: Rob Smith, Marketing Consultant, IBM, August 2002

Customer satisfaction has not only become one of the most popular metrics but also complex. Few sophisticated companies now just ask customers, on a scale of one to five, how satisfied they are. 3M, for example, computes satisfaction from 18 subsidiary measures.[3]

In essence, the general approach has two components: financial indicators from the profit and loss account and the adjustment for changes in brand equity. The financials are fairly obvious but there are some nuances most firms miss.

Financial metrics

For a single brand in a single market, three financial metrics (top line, marketing investment and bottom line) give an adequate overview of marketing performance provided brand equity is unchanged. Note that 'marketing investment' is the expenditure intended to build the brand equity asset. Some companies charge other forms of expenditure such as promotional discounts or price promotions that may be important to sales but do not build brand equity; these should be reported as part of sales, as distinct from marketing, management. Strictly speaking, it is illogical to compare the investment for future sales with current sales, but that is what companies almost universally do.

Showing metrics without comparative figures is as messy as serving spaghetti without a plate: they need a basis in order to be accessible. The two main bases for comparison, apart from prior year, are the business plan and competitive performance, i.e the market. Table 5.2 shows how these three financial metrics are often used.

To the extent that prior year performance is reflected in the business plan, metrics do not need to be compared with both. Similarly, if sales value and volume move in step, both should not be needed. The 'bottom line' for marketing is also a choice. Some companies take it all the way through to shareholder

Table 5.2 ◆ Standard profit and loss account metrics

Actual metric	% compared with plan and/or prior year	% compared with competition
Sales	Volume/value	Market share
Marketing investment	Period costs	Share of voice
Bottom line	e.g. economic profit	Share of profit

value, but more often firms accept 'brand contribution', i.e gross profit less marketing expenditure, as the place to stop.

But comparative figures imply that the comparisons should be fair. A chain of stores will usually adjust sales comparisons so that the same stores are compared year on year, i.e. newly acquired stores dropped from this year and disposals eliminated from last year's. All standard stuff, you may think, but we need to remember that the profit statements reviewed at the monthly Exec are not necessarily the same as those that should be used for marketing evaluation. Campbell's provides an example of P&L metrics being balanced with the marketing asset (*see box*).

We found market share to be one of the most used metrics, although

---

Campbell's Soup

Jeremy J. Fingerman is President, U.S. Soup, and responsible for Campbell's largest division, representing approximately one-third of overall company sales and one-half of its profit. Campbell's has operations throughout the world. As a longstanding world leader in its category and as a marketer, its systems are well developed.

The key measures of success are primarily sales volume and earnings. Then, looking more closely, key metrics are brand relevance, brand preference, consumer takeaway, market share, consumer satisfaction. The primary comparison is year-on-year improvement.

Although the tracking systems have changed over time, Campbell's maintain continuity for the metrics themselves. Metrics are aligned with the executive leadership team and are reported to the board of directors. The CEO reviews market metrics on a quarterly basis.

Campbell's refer to the marketing asset as 'Brand Relevance, Salience and Preference', and it is measured by top of mind brand consideration, key benefit perceptions and overall brand preference.

Source: Jeremy Fingerman, 28 October 2002

Shell, for instance, uses the share of consumer preferences brand by brand. This is more predictive than market share, but it is more an indicator of brand equity – see below.

The only part of the marketing investment that is usually compared with competition is advertising, i.e. 'share of voice'. Brand profits are rarely compared although the corporate bottom line, and especially the increase in shareholder value relative to defined peer, not necessarily competitor, companies is now used for top executive bonuses.

The frequency with which the Exec typically reviews these metrics usually decreases as one moves toward the bottom line: sales may be reviewed weekly, daily or even hourly if management is seriously paranoid, but expenses are usually monthly and a full shareholder value analysis may be quarterly. Brand equity information, however, may not be available more than twice a year because of the difficulty and cost of collection. Furthermore, marketing, i.e changing brand equity, is usually a fairly slow process. Crises aside, marketing performance should not normally be formally assessed more than twice a year. Accordingly, the Exec needs to distinguish its review of these financials as part of its normal control of the business from its less frequent but deeper assessment of marketing. In other words, informal marketing checks, such as listening to customers or monitoring sales figures, are rarely misplaced, but that should not be confused with a complete market review.

> Crises aside, marketing performance should not normally be formally assessed more than twice a year

Brand equity metrics

Having established the three conventional financial metrics, we now need to monitor changes in brand equity. Of the two groups of customers in Figure 5.2 (trade and end users) most market-oriented firms focus on the final consumers. Which is the more important is a matter of experience rather than ideology, but we will side with the majority here. Of course, retailers of goods and services have no intermediate customers although they usually do have branch managers who should be treated as quasi-trade customers. In other words, almost all large firms have these two levels to be concerned with and one has primacy.

Returning to marketing as the sourcing and harvesting of inward cash flow raises some basic questions:

◆ Are potential customers aware of this brand?

◆ What proportion of the intended market has bought the brand?

◆ How do they rate the brand's quality?

◆ How satisfied are they with their experience of the brand?

◆ Do they have the brand habit, i.e are they loyal?

◆ How easy is it to locate the brand?

Awareness is the first stepping-stone for a new brand; it is a necessary but insufficient stage to developing brand equity. Being aware of something does not make you want to do it. Second we need to know how many of the targeted customers have tried the brand at least once.

The next three questions are based on the three basic components of how our minds work: thinking, feeling and habits. The academic jargon calls them cognitive (strictly, 'knowing' but knowing and thinking are treated as one), affective and conative. Confirmed, perhaps surprisingly, by modern neuroscience, this three-way analysis goes back to Plato and Aristotle.[4]

Finally we need to check availability. If the brand is not in distribution, none of the other factors will add up to much.

These questions are almost universal and stem from marketing being seen as the begetter of cash flow. We need to understand how many end users there are, and the extent to which they will buy more, and more often and pay more. We can turn to how the answers can be quantified a little later but first we review how Accenture established its metrics (*see box*).

Accenture

On 1 January 2001 the Accenture brand was launched across 46 countries, in one of the largest scale and most successful rebranding exercises undertaken anywhere in recent years. Their brand measurement techniques were further enhanced and the proprietary survey from which brand data is sourced was conducted three times in the first year as Accenture so that progress could be monitored very closely. The Marketing & Communications (M&C) team found that by June 2002 unaided awareness on a global basis had reached 83 per cent of their former name awareness levels at their peak. In their main markets including the USA and UK, they had equalled or exceeded these levels.

In addition, Accenture's most recent brand equity score (a composite calculation based on attributes including image, awareness, consideration and preference) exceeds that of its former name, over just the relatively brief period of its existence. One-and-a-half-year-old Accenture is now fifty-third in the Interbrand/ Business Week's Global Brands Top 100 league.

▶

Metrics are embedded throughout the M&C group, both strategic and the operational. Strategic effectiveness is measured via a marketing scorecard at the global and country level. This not only includes brand and image metrics, but also takes in media relations, market development, relationship building and website measurement, amongst other areas salient to the sector. As well as this overview, each marketing programme is entered onto an online planning database and performance targets set at the programme level, reviewed each quarter. The scorecard is used within the marketing group and with the company's management committee.

From an operational viewpoint, Accenture has just completed a major restructuring programme within its M&C function, moving to a shared services model for the delivery of all marketing programmes across the world. The 'Marketing Services' group will be measured via a select number of key operational metrics on a monthly basis to ensure that it is realizing the efficiency targets it has been designed to achieve. These operational metrics include customer satisfaction, supplier discount targets and utilization, as well as the efficiency of specific new marketing processes, so they may be adapted and streamlined over time.

Accenture believes its marketing metrics architecture, tied directly to the company's business goals, will help demonstrate marketing success and 'Marketing ROI' in the tangible, quantifiable way which a consultancy culture understands and looks for.

Source: Sarah McMahon, Director of Marketing Strategy and Planning, Accenture, August 2002

The six questions above are closely related to the layout of the typical positioning statement: defining the product benefit, the target market, competitive advantage and distribution strategy. The concepts are more important than exactly how each metric can be extracted from the market, i.e the precise question that needs to be asked. The way each concept is quantified will vary according to sector and data availability. Let us examine these six and then consider some other candidates:

◆ Awareness

◆ Penetration

◆ What they think of the brand

◆ What they feel about the brand

◆ Brand loyalty

◆ Availability

Awareness

Among the US and international marketing companies polled by the Marketing Leadership Council, brand awareness proved to be one of the top two metrics when each was asked to name their top five.[5] The variety among those top fives confirmed the earlier observation of very little consistency over all.

Awareness is the most used marketing measure reported in our UK research at 78 per cent, but it appears on only 28 per cent of top Exec tables, and only 28 per cent of our respondents rated it as a very important measure. Research by Young and Rubicam shows that awareness is a vital indicator for new brands but, as they mature, awareness signifies little. Furthermore, it is implied by satisfaction/preference, since if one is not aware of it, one is unlikely to be satisfied by it. That, however, does not reduce the role of awareness as a diagnostic within satisfaction analysis.

Accordingly it was dropped from the general list in the first edition of this book on the grounds that it fell into the special case, rather than universal category. Since then, our brain scanning research with colleagues at the Open University revealed that salience, the term we gave to relative awareness, or rather familiarity, appeared to play a major role in the purchase decision.[6] To summarize this part of the research briefly, respondents provided familiarity figures for 270 supermarket products on a five-point scale. They then made a virtual shopping trip where they were presented with 90 triplets of competing products and asked to choose one or none just as they would normally. We took brain images throughout the video visit including these 90 decision points.

The brand's salience was quantified as its familiarity less half the sum of the familiarity of the other two brands in the triplet. In other words, if our brand scored an familiarity level of 4, and the other brands 3 and 1, the 'salience' of our brand is 2. We found that the right parietal cortex (a technical description of this is 'above the back of the right ear and in a bit') was activated in high salience conditions but not otherwise. Further the high salience brands were typically selected from the triplet. This research is exploratory but it seems likely that high salience stimuli relate to decisions in which the outcome is strongly consistent with some form of intention based on previous experience.

Although awareness is not likely to be a driver of intention to purchase, it may work the other way about[7]: salience indicates purchase intent and can therefore be a useful metric for mature brands as well as new. Note that the recommended metric is salience, or relative familiarity, not familiarity itself. In practice, the firm would therefore need to collect familiarity data for the brand's most immediate competitors (the 'consideration set').

Penetration

At its simplest, the firm should track how many customers it has and whether that number is growing or shrinking. It should know whether increasing volume and value sales are due to a larger customer base or to more demand by the same customers. A better measure, usually known as 'penetration', is the per cent of the intended market that has bought or experienced the brand in the last 12 months. This does not tell us whether they have bought again (repeat purchasers may be a more useful metric) but at least we know we have reached them.

Perhaps surprisingly, tracking penetration or the numbers of customers did not rate highly in the Marketing Leadership Council research with a strike rate of 11 per cent against 26 per cent for awareness and 27 per cent for customer satisfaction. In the UK, 47 per cent of our respondents used penetration metrics and about the same number, presumably the same people, gave it the top rating for importance.

Now we can explore what is in their heads about the brand.

What they think of the brand

Relative perceived quality has been shown to be superior to market share as a predictor of future profits.[8] The absolute indicator, 'perceived quality' or 'esteem', is used more often than the comparative. In our UK research, 64 per cent of companies used it, 32 per cent at Exec level, and 35 per cent of respondents gave it a top billing for assessing marketing performance. As with satisfaction, both the absolute and relative metrics should be interesting to the Exec, but the competitive indicator is likely to provide a better forecast of subsequent performance. Share of preference, which, as noted above, some see as a better indicator than market share, is likely to be highly correlated with relative perceived quality and may be a suitable near-match alternative. It is worth comparing the data.

Similarly we found purchase intent, 'heads converted' and 'brand persuasion' as other ways of measuring what consumers think of the brand. All metrics of this type accumulated to 11 per cent of the top five metrics in the Marketing Leadership Council research.

What they feel about the brand

Consumer satisfaction has been one of the fastest growing metrics worldwide. In the UK, 68 per cent of companies use it, 36 per cent of their top executives see it and 46 per cent of our middle management respondents rated it as a very important measure. In the US research it was ranked top with 27 per cent. 'Brand liking' is not the same as satisfaction but probably gives a similar measure of what consumers feel about the brand.

However, doubts have been raised about its sensitivity. When surveyed, some customers claim to be satisfied and then switch to another brand. Others claim dissatisfaction and stay loyal. Empirical US research has shown that a better metric is relative satisfaction, i.e. relative to market or key competitor(s):[9] however much consumers like Brand A, they may leave if they like Brand B more.

> Consumer satisfaction has been one of the fastest growing metrics worldwide

Inertia, lack of information, lack of product experience and the cost of changing all explain why consumers stay with Brand A even though they prefer Brand B, which is why relative satisfaction is a better measure than satisfaction alone. This is particularly important for financial services, such as banks, where consumers change only with reluctance.

Brand loyalty

The third in-the-head metric is probably the most important but easier to measure by behaviour. The brand habit is indicated by loyalty that in turn can be calculated as the share of category usage the consumer gives to your brand or the probability of buying next time. Retention and churn data are similar. In-the-head measures are complicated by some agencies seeking to trademark terms like 'engagement' and 'commitment'. Relevance to the consumer, purchase intention and 'bonding', a WPP metric, are all also seen as potential indicators of commitment. Telecoms companies use churn as the negative equivalent.

As usual, the particular measures and technicalities of data collection will be determined by business sector and data availability from research suppliers. Whatever best captures the extent the consumer loves or is addicted to the brand, or has the brand habit, is the metric that matters. Brand habit metrics indicate loyalty and thus the competition is already factored in. It is not usually appropriate to use relative (to other brands) metrics.

The problem with using behavioural measures for the brand habit is that they may reflect inertia rather than commitment. Utilities have high levels of loyalty when there is no alternative. UK retail banks in particular have maintained high retention from inertia, the feeling that all banks are the same and erecting barriers to exit. Medieval knights wooed their ladies and then employed chastity belts in much the same way.

Where behavioural metrics are used for the convenience of data collection, it would be wise to check them out against in-the-head or 'intermediate' measures from time to time. Otherwise your customers may leave when someone finds the key.

In our UK research, loyalty fell into the second rank in terms of the frequency of collecting this data but was seen as the most important brand equity measure. In the USA, it was part of the second group with 11 per cent.

Availability

Since AC Nielsen set up shop in the 1930s, distribution has been a key metric for the packaged goods and grocery products business. It was measured as the total stores carrying the brand expressed as a per cent of those who could but also as weighted by the size (turnover) of those stores. Obviously being in supermarkets matters more than availability in neighbourhood shops. Neither the UK nor US respondents across all sectors, however, rated it as very important. Accountants are especially unconvinced by this measure. It is also double-edged in the sense that more is not necessarily better. The required distribution has to be part of the brand's positioning. The majority view is that availability does not belong in the general shortlist. Despite this, I have retained it as a general brand equity measure for two reasons. No other metric represents the trade's contribution to brand equity. More importantly, if the consumer cannot get access to the brand, that factor must down-weight brand equity overall. After all, the most significant Coca-Cola strategy since World War II has been putting the brand within reach of every consumer around the globe.

Increased sales and static measures of relative satisfaction, commitment and preference would imply success but may be explained by growing availability without any consumer uptake. More sophisticated distribution measures take the extent of the brand range into account. For example, if each brand has ten flavours available in three sizes, it has 30 stock-keeping units (SKUs). If 100 per cent of retail outlets handle just one flavour in one size, this is probably less attractive than 50 per cent of outlets each handling the full 30 SKUs. The arithmetic here can be complex, as it turns on the relative sales potential of each SKU in each store. Non-moving SKUs have only the negative aspects of keeping competitors off the shelf and increasing brand visibility.

Other candidate metrics

Relative price has a strong claim to be included where it can be calculated but in many sectors, e.g. financial services, that is well nigh impossible. The simplest estimate is the annual market share (value) divided by the market share (volume). That eliminates monthly distortions, such as promotions, but it depends on how reliably the market can be defined. Many firms trade in several different markets at the same time.

In UK research, relative price was one of the favourite indicators: seventh among all marketing metrics and third among non-financial metrics. It was used by 70 per cent of companies, 34 per cent at Exec level, and 37 per cent of respondents saw it as a top performance metric. In the USA, however, it barely registered in the top group.

Relative price should match perceived quality and, if all is well, should be redundant. Where, however, perceived quality and relative price are out of line – especially if quality is falling while price is rising – a major problem exists. If it has not yet hit sales revenue, it will.

Similar arguments to availability can be applied to pipeline (the number of days of stock in trade, i.e. sold by the brand owner but not yet bought by the consumer). Marlboro Friday immortalized one of the most dramatic price cuts of all time. On 2 April 1993, Philip Morris cut their leading cigarette prices in the USA by 20 per cent and the share price fell pro rata. While the relative price had been allowed to creep higher than perceived quality, the latter was the bigger problem. Philip Morris had allowed the pipeline – which they were not tracking at senior levels – to be overstocked. Tobacco has a short shelf life. The pipeline metric has, nevertheless, been excluded as not being relevant to services which today accounts for the larger share of developed countries' GDP.

General shortlist summary

Table 5.3 brings the general metrics together before we move on to the tailored approach.

The importance of consistent market definition, noted after Table 5.2, applies here too, as does the need for consistency in defining the end user segment. When metrics are presented at Exec level, the brand market segment unit of analysis should be reaffirmed and any variations treated as outlined above, i.e. both sets should be presented until the transition is complete.

Table 5.3 ◆ General brand equity metrics

Consumer metric	Measured by
Familiarity	Salience, i.e. familiarity relative to the other brands in the consideration set
Penetration	Number of customers or the number of active customers as a per cent of the intended market
What they think about the brand	Brand preference as a per cent of preference of other brands within the consideration set or intention to buy or brand knowledge
What they feel about the brand	Customer satisfaction as per cent average for the consideration set
Loyalty	This may be behavioural (share of category requirements, repeat buying, retention, churn) and/or intermediate (commitment, engagement or bonding)
Availability	Distribution, e.g. weighted percentage of retail outlets carrying the brand

Thus our six measures of brand equity must be seen as the year-on-year change in the marketing asset. This change adjusts the performance revealed by the three financial measures when compared with the internal goals for that marketing unit and competitive benchmarks. This general three plus six (financial plus brand equity) approach has drawn on universal marketing basics. Interestingly, the length of this list matches the size of dashboards in the Marketing Leadership Council findings.

The tailored approach

Now we put the general list aside and consider how to derive metrics from the firm's strategy and business model. Four sources of tailored metrics are available to a company starting from scratch. Unfortunately the process is demanding and, typically, few Execs give it that much time. In the hope of promoting a change of mind, the next section discusses why that time investment is worthwhile. The tailored approach is not, of course, essential for running a business. As we saw in the last chapter, many firms get by without any market metrics and others can take the general three plus six above or draw a quick list from some other source. If that is your preference, skip the rest of this chapter, but one day you may find yourself wondering where and when your business parted with the rest of the world.

The four sources of tailored metrics

If we can identify 'success' then the metrics we need are the milestones toward that success. One useful technique is Professors Kaplan and Norton's 'success mapping'.[10] The medium-term, say five-year, goals are agreed and quantified. The question then is what needs to precede each goal in order to achieve it. For example, if the company wants a portfolio of six successful products and can only launch one a year, then it must get to five before six, four before five, etc. By working backwards from each goal to the status quo, two products in this example, the Exec defines a success map which routes the immediate actions they need to take and the performance metrics, the milestones, they will need to have (see Figure 5.3).

In this example, the company has identified seven quantified goals. The second one is quickly achievable and only needs one step beyond next year's plan. The third goal only needs two more stages but the first one is a major challenge. The last four goals have yet to be mapped back to the present situation. Once the map is complete, the key metrics can be deduced. For example, if G4 requires higher customer retention rates, and they in turn require better customer service, then retention and customer service metrics need to be reported to the Exec.

The second starting point for tailored metrics is the firm's strategy. Obvious? It is not what happens. Now that specialist departments have

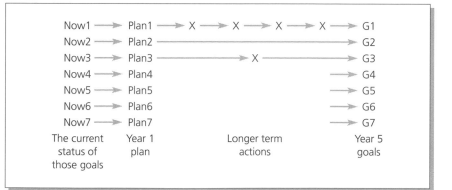

Figure 5.3 ◆ Success mapping

mostly disappeared, strategy is usually set by the Exec, plus a few directors and minders, at their annual retreat in some salubrious watering hole surrounded by a golf course or two. They return refreshed, but rarely accompanied by metrics. That is the province of financial planning, not strategy. Business school strategy professors teach executives not to shackle strategic creativity with arithmetic. The usual sample size for empirical testing is n = 1. Yes, the corporate minders do try to link the strategy with the financial plans but market metrics are rarely considered, still less included.

I should not make fun of corporate strategy making because, as Professor Henry Mintzberg has long shown, most firms' strategies are only apparent after the event.[11] Calling them 'emergent' is polite because it is hard to see how a post-hoc strategy could have been a strategy at all; it is simply the way the firm does business, or its implicit business model. A deliberate strategy requires an explicit business model.

Deriving key metrics from strategy or strategy from key metrics

This leads to the last two starting points. The firm's business model, if sufficiently explicit, should indicate the key issues and therefore what should be measured. More likely, the model is not that explicit but it can be inferred from what management considers the critical issues to measure. In other words, the process can begin from either end: the metrics considered important or the strategy itself. The Exec can share ideas and sketch out the links between what the company does (inputs) and the effects those actions have on the minds of trade customers and end users (intermediate metrics). We will come to employees in Chapter 7. Then the effects on customer behaviour can be measured and finally how those translate into the company's financial figures. Starting from the other end, the Exec can select from their experience the metrics they have found to be really important in driving the business. Pool and discuss those metrics and a picture of the firm's business model will begin to form.

If the firm's own selection of metrics needs nudging, research the metrics used by exemplar firms, whether they be immediate competitors or those similar enough to provide useful lessons. The metrics used by exemplar firms will reveal their implicit models of how shareholder value is extracted from their marketplaces. This competitive intelligence should not only refine your own firm's model but also help develop differentiation, and thus competitive advantage.

If competitor metrics cannot be discovered, then choosing from the existing popular favourites is practical but not profound. In the absence of something more radical, this good starting place should promote questions such as 'Would more be better for us?' For example, increasing awareness for a small new entrepreneur would almost certainly be primary even if the reasons for the awareness are not. The first stage is just getting known. On the other hand, many people only became aware of Monsanto as a result of the genetically modified foods scare. The increase in awareness was not only unnecessary for such a well-established firm that was already held in high regard by its target markets, but so damaging that the company considered changing its name.

Similarly, most managers regard more market share as better, but they may be wrong. More share bought at the expense of reputation, e.g. through price promotions, can damage the brand's health permanently. The French have established special skills with prestige brands, such as particular fashion items, perfumes and alcoholic beverages (e.g. cognac). Any of these brands could double their market share if they wished, but through 'vulgarization'. In other words, if the brands become too popular, they lose their cachet, and ultimately their raison d'être.

> So run the firm's strategy trolley round the metrics supermarket and see which metrics fit in

So run the firm's strategy trolley round the metrics supermarket and see which metrics fit in. That preliminary analysis should quickly inform the Exec about some incremental improvements that could be made both to strategy and to the metrics in use. The more profound question is perhaps for the Exec's next annual strategy retreat: does this match of strategy and metrics fully describe the success we are seeking? Inevitably some things will be missing and some things will need to be changed, but the point here is that the tailored approach to metrics and strategy formulation is interactive: metrics are not just an afterthought.

The application of strategic metrics

An example of the significance of determining the individual company's goals before deciding the metrics is the research study commissioned by the UK Chartered Institute of Marketing to establish the efficiency of marketing expenditure in the financial services industry.[12] Neither the firms themselves nor we could do this, not because of missing data but because the firms had different goals. Most firms were achieving the targets in their plan. This was not a zero-sum game; competitive firms were winning because they had different targets. We could judge effectiveness but not efficiency because the latter implies that short-term profit is the only goal that matters. In the UK metrics research three years later, we found that management is increasingly assigning more importance to effectiveness than efficiency.

As a further illustration of the practical impact of using tailored metrics at Exec level, consider advertising. Millions of dollars are spent on advertising by many firms without any clear idea of what they will get for their money. Setting ad budgets as an act of faith can be compared with weekend church or synagogue collections: if you can spare the money, it could be a good investment. If the firm has an explicit business model, then they should know how inputs (the various possible advertising campaigns and their costs) link to intermediate effects (in-the-head) and those in turn to changes in consumer behaviour. If the model is implicit, then the ad agency can be pressed to forecast the intermediate and behavioural outcomes from the campaign they expect to present. After all, the ad agency is supposed to understand more about how their ads work than the client can be expected to know.

Times are changing and companies are increasingly paying advertising agencies by results which has the great merit that the expected results have to be pre-specified. Nevertheless few client–agency standard briefing formats for new advertising campaigns do not include space for what measurable effect(s) the advertising should achieve.[13] They do detail the media to be used and what the ads should say, but that is like telling a plumber what tools to use without telling him where the leak is. The client–agency agreement should specify what the advertising should achieve in terms of which metrics should change and by how much.

Where advertising is the majority of the marketing budget, that brief should be agreed by the Exec. I am not suggesting that the Exec should approve the advertising campaign, heaven forbid, but only that, in a professional marketing environment, the expectations of the Exec, the client marketers and the agency should be aligned.

In the same way, the marketing plan, or the business plan if there is no separate marketing plan, should show how the market metrics, not just the financial indicators, will change as a result of the plan. Our UK research showed metrics were typically reported to the Exec versus the prior year because plans forecast financial, not market, metrics. In the Marketing Leadership Council research, although 75 per cent had marketing metrics, only 39 per cent compared them with plan. Significantly, 43 per cent of those who were satisfied with their system compared metrics with plan, versus 37 per cent of those who were dissatisfied. Whether for advertising or the marketing plan as a whole, the Exec should agree the goals ahead of time and then see results compared with those goals.

This chapter proposes that metrics should flow directly from the firm's strategy and business model. The number of metrics that will emerge depends on the complexity of the strategy and business model. It may be 5 or 50; the number at this stage does not matter as we will form the dashboard later. What does matter is that these metrics are tailored to the individual business: they should fit your business and no one else's.

The tailored approach is perhaps the antithesis of the general. To succeed, a firm must have a different strategy and, to some extent, that implies different metrics. If it chooses the same measures as everyone else, its thinking risks becoming standardized.

> This chapter proposes that metrics should flow directly from the firm's strategy and business model

ACNeilsen sells syndicated information to direct competitors who are more likely to respond in similar ways, precisely because they see the same information. Competitive metrics like market share and share of voice help to show who is winning, but the thinking is still trammelled in the conventional. Raising consumer satisfaction may be a fine target, but if everyone is doing the same, the returns are likely to be low.

The extremes of conventionality and differentiation are both suboptimal. Consumers want their products to be familiar and easy to use and yet different enough to be distinguished and better. Marketing conformity is likely to increase if management has close social ties with others in the same sector. For example, should they spend more or less time with trade associations? Economists since Adam Smith have viewed these associations with suspicion, but leaving market fixing aside, do those social contacts promote conventional marketing? Professors Marta Geletkanycz of Boston and Donald Hambrick of Columbia found that they did, along with other forms of social relationships within that business sector.[14] The strategic conformists' (association attenders') companies did better under trading conditions of high uncertainty whereas more stable environments suited the differentiators.

Thus the extent of strategic differentiation/conformity should be a matter of conscious Exec choice depending on the trading environment and competition. And maybe that is something they should measure.

Why the tailored metrics effort is worthwhile

Most of us drive our cars and our computers with very little idea of how they work. So long as they perform, our time is better spent on giving these machines what they seem to crave and ensuring they get where we want to be. Many businesses work the same way. Executives are drafted in with good driving and signalling skills. The culture ensures that predicted targets are achieved. So why, as the tailored approach asserts, should they get out and maybe get under the hood?

The three main reasons are discovering themselves in an unfamiliar landscape (the environment has changed), engine failure and a wish to reconfigure the business to achieve more radical goals. Any of them requires a new level of organizational learning. It means a deeper understanding of why the business works, what could be improved and what should be left alone. Most of all, the Exec needs to understand the firm's differential advantage.

At this point, I may be trapped with my own metaphor. When the car or computer goes wrong, we do not get under the hood but call in a technician. In practice, most Execs, once they get involved at all, agree that the process of identifying tailored metrics is worthwhile but they appoint a task force or consultants to do it. They ask to be given a new dashboard, and any insights or any tips on driving in future.

Second prize it may be, and not to be sneezed at, but my challenge to the Exec remains. 'Understanding the business', in this context, means knowing where cash comes from, and why, and how inward cash flow can be increased. It means recognizing the relationships between what the firm does and the consequences for customers and costs. The detail, I accept, should be left to technicians but the metrics that go to the Exec should be the key indicators of business health. Should the Exec delegate that understanding?

The four starting points in the previous section had one thing in common: they were ways to make the firm's business model and strategy more explicit. If this is not the type of organizational learning that should concern the main Exec, then what is? The process pushes the CEO to be clearer about what s/he wants and how that can come about. The key forward-looking question is also the simplest: how will we recognize 'success' when we see it?

The discussion thus far may have given the impression that metrics are merely a control device: having determined the forward plan, the metrics dashboard provides the guidance for corrective action when needs be. That is a false perception because, unlike our cars and computers, businesses are not inanimate. The direction given by clear performance metrics is far more important than their control function. Indeed, leadership, direction, strategy and measurement are all aspects of the same concept. Alignment prevents the confusion of signals. The overriding justification for metrics is their value as pointers to what the company seeks to achieve and as milestones along that path.

Determining goals and then measuring and reporting on success against them is a key part of organizational learning. Failures, as always, are more valuable for this purpose than success. And multinationals have the extra advantage of sharing this information globally. McDonald's gives a good example of a disciplined and advanced approach to measurement as the primary basis for global learning. It believes in keeping with the basics but building its database to provide sophisticated forecasts and diagnostics (*see box*).

McDonald's

Marketing in McDonald's UK controls all the classic four Ps and drives the business with the support of other departments. There are four key areas for metrics. Sales transactions have equal priority with customer satisfaction and functional elements such as value for money and cleanliness. The second set contains market share and brand equity measures such as awareness and advertising recall and mystery diners who assess their whole visits. Brand equity was introduced five or six years earlier and is becoming increasingly important.

Marketing is assessed quarterly by top management against pre-set targets for these measures. The future looks to better models using better segmentation and providing more actionable and precise information. Accordingly, the company is moving to the 'scientific' stage.

Source: Metrics interview April 1999, updated June 2002

In short, the argument here is that every Exec ought to determine its own ideal set of market metrics as part of its learning so that it can give optimal direction to the business as a whole and, albeit of lesser importance, share a consistent set of control indicators to keep the business on its strategic course.

So far we have been building the long list of potential metrics. Before we change gear from addition to elimination, we need to make sure we have all the candidates. For example, should we be considering the absolute metric, e.g. customer satisfaction, or the comparative, relative satisfaction? Two categories can, however, be excluded: trends and diagnostics. Trends are excluded because all metrics will be presented as trends in any case and diagnostics, e.g. penetration by segment, merely explain variances in metrics.

Merging the two

If your firm has followed the process thus far, you have assembled three financial and six brand equity metrics from the general list, but because some of the concepts can be measured in different ways, there may be more than nine. In addition, you have somewhere between 5 and 50 external market metrics from the tailored approach. This section considers how the shortlist, which will form the Exec dashboard, can be chosen from this long list.

Overall, there must be well over a thousand different kinds of marketing measures. In practice, few Execs can cope with more than, say, 20. Diageo uses rather more than that and presentation does make a difference. Listing the metrics in the first column and using a traffic lights system for displaying the good, not so good and neutral news in the other key market columns allows a wider range than the dashboard presentation of dials. As noted above, the Marketing Leadership Council research found that most firms used about eight and considered ten ideal. That may be a consequence of the dashboard layout but, for a large firm, it is probably too few. Figure 5.4 shows the Brand Equity Monitor used by Burger King in the 1990s. In this reproduction, pale gray, dark gray and black have had to be used in place of the green, amber and red traffic light system which loses some of the effect.

The issue is determined, trivial as it may seem, by what fits onto a single page or slide for Exec consideration. Showing marketing performance, or brand equity, as a single number, be it a financial valuation or index, loses too much information but, on the other hand, the full picture does need to be seen at a glance. This frames what can be used at a typical meeting. Internal metrics, covering employees and innovation, need a separate page and we will come to that later.

The first step is to divide the assembled metrics into two types: financial and brand equity. The former group is the easier. Some tailored metrics may

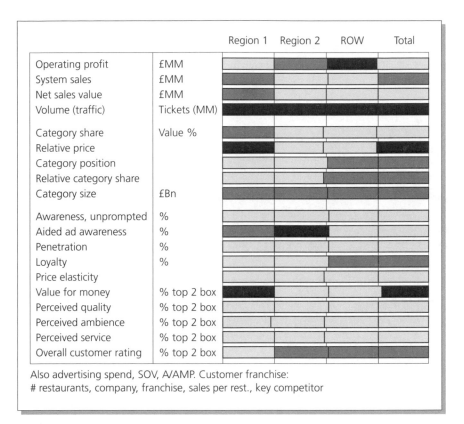

		Region 1	Region 2	ROW	Total
Operating profit	£MM				
System sales	£MM				
Net sales value	£MM				
Volume (traffic)	Tickets (MM)				
Category share	Value %				
Relative price					
Category position					
Relative category share					
Category size	£Bn				
Awareness, unprompted	%				
Aided ad awareness	%				
Penetration	%				
Loyalty	%				
Price elasticity					
Value for money	% top 2 box				
Perceived quality	% top 2 box				
Perceived ambience	% top 2 box				
Perceived service	% top 2 box				
Overall customer rating	% top 2 box				

Also advertising spend, SOV, A/AMP. Customer franchise:
restaurants, company, franchise, sales per rest., key competitor

Figure 5.4 ◆ Burger King Brand Equity Monitor (1990s)

be needed in addition to the general three, e.g. the percentage of sales on promotion, but they should form the minority of the total. Four tests will help decide whether either type of metric should be added:

◆ Does the candidate metric rarely change?

◆ At the other extreme, is it too volatile to be reliable?

◆ Does it add anything to what we already have? In other words, if it moves in sync with an existing metric, it is redundant. For example, if the sales on promotion, or marketing investment, are always the same proportion of total sales, those metrics will add nothing to the Exec's understanding of marketing performance.

◆ Does the indicator simply explain the change in a higher level? For example, sales by segment will explain the changes in sales but they are diagnostics, not metrics.

Professors Agarwal and Rao found that ten popular brand equity measures (such as perceptions and attitudes, preferences, choice intentions and actual choice) were convergent.[15] Perceptions, preference and intentions (five in all) predicted market share but 'all these brand equity constructs may be necessary to fully explain choice'. In other words, they were not similar enough to allow measures to be dropped altogether.

The ensuing process resembles an Agatha Christie whodunit: the survivors are all suspects. For the purpose of illustration, let us assume a firm began with 40 brand equity metrics (6 general plus 34 tailored). Eight failed one or other of the four tests but, on reflection, they decide to keep two of the volatile ones. Unreliable as they are, the metrics are tracking key aspects of the market. That leaves 34 in total. They have settled for 4 financial metrics and are shooting for 20 in total so the firm needs to find a way to get the 34 down to 16.

The next eliminator is pragmatic: are the data available? A metric may be fine in theory but if we cannot obtain the data, or we cannot afford the research, then it has to go. For our example, we will assume that the data for six metrics could not be obtained so the 34 are now down to 28.

Before losing any more, the firm needs to think about the balance between the different customer segments. For example, what is the balance of importance between the immediate trade customers (or retail branch managers or franchisees) and the end users? If the business is dominated by trade customers, then however much the textbook counsels end-user orientation, reality should prevail. Most of the remaining space on the page should go to the segment that matters most. Staying with our example, of the 28 remaining brand equity metrics, only four reflected the trade customer contribution but the trade is estimated as being responsible for 30 per cent or so of brand equity. So the firm keeps those four trade metrics and now concentrates on reducing the 24 end-user metrics to the 12 spaces left.

If the back data are available, they can now regress the brand equity metrics from the immediate past period(s) on the current year's sales and/or profit results. When not searching for additional metrics but finding a rationale for reducing their number, multivariate techniques are appropriate. These techniques do not tell you which variables are missing, only their significance. Remember too that we are less interested in measures of health than ill-health. We need as many indicators as there are likely causes of failure. So the better test is not which measures predict success but which reveal symptoms of trouble to come. The regression can be run for predicting both success and failure. Those metrics that were not predictive in either sense are candidates for the chop.

Due to technical problems in the data, e.g. different time periods, full quantitative analysis is rarely as easy as it sounds. The alternative is for the Exec (or the task force) to use their collective experience. A variety of techniques, e.g. Delphi,[16] are available for this. The process, broadly, is to identify upward or downward change points in the brand's progression and then to look back to identify the early warnings. Although the database may not have exact information, those who were there at the time, or in similar circumstances elsewhere, will have opinions on what the leading indicators were, or should have been.

Formally with multivariate methods, or less formally, the firm has finally reached the point where six of our remaining 24 metrics are indicative of success and eight may be symptomatic of other failures, i.e not just the opposites. The other ten can now be dropped. They were seeking a reduction to 12 but pragmatism should prevail. The remaining 22 metrics are made up:

◆ 4 financial

◆ 4 trade customer brand equity

◆ 14 end-user brand equity

We have seen a diversity of ways to generate a long list of metrics and then reduce them to the final choice. Do we need this diversity? Why not just take one route and keep it simple? Unfortunately, marketing is not a precise science; confidence comes from triangulating the possible solutions to establish the degree of convergence. When Shell was faced by justifying the considerable cost of Formula One sponsorship, they too used a variety of approaches (*see box*).

Figuring the Ferrari sponsorship

How much Shell spends on sponsoring Ferrari for Formula One is a closely guarded secret. Needless to say, Shell's top management is keen to know the financial justification for this expenditure. Prior to signing a new five-year sponsorship contract, Shell evaluated the costs and benefits in a number of different ways. They took the view that no one method could give an exact answer, but that a range of methodologies taken together would provide the range of answers.

▶

In principle, sponsorship is similar to advertising, so their first approach was to compare the attitudes towards the Shell brand of those who were aware of the Ferrari link with that of those who were not. There are two assumptions here, which probably cancel each other out. Reporting awareness underestimates those who were, in fact, influenced by the sponsorship but have since forgotten about it. On the other hand, those already favourable to Shell are more likely to be aware of the promotion. Using existing conversion rates, this difference in attitudes could be translated into extra sales and then profits. Specifically, share of preference was converted, for those calculated to have shifted, to the total effect on share and then sales and incremental profit.

The second method was similar but used the measured change in purchasing behaviour rather than the shift in attitudes.

The third methodology involved an independent assessment by a brand valuation expert. This included branding, sales, price premium and advertising effects.

The fourth approach is perhaps the most interesting. Different Shell companies had merchandised the sponsorship to varying extents in their different countries. If the sponsorship was essentially profitable then those who used it more fully should have reaped more profit. Conversely, if it was intrinsically unprofitable then the more they spent on it the more they should have lost. These country-to-country comparisons revealed a positive picture, i.e. the investment paid off, as well as showing that the laggards should be more forward in future.

The final method was a form of the Delphi technique. Managers were surveyed for their opinions based on their experience but without being given any new evidence. This showed they were highly skewed, rating the sponsorship very high or very low in terms of their perceived return on investment. They were also asked for their arguments for and against the sponsorship. These responses were used to help guide the market research in terms of the questions to be answered. In a second wave, managers were provided with the evidence from the market research and the for/against question was asked again. Other than in some technical areas such as aviation (not so relevant), the responses were now overwhelmingly favourable.

The results of all these approaches were drawn together in a short slide presentation for the top executive team, who then approved the new five-year contract.

Source: Raoul Pinnell, Global Brands Director, Shell, March 1999

Executive minutes

1 Chief Financial Officer to comment on the usefulness of general financial metrics, in evaluating marketing performance. In this business are others more insightful? Are these metrics compared with plan and competition now? Should they also be compared with prior year?

2 Chief Marketing Officer similarly to comment on the six general brand equity measures (Familiarity, Penetration, What they think of the brand, What they feel about the brand, Brand loyalty and Availability) and report on whether the general measures are adequate. If not, what should be added/subtracted? Will the marketing team accept them as their own measures?

3 Exec, or a task force, to prepare a long list of candidate metrics.

4 Exec to consider the long list against the firm's strategy and business model. Any missing metrics based on that, or their wider experience, to be added.

5 Task force to reduce list according to data availability and to balance the list as between financial, brand equity and trade and end-user crucial segments. Stable, excessively volatile and those not symptomatic of future success or failure to be eliminated.

6 Exec to consider the resulting shortlist. Will these metrics provide direction for the whole firm as well as control?

Notes

1 Barwise, P. and Styler, A. (2002), 'Marketing Expenditure Trends', Havas and London Business School (December). The study was commissioned by Havas and conducted by a team at London Business School directed by Professor Patrick Barwise in collaboration with Alan Styler of EHS Brann. The data, telephone interviews with 700 chief marketing officers, were collected by Kudos Research in July/August 2002.

2 A brand positioning statement lists the proposition (i.e. primary brand benefit to the end user), the target consumer market, the primary competitor, why the brand is different and why it is better. It is not enough just to be different or better. Where a specific distribution and/or pricing strategy is intended that may be included.

3 In stock service levels
On time delivery
Order completeness
Emergency response time
Condition of product on delivery
Ease of dealing with supplier
Ease of contact with customer service department
Understanding of my needs as a customer
Flexibility and responsiveness of supplier
Complaint handling
Communication with sales representative
Accuracy of shipment
Order cycle time
Fulfilment process
Reliability of delivery
Meeting my special invoicing needs
Product quality and performance
Overall attitude to me as a customer (Shaw, R. and Mazur, L. L. (1997) *Marketing Accountability*, London: Financial Times).

4 McGuire, W. J. (1968) 'The nature of attitudes and attitude change', in G. Lindzey and E. Aronson (eds) *The Handbook of Social Psychology III*, Cambridge MA: Addison Wesley, 155.

5 Marketing Leadership Council (2001) *Measuring Marketing Performance*, (supporting data), August, Washington DC: Corporate Executive Board.

6 Braeutigam, S., Stins, J., Rose, S., Swithenby, S. and Ambler, T. (2001) 'Magnetoencephalographic signals identify stages in real-life decision processes', *Neural Plasticity*, 8 (4), 241–53.

7 I do not want to complicate this but one cannot assume that the brain works in conventional linear time: perceived effect can precede its perceived cause which brings the whole issue of 'free will' into question. For example, see Haggard, P., Clark, S. and Kalogeras, J. (2002) 'Voluntary action and conscious awareness', *nature neuroscience*, 5, 382–5.

8 Gale, B. T. (1994) *Managing Customer Value*, New York: Free Press.

9 Ryan, M. J., Rayner, R. and Morrison, A. (1999) 'Diagnosing customer loyalty drivers', *Marketing Research* 11 (2), 18–26.

Varki, S. and Rust, R. T. (1997) 'Satisfaction is relative', *Marketing Research* 9 (2), 14–19.

Vredenburg, H. and Wee C. H. (1986) 'The role of customer service in determining customer satisfaction', *Journal of the Academy of Marketing Science* 14 (2), 17–26.

10 Kaplan, R. S. and Norton, D. P. (2000) 'Having trouble with your strategy? Then map it', *Harvard Business Review*, 78, 167–76.

11 Mintzberg, H. (1994) Rise and fall of strategic planning, Englewood Cliffs, NJ: Prentice Hall.

12 Swartz, G., Hardie, B., Grayson, K. and Ambler, T. (1996) 'Value for money? The relationships between marketing expenditure and business performance in the UK financial services industry', *Chartered Institute of Marketing*, April.

13 Survey of UK advertising agency creative brief proformas, April 2000.

14 Geletkanycz, M. A. S. and Hambrick, D. C. (1997) 'The external ties of top executives: implications for strategic choice and performance', *Administrative Science Quarterly* 42, 654–81.

15 Agarwal, M. K. and Rao, V. R. (1996) 'An empirical comparison of consumer-based measures of brand equity', *Marketing Letters* 7 (3), 237–47.

16 In the Delphi technique, a group of experts separately provide solutions (often forecasts), which are then merged. The group discusses the similarities and variances, and the reasons for those differences. Then each expert independently provides a solution and the merger and discussion cycle takes place again. In theory this leads to robust convergence to the 'best' answer. It is similar to IGI (individual, then group, then individual) brainstorming.

6

Using metrics to improve innovation performance

THESE NEXT TWO CHAPTERS CHANGE GEAR from the external market to the internal. We move from assessing the motivation of customers to that of employees. Some argue that if top management optimizes its internal brand equity, then the staff will optimize the external: enthuse your staff and they in turn will enthuse the sources of cash flow. Consumers may be the ultimate focus for top management, but in terms of the sequence of events, employees come first. The brand will never reach end users unless the firm's own staff has the message first. The next chapter considers employee-based brand equity beyond innovation.

> The brand will never reach end users unless the firm's own staff has the message first

Nearly all our respondents rated innovation as a top priority. Although measures were aplenty, confidence in overall innovation assessment fell short. The Marketing Leadership Council research found that 78 per cent of respondents tracked new product development pre-launch and 90 per cent post-launch.[1]

By 'innovation' I mean management inspired changes that alter the firm's position in the market. Such innovation may be introducing new brands and products, finding new customer segments for existing products, perhaps overseas, or new ways of selling, servicing or using the brand. Innovation also fuels R&D, major cost reductions, business reconstruction and mergers, but this book deals with market-changing innovation. I am also distinguishing what my colleague, Professor Arvind Sahay, calls 'market driving' from 'market driven'.[2] In other words, we are seeking to understand and then measure the characteristics of the firm that leads the market as distinct from one that merely reacts to competitive activities.

Some marketers told us that their attention had switched from ever smaller product variations to major ways of delivering customer satisfaction. Producing yet another flavour of potato snacks was boring the consumer. Indeed, lack of real innovation paradoxically arose from an excess of innovation, often called initiative overload. So management has two fights on its hands: reducing initiative overload and providing the climate in which market driving innovation can flow. They need to begin with the first. Figure 6.1 gives an overview of this chapter, which addresses these issues:

◆ The market gap myth: innovation springs from within the firm, not from the market.

◆ What causes market-driving innovation, what blocks it and what helps it along? We need to understand the roots before we can identify the indicators of a firm's innovation health.

◆ Strategic leadership is the key driver. Within this, the innovation goals need to be clear.

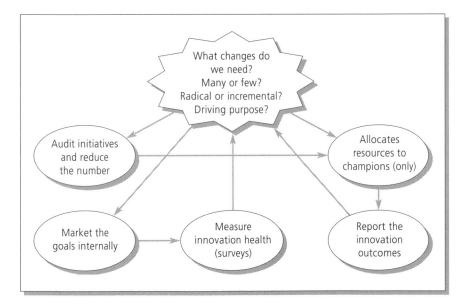

Figure 6.1 ◆ Innovation health metrics

◆ Clearing the decks: auditing and reducing initiatives and streamlining processes.

◆ Cultural enablers: the creation, development and implementation of radical innovation require different, perhaps even competing, skills.

◆ Deriving a shortlist of innovation health metrics.

The first two sections provide a model of how radical innovation happens. Culture and process are not drivers so much as enablers or, more often, disablers. The right culture and process will not guarantee innovation, but when they are wrong, innovation will be blocked.

The third section states what you may consider obvious: the firm will tend to achieve what the CEO is determined to achieve. The consequences are sensitive. Few firms want to have researchers collecting and presenting data on their CEO. While leadership is ultimately an individual matter, pragmatism requires us to depersonalize this crucial driver of innovation.

The next stage is to examine the blockers of innovation. Large firms would be well advised to junk much of the bureaucracy that hinders the generation of new cash flow. These 'stage-gate' systems can be long on nay-saying opportunities and short on enthusiasm for the unexpected. The message here is slightly equivocal. Some process is essential for organizational learning and control and the exact transition from there to bureaucracy is hard to judge. Since measuring bureaucracy is itself bureaucratic, it is usually simpler to prune it heavily.

> Since measuring bureaucracy is itself bureaucratic, it is usually simpler to prune it heavily

On the other hand, we need to look kindly upon and measure the enablers, so that management can enhance the climate for the kind of innovation they want at each of the three crucial stages: creativity, development and implementation both before and after the introduction of innovations. Transferring attention from whatever has just been introduced to the next one coming along is a sure-fire way to damage performance.

The last section extracts a shortlist of innovation metrics from the many possible. We need to distinguish between tracking individual innovations and assessing the innovativeness of the business. Maybe the monitoring of individual innovations needs to be part of that, but here we are concerned with the cannon, not the cannonballs. In this chapter, therefore, we focus on measuring the innovation health of a business as a whole, while Chapter 9 considers individual innovations.

One conclusion from our research was that top management should be less directly concerned with individual innovations. They should agree the menu, ensure the kitchen has what it needs and then get out of the heat. Professor Christina Shalley and her PhD student Jill Perry-Smith used experiments to show that creativity was inhibited by rigorous senior management examination but aided by supportive learning.[3] No surprise there. More interestingly, managers who provided plenty of help, e.g. previous examples, were likely to stultify innovation. Their advice to senior management was 'to stop getting in the way'.

The concern with monitoring innovation health is not universal. Amongst those we talked to, the outstanding innovators create so naturally that they were amazed by our questions. To them, innovation health is the oxygen in the air: you breathe it, not measure it. At the other extreme, the stick-in-the-muds see change as a threat. They will not consider innovation, still less measure it. This chapter, then, is addressed to those who want innovation to improve performance and to use measurement as part of that.

The market gap myth

Too many MBA students are convinced that innovation springs from the marketplace. 'Just ask consumers what they want and then make it' seems rational but is usually disastrous because consumers rarely know what they want, or know how to give expression to it, and if they could competitors would have the same information. Despite the evidence of history, the conviction remains that research should be employed to detect a market gap so it can then be filled.

Where a gap can be found, a good reason for its being a Bermuda Triangle also exists but may be less obvious. Market gaps are only evident with hindsight, much like the wake of a ship. The gap in the water made by the ship was obvious looking astern but the 'brand', so to speak, made its own gap. Always true? No, exceptions exist but this section comes first to dispel the notion that innovation opportunities can be measured in the market. Mostly they are driven by the firm's internal situation.

In industrial markets, customers supply and even drive their suppliers' innovations. So do retailers for their own brands (private label). Mary Sonnack, Division Scientist at 3M, has worked with innovation expert, MIT's Professor Eric von Hippel, using his depth interviews of 'users in the extreme'.[4] As with consumer research, 'routine users' cannot imagine what innovations they will like. Superficial research will only reveal the obvious, which, in turn, is most likely to fail. Von Hippel and other top innovators get much deeper into understanding the problems the firm's and competitors' products solve and how they might be improved. Furthermore, innovation now deals with the way the goods and services are delivered, to make end use easier and/or more enjoyable.

In other words, the ideas may come from the market, but only because the inside team have tuned in. Bill Gates built his Microsoft empire from scratch not by formally researching customers' wants and needs states, but by empathizing with end-user experience and building software that would please himself. Shell's new fuel 'Optimax' provides an example of a large company tuning in to the users' unstated needs (*see box*).

Optimax

Shell Optimax won the 'New Brand of the Year' category of the awards sponsored by The Marketing Society and the trade magazine *Marketing* in 2002.

Fierce price competition between supermarkets and reduced marketing support from the major petroleum corporations have led many motorists to view petrol as a commodity. In response, Shell made use of market research that identified several emotionally different customer segments to create Shell Optimax.

Launched in 2001, it targeted 'real drivers' willing to pay a premium for a fuel offering extra performance and engine protection. With the technical task of product development, came the need to re-engage customers.

Optimax was given a £5 million budget, with the advertising's innovative fish theme rigorously adopted in all through-the-line communications. By the end of 2002, Shell Optimax will have been rolled out to all 1100 Shell service stations in the UK. It has met and exceeded all its targets, including winning new customers, upgrading existing customers, and improving margins. The planned pay-back period of 15 months was achieved in eight. The judges applauded Shell's unified approach to marketing. A cross-functional project team put the new brand at the heart of the business development process.

Shell now has a number of differentiated fuel brands, offering benefits such as improved performance, engine protection and environmental
benefits, depending on what the consumers want and are willing to pay
for. One or other of these has now been launched in 46 countries worldwide. This programme of differentiated fuels now makes up a material
part of Shell fuels' market share which is one of their measures of success.

Sources: Venetia Howes, Global Brands Strategy Manager, Shell, October 31
2002; 'New brand of the year, *Marketing*, 5 June 2002, 8

The distinction is subtle but asking the customer for the answer to a
problem she does not know she has, differs from the insider spotting a
problem that could be better solved and getting into dialogue, as von
Hippel suggests, about solutions. Innovation needs to lead the end-user, just
as my cat leads me to her food dish, by being slightly, but not too far, ahead.
The active party here is the innovator, or my cat. For that reason, the rest of
this chapter will focus on internal metrics of innovation health.

The roots of market-driving innovation

Innovation is under the spotlight. John Kearon, a founding partner in
Brand Genetics, one of the UK's leading innovation agencies, claims that
'large companies no longer have the ability to originate the sort of new category brands that made them successful in the first place'.[5] Others have
similarly concluded that innovation processes in large companies stifle
exactly those radical developments which the firms seek.

Yet there are more product launches, new media, new advertising and
promotion campaigns than ever before. The profusion of marketing offerings is expanding faster than consumers can absorb them. In the last ten
years, more organizational initiatives were created each year than in previous
centuries. Initiative overload in large companies, fuelled to some extent by
empowerment, creates constipation. The net result is less innovation, not
more. Yet change in the world is widely perceived as accelerating. Whether
such acceleration is real or perceptual, more firms are recognizing that they
need real innovation, and need it fast.

The innovation we most want gives marketplace advantage, which in
turn puts a generous dollop on the bottom line. We would all like to be able

to distinguish, early on, the winning initiatives from the duds. Unfortunately, although sophisticated analysis can help spot certain losers, measurement can do little to identify winners. The telephone, the Beatles, the PC, the automobile and many, many other great innovations were derided early on. The absolute maximum size of the US car market was once established to be 20,000 since that was the number of those who could afford chauffeurs. Market research has a valuable role in assessing incremental improvements but has proved unreliable for radical market-driving ideas. Baileys Irish Cream now dominates the global liqueurs market, but when it was introduced in the mid-1970s it had already been rejected in all market research tests. Luckily, the Baileys marketers had learned to interpret that as an encouraging sign.

So if we cannot identify winners early on, what do we measure? We have found no companies confident they have the answers. The most popular metric, led by 3M, is the proportion of sales represented by products launched in the last three or five years. But this measure looks back, not forward: companies need to know how they stand today – and particularly what can be changed today to improve performance tomorrow. At the same time, past successes are valuable indicators of continuing health. Sharwood's follows this approach (*see box*).

Sharwood's

Sharwood's is part of Centura Foods, itself part of RHM, one of the largest food companies in the UK and Ireland. Centura also markets Robertson's, Paxo, Saxa and Bisto. Hovis and Mr Kipling are within the RHM portfolio.

Sharwood's are experts in Indian and Oriental food and offer a wide range of ambient and frozen products – jarred sauces, accompaniments, ingredients and ready meals.

Sharwood's brand leader status has been cultivated through rigorous consumer insight and a company culture that places the brand and the consumer right at the heart of the organization. With this in mind, marketing accountability is both comprehensive and closely tracked and discussed right up to the board of directors.

'Brand equity' is a bundle of measures used to indicate the strength of Sharwood's consumer franchise. It is made up of marketplace performance, consumer penetration, loyalty, perceptions (disposition, awareness,

▶

image statements) and financial values. ACNielsen, Millward Brown and internal systems are used to track these measures and all are benchmarked against historical data and the key competitors.

A systematic approach is also used for innovation where the process has been designed to balance the development of class-leading new product with the need for close scrutiny and sponsorship of projects at the highest level. Key measures for innovation at Sharwood's include the percentages of revenue and profit delivered by new products.

Their other measures cover:

◆ Actual performance of each new product versus target (total and incremental after cannibalization)

◆ Forecast incremental value and number of new products in process but not launched

◆ Process efficiency – measures such as time to market and number of new products which do not get to market

◆ Benchmarking of efficiency and effectiveness of Sharwood's innovation verseus the competition and category average (ACNielsen)

Source: Sue Knight, Deputy Brands Director, Centura Foods Ltd, 5 November 2002

Debating innovation at the London Business School faculty lunch table showed that we each approach innovation with our own habitual way of thinking. As a marketer, I know the issue is driving the market, but colleagues in strategy, organizational behaviour and logistics assured me it was all a matter of strategy, culture and supply chain processes respectively. Had I consulted financial, R&D and IT colleagues, shareholder value, R&D and information would have been identified as the drivers. A year of dispute provided Figure 6.2, which brings the key components together.

Innovation cannot be understood in isolation but as a natural output from a well-functioning firm. A tree puts out a new branch because it is healthy. A botanist can go round counting branches (innovations) but will learn very little. Understanding the attributes that distinguish the healthy from the unhealthy tree is the first stage. Measuring them is the second. The answers, of course, lie in the roots of which we found three types: strategy, culture (how people interrelate) and the business processes (what they do and the approvals they need). Transplanting 3M's metrics into a firm without similar strategy, culture and processes will be a waste of time.

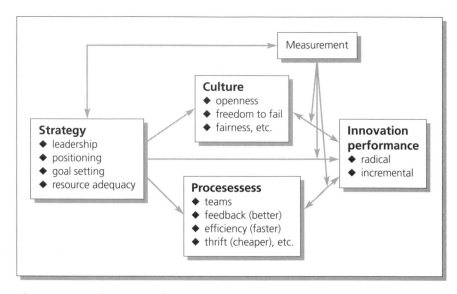

Figure 6.2 ◆ The roots of innovation

Thus, in Figure 6.2 strategy is the primary driver of innovation whereas culture and processes are the enablers. In other words, culture and processes will not cause innovation to happen but if they are sick, which typically means too dense, innovation can be expected to fail. Yes, innovation can arise in the most unlikely places; luck and serendipity are key factors but they are also immeasurable. Here we are looking to assess a system that will reliably beat the odds for producing successful innovation.

Compare Figure 6.2 with the Arthur D. Little framework reproduced here as Table 6.1.[6] This too sees the key components as strategy, process and culture. The definition of strategy in the next section includes resources. For each of these, they suggest metrics that may lag, lead or be contemporary (real time) with innovatory activities. In total they suggested the eight metrics shown.

Modern business is riddled with buzzwords like 'drivers' and 'strategy' to the point where we forget what the words mean. Financial metrics or abstract nouns are invested with importance they simply do not have. McKinsey, for example, defines a value driver as 'any variable that affects the value of a company'.[7] Thus a value driver is any old accounting metric. A serious look at innovation requires us to be reminded that the only drivers of value in any business are the management; sometimes with help from the other stakeholders. People drive businesses and metrics do not.

Table 6.1 ◆ The Arthur D. Little innovation metrics framework and representative metrics

	Lagging	Real time	Leading	Learning
Stakeholder strategies	Gross contribution of new products	NPV of idea portfolio		
Processes		Milestones completed on time		Take-up rate of new processes
Resources			External alliances being pursued	
Culture/ organization	Staff turnover rate		Innovation climate	Level of enquiry

The next section takes a look at how this driving works and then the chapter moves on to what assists and what blocks successful innovation. In all of these, we are seeking useful measures.

Strategic leadership is the key driver

Most academics use the word 'strategy' to mean whatever they want it to mean.[8] The original Greek meant 'what generals do', which are just four activities: leadership; positioning (selecting the battleground and the broad strokes for gaining advantage); goals; and adequate resourcing (people, logistics and money). Tactics (the battle plan) follow on from strategy and are largely left to junior officers.

Most generalship takes place before the battle. Implementation and tactics may alter in the light of changing circumstances, but the strategy should not. Business, however, is conducted with goals and plans that are implicit as much as explicit. Unlike warfare, business cycles have no clear beginning and end. For convenience we chop time into annual pieces. In the typical annual plan, the financial figures are clear enough but purpose, direction and goals may be implicit. In business as in battle, the main purpose of the plan is to ensure everyone knows what they are supposed to do. However informal, some sense of direction and purpose is essential. Strategy writer Gary Hamel calls it 'strategic intent'.[9] To head west in sunlight you need only the time of day, not a detailed map.

Strategy in this model has four measurable components: leadership, positioning, goal setting and resource adequacy. Goals need to be defined with sufficient clarity to drive, and to be compared with, performance, but not be so detailed as to inhibit opportunism. Our research indicated very clear financial goals but less specificity about non-financial innovation goals.

Leadership, which is probably the most important of these four, primarily entails the motivation of the business unit to achieve the goals that the leader has set. US General Chuck Krulak uses the view of leadership as getting ordinary people to achieve extraordinary things.[10] Awareness is not enough: commitment needs to be researched too. Metrics can play a key role in communicating and securing commitment to goals, e.g. the Balanced Scorecard. In particular, managers need to know what kind of innovation is required. What should be the balance between continuous small improvements (kaizen) and radical innovation? For example, the Japanese development of laptops was characterized by a constant stream of small, incremental innovations whereas their US competitors implemented fewer but larger changes. Which parts of the business most need innovation?

> Strategy in this model has four measurable components: leadership, positioning, goal setting and resource adequacy

Many different leadership styles have proved effective. The search for a one-fits-all has been unproductive and is probably foolish. The context of the market, the competitive environment and corporate culture determine what type of leadership is appropriate. At the same time, leadership depends on the plausibility of the other three components. Given this positioning and these resources, does the staff believe the goals to be realistic? Or are their careers likely to be sacrificed in a vain cause?

In warfare, 'positioning' refers to the location of the general's troops relative to the enemy and marketing carried this idea into the mental warfare fought between brands. Typically a brand prefers the high ground and to be well dug in. Defence tends to be cheaper and more certain of victory than attack, customer retention being a case in point. A general or a CEO should ensure the troops understand their positioning as it determines what they should do.

For innovation, unusually, I am using positioning in the geographic sense of location as well as the brand warfare sense. Professors Michael Porter and Scott Stern, amongst others, have researched why small locations have proved hotbeds of innovation – Silicon Valley for example. While one might expect specialist firms to be spread across the globe to insulate themselves from competition and each to dominate its own market, this is not the usual pattern. In practice the experts cluster together and innovate faster and better as a result, leaving the dispersed manufacturers to fall behind and fade away.

The reasons for this include the sharing of skills through informal networks and experts moving jobs but staying in the area. Why clustering happens matters less than the fact that it does. The implication for the CEO looking for outstanding innovation is clear: if the business is not located in the relevant hotbed, a large (and autonomous) part of its R&D needs to be. As a long-term strategic issue, rather than a year-to-year metric, location is noted only for completeness.

No company has all the resources for the innovation it could undertake and allocation is part of the process consideration below. At the same time, there must be some broad sense that there is enough slack in the treasury and human resources to invest in the future. A firm that talks long term but routinely axes projects without short-term payback will soon run short of strategic initiatives. Managers' perceptions may give enough measures. If those who have to achieve the goals think there are adequate resources, there probably are. On the other hand, the perception of inadequate resources may be due to poor communications, reluctance to innovate, or 'not invented here'. Positive managers will narrow the objective to the point where the limited resources can be effective against the smaller target or they will fight to get more. Montgomery was right not to attack a better general at Alamein in 1942 until he had superior resources. Inadequate resources are not an excuse for inaction.

A survey of 33 companies making up the 'Innovation Exchange' at London Business School revealed these best and worst practices for leadership, strategy and vision.[11]

Best

◆ Leader's demonstrated commitment to innovation.

◆ Clear and timely communication.

◆ Common purpose.

◆ Inspirational and involving with emotional connection.

- Experiment encouraged.
- Failure tolerated.
- Strategy developed from the future, not the past.
- Alignment of innovation and overall company strategy.

Worst

- Blame when something goes wrong as distinct from seeing it as a learning opportunity.
- Delegation of responsibility but not authority.
- Secretive, suspicious and critical.
- Focus on day-to-day activity.

These various components of strategic leadership and practices suggest a wide list of possible metrics but that can be reduced if we do not consider what the Exec does but how those actions are received by the internal customers, the staff. That may require only two questions: to what extent do they understand what has to be achieved (the goals)? And to what extent are they committed to achieving them? Poor metrics may be attributed to poor leadership, or unclear positioning, or poor goals, or inadequate resources, but that analysis should be triggered by these simple questions.

Of course, leadership should drive the firm's innovation process but that is now considered separately.

Clearing the decks: streamlining process

In reviewing the different processes that firms use to nurture or destroy innovation, we looked for factors that excite the few successful Big Ideas, not the myriad initiatives which get in the way. Procter & Gamble found that the big winners were conceived and championed by a small number of key executives who were distinguished by their energy and a very high bandwidth of interests. Such creativity seems to be associated with 'outsights' (the opposite of tunnel vision), which are the peripheral associations most of us do not make.

3M, where the champion concept was born, supplies many examples of its importance. Champions are motivated by passion, not financial rewards, and a 'maverick' on the main Exec champions the champions. The successful champion is funded to travel the world to spread the gospel. In the alcoholic beverage industry, Baileys Irish Cream and canned draught Guinness are two other examples of successful use of the champion concept. The Exec may not be able, or wise, to measure the DCF of their creative ideas; but it can measure the number of true champions, defined as people who do not clear hurdles so much as crash through them (*see box*).

Professor Chris Voss, of London Business School, has reduced process characteristics to three groups: better, faster and cheaper.[12]

Novartis

Novartis was created by the merger of the Ciba Geigy and Sandoz groups in 1996 and covers healthcare products (60 per cent of turnover), nutrition (Gerber), medical and food supplements and agribusiness. Professor Walter von Wartburg is Head of Communications.

Perhaps its biggest challenge has been to rise above its long history and take 100,000 people through a radical culture change to become an organization that is flexible and fast moving. 'You have to find the right balance between empowerment and control,' von Wartburg says. 'On the one hand you have to let loose, but on the other you have to have a tight rein. But where do you let loose and where do you have a tight rein? That is basically the art of management.'

A formal programme identifies and nurtures the next generation of managers and recruitment brings in bright young people even though there is no obvious career path. Novartis also spots the best research talent through a programme of prizes and recognition, where the three most innovative people are selected from the 5–6000 strong research community.

Measurement covers both hard and soft areas. The hard include the number of products going from stage to stage and number of new patents, registrations and market launches. Soft measures deal with the way employees achieve results and whether behaviour matches the firm's core values.

Source: Laura Mazur interview with Professor von Wartburg, November 1998

▶

Better

- Formality: all innovations have to follow the same broad process and everyone knows what it is.

- Organization should be flat and informal.

- Incentives, not necessarily financial, should be seen to reward success; for example, innovators are promoted.

- Delegation: once the targets are agreed, senior management should get out of the kitchen.

- Diversity: multifunctional teams should have a wide mix of skills, personalities and backgrounds. The mixed evidence on this shows diversity to slow the process at least initially. Accordingly diversity should be set by the nature of the required innovation and not by political correctness.

- Supplier and customer involvement: retailers often lean heavily on their suppliers for innovation. Conversely, in business-to-business marketing, innovation is usually inspired and assisted by customers.

- Commitment to quality: the process needs feedback loops at each stage to ensure quality assurance.

- Relative state (to chief competitors) of technological development: innovation, to some extent, is self-fuelling. Being ahead creates a pressure to stay ahead.

- Fewer: however they may do it, businesses need to focus resources on those innovations likely to perform best.

Faster

- Stretch time targets: whilst artificial deadlines tend to be counter-productive, a shared sense of immediacy can focus minds.

- Frequency of meetings: many of us have a just-before-the-next-meeting approach to prioritization. The content or quality of the meeting matters less than the fact that it is happening.

- Action orientation: analysis paralysis exemplifies excellence as the enemy of the good. The modern trend is for 90 per cent today rather than 99 per cent next year but, again, that must depend on the nature of the innovation required.

Cheaper

◆ Thrift: poverty may not be the father of invention but imagination can be crippled by indulgence. The father of atomic research, Lord Rutherford, put it thus: 'We haven't the money, so we've got to think.'[13]

◆ Recycling: using what exists rather than buying everything new. This also promotes learning from the past.

◆ Benchmarking competitors' costs.

Comprehensive as this is, our research found none of them on our respondents' shortlists of the key innovation health metrics; quite the reverse. In large companies, process tends to inhibit innovation. The more rational it seems, the more complex it becomes and the more the process destroys its own children. Each step is an opportunity to say no. Of course no-hopers should not be allowed to waste scarce resources but the objective is to stimulate winners, not identify losers.

Process, in short, is painted here as a begetter of blockers to innovation. Joseph Bonner and colleagues looked at management control of product development and concluded that 'less appears to be better'.[14] Process is essential for organizational learning and control but a well-ordered firm will regularly take a machete to its existing processes. Bureaucracy grows like ivy on an oak tree. Unchecked it will destroy the tree and, such is its regenerative ability, you are very unlikely to prune excessively. Furthermore, fresh attention to learning is likely to be more fruitful than the old routines. Be that as it may, the conclusion here is that, once the streamlining has taken place, no continuing process metrics are required.

Culture

Culture can enable all three stages of innovation: creativity, development and implementation. The stages themselves are each different and make separate demands on the way the firm operates. Creativity may get the most attention but the more prosaic aspects of converting the idea to reality and market launch are just as crucial. The mechanics of all three could be seen as process rather than culture, but the mechanics turn out to matter less than the climate within which they operate.

Let us begin with creativity. Professor Teresa Amabile and her colleagues at Harvard have developed one of the best models thus far of corporate culture and creativity (Figure 6.3).[15]

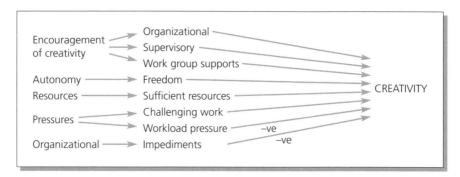

Figure 6.3 ◆ Conceptual model (KEYS)

Source: After Amabile *et al.* (1996)

In this view, creativity is a sensitive flower that needs to be encouraged at organizational, immediate supervisory and peer group levels. Like autonomy and resource adequacy, this encouragement has a positive effect on creativity. As we move down the left side of the chart, the picture becomes more mixed. Challenging work has a positive motivational effect, but not if it is excessive. Too many pressures, organizational blockages or approval hurdles become negative, shown in Figure 6.3 as '–ve'. All the factors in this model are positive except workload pressures and organizational impediments.

These and similar models have been tested and represent some degree of consensus both in academia and with our practitioner discussants. Key performance indicators, and measurement in general, were seen as examples of organizational impediments and thereby negative. Cross-functional teams should be given considerable autonomy to devise their own targets, within broad strategic direction, as well as processes and procedures. Their findings applied to both incremental and radical innovation.

This picture may be too utopian. No company can grant freedom to all managers to be creative and change everything all of the time: the change imperative fights with the consistency imperative. Something somewhere has to apply the firm's existing knowledge and disciplines to achieve focus. While less process is better, the culture must include opposition. Innovation is unlikely to succeed in the external marketplace if it has not been thoroughly tested in the internal one first.

Part of the answer lies in the cross-functional nature of innovation teams. Divergent perspectives within the team should hammer the innovation into shape before it sees even internal light of day. In particular, one or more team members need to play the part of the recalcitrant customer. All the

Dell

Michael Dell attributes much of his success to well-hired people, all of whom have a sense of personal investment. He provides eight tips:

◆ Learn voraciously

◆ Teach innovative thinking

◆ Encourage smart experimentation

◆ Beware the perils of pride

◆ Do not try to perfume a pig

◆ Communicate fast and deeply

◆ Stay allergic to hierarchy

◆ Mobilize people around a single goal.

Together these amount to responsibility, accountability and shared success but people have to feel it is safe to fail. Giving them the knowledge and permission to do what they do best, ensuring that staff see themselves as owners, brings more success to a company, according to Dell, than anything else he has found.

Source: Dell, M. (1999) *Direct from Dell: Strategies that Revolutionized an Industry*, New York: Harper Collins

positive parts of the Amabile model (learning) need to be challenged by the harsh reality side of culture (knowledge). The innovation teams need to be experienced in all parts of the business. Too many CMOs put the latest recruit in charge of innovation because it has the lowest budget, although newcomers should certainly be encouraged to challenge the prevailing wisdom. The more that organizational knowledge can be applied within the team, the less friction will have to be applied when it gets into the wider internal market. But the harsh side can be expressed positively: knowledge can be enforced or it can be actively sought by team members. They can 'learn voraciously', as Dell puts it (*see box*). Assimilated knowledge means someone else never having to say 'no'.

Creativity is only the first part of the story. Innovation performance requires creativity and effective development skills and good implementation to deliver the innovations. These cultural characteristics may be in conflict: the freedom to create may not fit well with the discipline required to deliver.

One solution to this is to separate these roles, by, for example, giving the role of creating initiatives to one task force, or outsourcing it, and giving development and implementation to others. This has the superficial advantage of specialization but experience does not support it. New concepts are not neat parcels that can be passed from group to group, but ill-defined, unwrapped intuitions, which a team can hold and believe in passionately but which will fall apart when they are passed to unbelievers. GrandMet's portfolio of adult soft drinks (Dexter's, Aqua Libra and Purdey's) pioneered the category but lost its way with changes of management.

Our research has found overwhelming support for cross-functional teams with high levels of autonomy to see the whole project through. The

The Phoenix process at Fluke Corporation

The Fluke Corporation has a $500 million turnover in compact professional electronic test tools such as handheld multimeters. In 1992, their peace dividend was negative: most of their business was tied up with the military. Phoenix was the name for the new process that started with a blank board. Joe Martins, Fluke's Business Development Manager, sees creativity as only a catalyst: a small amount of substance that speeds things up but is not consumed in the process. Other key ingredients are the commitment and enthusiasm of the teams that were initially made up of volunteers with little to lose – not the high-flyers.

Practical team details included two weeks to form a group of four to eight people, full time, with a team manager, rules and analysis style, interaction with the rest of the organization and a project plan/milestones/reporting. Martins sees team identity as important. Each had a name, a mascot, rituals and a war room. They brought their hobbies into the process.

Rather than building a strong team spirit that might get in the way of adopting ideas from outside, they looked for affiliative characteristics, i.e. how people got along. The de-emphasis above on creativity should not be taken literally. Fluke ran creativity training sessions and whenever minds got 'locked up' introduced 'crazy discussions about why the sky is blue or why is the grass green'.

Using the Phoenix process, four innovations, including two acquisitions, will soon account for about half of Fluke's turnover.

Source: Martins, J. (1999) 'The Phoenix process at Fluke Corporation', *Business Strategy Review* 10 (1), 39–56

▶

Innovation Exchange survey used Kuczmarski's questions, where the third deals with the use of multi-functional teams.[16] This had the most positive response with 80 per cent of firms already doing so and the other 20 per cent planning to.

As well as enabling all functional issues to be considered early, the sheer cost of these teams, especially full-time teams, forces top management to prioritize initiatives. The Fluke Corporation provides an example of how team-centred innovation can be set loose (*see box*).

The Fluke Corporation experience is mirrored in that of the innovative companies responding to the LBS survey mentioned earlier. In the words of the report 'innovation cultures are characterized by fun, focus, freedom to fail and flexibility'. (p.5). Best practice includes a restless search for learning, finding better ways of doing things and experimentation. The attitude to risk is 'if in doubt, do it', although any sensible firm tries to keep the risks small.

In this literature, the reader soon finds paradoxes. First he is expected to reduce initiative overload and then exhorted never to kill a project. The centre must control innovation for global consistency and yet the locals must be free to experiment. The innovative company does not try to resolve these paradoxes, an undesirable if not impossible task, but to enjoy them. In a sense, each successful innovation is a new solution to an old paradox. Is that wimping out of the contradictions? Maybe, but the fallacy lies in thinking they have solutions. Command and control companies seek to make the choices at the top but the more modern alternative is to recognize the problems and then provide the climate in which junior and middle managers can find new paths. In particular, initiatives must be allowed to wither when management has better things to do.

Before we move on to refine a shortlist of key metrics, one Silicon Valley example illustrates the importance of culture in strengthening or destroying innovation health. Professors Baron, Hannan and Burton were able to allocate 54 per cent of the 167 small companies they studied into five types.[17] The majority of those fell into the 'engineering model' with strong challenges and peer-group control. The professional, bureaucratic and autocratic models were as unsuccessful as you would expect. Far the best performer was the fifth, 'commitment model', with about 7 per cent of the total sample. This was characterized as having strong emotional bonds as the basis for staff retention. Cultural fit is a key consideration in recruitment and formal (rational) controls are light. But commitment was not a one-way street: the top managers had to demonstrate their own commitment and shared values with the rest of the team. These had to be in place from the beginning:

patching this happy valley model onto a previous alternative did not succeed. Innovation is likely to flower when we do not see ourselves as coming to work so much as enjoying playing together.

Research into culture, innovation, organizational learning and knowledge is immense. The number of possible metrics is likewise too extensive for our purposes.[18] The three key enabling factors that emerge from the above culture summary are: freedom to fail, autonomy for the innovation team and a willingness to change by the firm as a whole. These need to be balanced by the application of knowledge. The friction, or interaction, between the encouraging and harsh sides of culture provide the spark for effective innovation. Put positively, it can be expressed as the appetite for learning. The freedom to fail comes with a responsibility to exploit what the firm has already learned.

> The three key enabling factors that emerge are: freedom to fail, autonomy for the innovation team and a willingness to change by the firm as a whole

Deriving a shortlist of innovation health metrics

Innovation is only part of the manageable list of marketing metrics for regular Exec review. If we only need five to describe brand equity, what is appropriate for innovation health? Table 6.2 provides nine, which seemed a reasonable starter list. Individual firms may need more, or less, or different metrics but their next question should be the relative importance of tracking

Table 6.2 ◆ Innovation metrics shortlist

Strategy	Awareness of goals (vision)
	Commitment to goals (vision)
	Active innovation support
	Perceived resource adequacy
Culture	Appetite for learning
	Freedom to fail
Outcomes	No. of initiatives in process
	No. of innovations launched
	% revenue due to launches during last three years

the key driver (strategy), enablers/blockers (process, culture and measurement) and outcomes (results).

In this model, two enablers/blockers do not get a mention: process and measurement. I argued earlier that process needs modernizing infrequently and does not need routine tracking meanwhile with one exception. The Exec probably should monitor the number of initiatives. This appears here as one of the outcome metrics. The strategy should have indicated if the firm was seeking a large number of incremental innovations or a small number of radical ones. They are unlikely to be able to manage both. As already noted, most large firms suffer from an excess of initiatives and this is one way the Exec can keep the reins on distraction.

Measurement could be seen as part of process but it is more subtle than that. What the CEO chooses to have measured and then reviews is a powerful indicator of his interest and commitment. The act of measuring innovation health and, better, sharing the results communicates active support and an appetite for learning. This is why Figure 6.2 showed measurement as a moderator of both strategy and culture.

So the metrics are a key part of promoting innovation health as well as a means of control. On the other hand, having metrics to monitor metrics usage would, in my view, be taking managing by numbers a step too far.

The strategy and culture metrics are synthesized from the sections above. Awareness of, and commitment to, innovation goals can be measured directly from staff surveys, as can the general question 'Are resources adequate for these goals?' On the other hand, they can also be seen as summary or index metrics built up from a greater number of more detailed questions, e.g. adequacy of finances for particular innovations. Note that the perception of resource adequacy probably matters more than the reality.

We have not previously considered the other outcome metrics. The number of innovations getting through process into the marketplace, which can also be expressed as a percentage of those in process, provides some indication of productivity. The list concludes with the most popular innovation metric: the share of sales revenue due to recent innovations. Perhaps the Exec could manage with outcome metrics alone, as many companies do. This chapter has argued that understanding the roots of innovation is the better alternative.

The selected metrics look at innovation as a whole and not the separate stages of creativity, development and implementation, each of which makes different demands on management. If we had a satisfactory metric for creativity per se, it would have been included. As it is, we can measure only the climate in which it could grow. For development and implementation too, culture and process are after all only enablers. The wish to learn is an indicator of high-bandwidth people likely to be innovators, and the freedom to fail also represents all kinds of autonomy. A higher level 'innovation freedom' metric constructed from several indicators would be an alternative. On the other hand, if invigorating innovation is a priority for the firm, a more extensive study of these three components separately may well be called for.

Executive minutes

1 If Exec is not satisfied with general state of innovation health, a full audit of strategy, culture, process, outcomes and internal communication should be put in hand. This will need closer to 90 than the 9 metrics suggested here for regular use.

2 Use such an audit to weed out the blockers, notably complex processes.

3 Re-establish corporate and innovation goals, metrics (adapted from the nine above) and performance benchmarks.

4 Ensure that a vigourous two-way international communication programme is in place to achieve awareness, commitment and an effective balance between resources and focus.

5 Review all initiatives in progress with champions. Cull those where enthusiasm is waning or reinvigorate them, perhaps with new champions.

6 Ensure major innovations have cross-functional teams who can balance zest for learning with harsh experience before initiatives are exposed to similar tests in the wider company, where they will still have to compete for resources to gain approval for launch.

7 Finance director to report metrics to Exec once or twice per annum, in addition to any individual applications for resources. Metrics to be compared with benchmarks, prior year and competitor information, as far as possible.

Notes

1 Marketing Leadership Council (2001) *Measuring Marketing Performance*, (suporting data), August, Washington DC: Corporate Executive Board.

2 Sahay, A., Kohli, A. K., Jaworski, B. J. (2000) 'Market driven vs. driving the market: conceptual foundations', *Journal of Academy of Marketing Science*, 28 (1), 45–54.

3 Shalley, C. E. and Perry-Smith, J. E. (2001) 'Effects of social-psychological factors on creative performance', *Organizational Behavior & Human Decision Processes*, 84, 1–22.

4 *Marketplace*, Institute for the Study of Business Markets, Fall 1998, Penn State, 1.

5 Kearon, J. (1999) 'Innovation at a crossroads', *Market Leader* 6, 32–37.

6 Collins, J. and Smith, D. (1999) 'Innovation metrics: a framework to accelerate growth', *Prism*, first quarter, 33–47.

7 Copeland, T., Koller, T. and Murrin, J. (1996) *Valuation: Measuring and Managing the Value of Companies*, 2nd edn, New York: Wiley, 107.

8 See 'In search of strategy', *Sloan Management Review*, special issue, 40, 1999. The various authors in this tour d'horizon of academic understanding of 'strategy' come to quite different conclusions, or perhaps begin with quite different preconceptions, of what the word means.

9 Hamel, G. and Prahalad, C.K. (1994) 'Seeing the future first', *Fortune*, 5 September, 64–8.

10 Speech to Financial Services Forum, London, 29 October 2002.

11 Von Stamm, B. (2001) 'Innovation best practice and future challenges', Innovation Exchange, London Business School working paper.

12 Voss, C.A., Johnston, R., Silvestro, R., Fitzgerald, L. and Brignall, T. J. (1992) 'Measurement of innovation and design performance in services', *Design Management Journal*, winter, 40–46.

13 According to Professor R.V. Jones in his Brunel Lecture, 14 February 1962.

14 Bonner, J., Ruerkert, R. W. and Walker, O. C., Jr. (1998) 'Management control of product development projects', Cambridge MA: Marketing Science Institute report, 98–120, summary page.

15 For example, Amabile, T.M., Conti, R., Coon, H., Lazenby, J. and Herron, M. (1996) 'Assessing the work environment for creativity', *Academy of Management Journal* 39 (5), 1154–84.

16 Kuczmarski, T. (1996) *Innovation – Leadership Strategies for the Competitive Edge*, New York: NTC Business Books. His ten questions are:

   1 Do you accept failure as an intrinsic part of innovation?
   2 Do you develop a new products strategy?

    3 Do you establish multi-functional teams with dedicated members?

    4 Do you define a systematic new product development process?

    5 Do you design compensation incentives that stimulate an entrepreneurial environment?

    6 Do you foster top management commitment to innovation?

    7 Do you track the results of innovation?

    8 Do you develop a balanced portfolio of new product types to diversify risk?

    9 Do you identify customer problems and needs before generating new product ideas?

    10 Do you define new product team values and norms to guide behaviour and communications?

17 Kwak, M. (2001) 'Commitment counts', *MIT Sloan Management Review*, summer, 8–9, reporting on the Stanford Project on Emerging Companies: *http://www.gsb.stanford.edu/spec/research_findings.html*

18 For example, 24 factors are listed in DiBella, A. J. and Nevis, E. C. (1998) *How Organizations Learn*, San Francisco: Jossey-Bass. These barely overlapped with the 38 metrics reported to us by respondents.

7

Employee-based brand equity

AS MENTIONED AT THE START OF THE LAST CHAPTER, a firm's first customers are its own employees. If the staff understand and wholeheartedly endorse the firm's marketing goals, they will take care of the external customers and ultimately the end users. Research suggests a close link between the happiness of customers and that of employees.[1] For this reason, companies have become increasingly interested in creating success in the external marketplace by first doing so internally. And success is made more probable by finding, and then tracking at Exec level, the key metrics.

To some extent, the concepts of employee and customer are interchangeable. A well-ordered firm wants its external customers to consider themselves part of the family and its staff to feel that they are respected and their needs are met. Brand equity is the same but carried around in different heads.[2] The metrics, however, are not quite the same. This chapter discusses which metrics appear, in general, to be appropriate for employee-based brand equity and whether they will also track the innovation health considered in the last chapter. At the least, they overlap.

Internal marketing is not more important than external but the differences arise more from the separation of the human resources (HR) and marketing silos than from what needs to be measured. The similarities and market-driving potential of employee-based brand equity should encourage HR and marketing to swap notes, but such synergy is rare. Contentious as this may be, the conclusions from previous chapters still apply: the 'customer segment' carries over to the employees and the brand is the corporate, or employer, brand. Employee-based brand equity needs to be motivated and maximized. In this chapter, 'employer brand', 'corporate brand', 'internal brand' and 'employee-based brand' are synonyms. Figure 7.1 provides an overview of the chapter, which is organized into these sections:

◆ The increasing recognition of internal branding in the USA and Europe.

◆ Employee 'buy-in' introduces another approach to measuring internal brand equity.

◆ The link between company performance and employee attitudes.

◆ Internal brand measurement in a single-brand, single-business-unit company.

◆ The multi-brand business.

◆ The multi-unit business, e.g. a retail bank with multiple branches.

First, we need to note an important difference: for the external market, the unit of analysis is the brand market segment, but for innovation health and for the employer brand, the business unit applies. In a complex organization with a portfolio of brands and a variety of trading names, the 'brand', so far as individual employees are concerned, may vary across the organization. Simplicity requires a single employing entity, even where there are multiple consumer brands, e.g. as for Unilever.

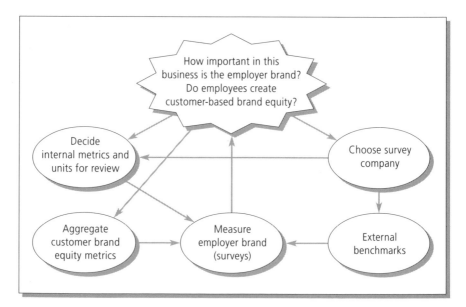

Figure 7.1 ◆ Employee-based brand equity

The increasing recognition of internal branding in the USA and Europe

Hewitt Associates surveyed a cross-section of about 250 US employers in 2001.[3] Almost all respondents considered the company had an external brand but while 72 per cent of corporate communications specialists believed that their company had an internal brand, only 51 per cent of human resources (HR) managers did so. Similarly, two-thirds of the corporate communicators, but only 41 per cent of HR managers, regarded their external and internal brands as identical or at least very similar. Only 1 per cent believed there were no benefits in employer branding. Table 7.1 sets out the five key benefits as seen by respondents.

Table 7.1 ◆ Benefits of employer branding from Hewitt 2000–1 survey

Benefit	Per cent of respondents agreeing
Retains current employees	93
Increases employee engagement/satisfaction	91
Attracts job candidates	90
Motivates employees in their work	79
Leads to improved business results	71

Although only half the sample responded to measurement questions, 72 per cent of respondents used financial performance as an indicator and another 13 per cent felt that it should be used.

The UK consultancy firm, Maritz, was commissioned by the Chartered Institute of Marketing to research the effect of employee brand equity on the bottom line.[4] Their results were consistent with the other findings reported in this chapter. Respondent companies included Barclays and HSBC in financial services, McDonald's and Whitbread in leisure, Safeway and Tesco in retail, and Unisys and Xerox in IT. The results were enshrined in eight principles, the last being measurement which concentrates on what is most important for the brand. Key to gaining the benefits was the way the metrics were reported back to frontline staff.

Tesco uses a version of the Balanced Scorecard, with 'steering wheels' showing employee, customer and financial metrics. HSBC is seeking to link employee with customer satisfaction. External benchmarking is less important than comparing these measures across branches. Whitbread also aims to 'measure every which way', including mystery shopping, customer panels and focus groups and satisfaction monitors. The Marriott hotel chain has a similar approach and the UK consultancy, Circus, explored the relationship in financial services (*see box*).

Brand Engagement

Brand Engagement is a registered trademark of Circus, a UK media-neutral brand consultancy. Circus believes that brands with consistent actions and behaviours have a much higher reputation across all stakeholders, and achieve a higher degree of loyalty among those stakeholders. Six financial services companies with a cross-section of cultures formed the pilot for empirical research.

The method involved matched, parallel surveys of customers and employees. The alignment of a brand's behaviours behind a clear purpose emerged as a driver of both employee and customer satisfaction, and also of personal identification with the company.

Far the largest driver of customer satisfaction was brand performance being in line with promise. The second biggest factor is how they perceive that brand to be treating its employees. In other words, Circus found a direct link between the loyalty and satisfaction of different stakeholder groups. Customers care about the ethos and internal culture of the brands they use.

Similarly, the highest factor in driving employee satisfaction is whether a company keeps its promises to them. This is twice as important as salary. In terms of employee engagement, the survey indicates that a company should deliver a balanced triumvirate of goals relevant to employee values, distinctiveness of culture and clarity of purpose.

Circus concludes that the external and internal reputations of a brand are inextricably interlinked, and therefore human resources should be treated as internal marketing and given the same skill and content as external marketing.

Source: Paul Twivy, Consultant to Circus and Chief Strategic Planning Officer McCann-Erickson, EMEA; and Mark Hutchinson, Partner, Circus, 8 November 2002

The HR consultancy Watson Wyatt's fourth iteration of their Human Capital Index™ (HCI) research that studied people management practices in over 600 companies from 16 countries across Europe and combined this with independent financial data. It showed a clear link between specific people management practices and financial performance (Table 7.2). Similar results have been found in Watson Wyatt's North American and Asia-Pacific HCI studies, which together with the European participants, have respondents from over 1500 of the world's leading companies. They have found a strong link between effective human capital management (including employer branding) and shareholder value. Companies with the best people management deliver nearly twice as much value to their shareholders as their average competitors.

Table 7.2 ◆ European 2002 HCI study

HR practice	Contribution to shareholder value %
HR function effectiveness (alignment of HR to the business, cost management, and leveraging technology)	21
Clear rewards and accountability (rewarding employees for good work and refusing to accept sub-par performance)	21.5
Recruiting and retention excellence (getting the right people in the right jobs and keeping them)	14.6
Collegial flexible workplace (integrated leadership, cooperative, flexible)	11
Communications integrity (two-way sharing of information, employee participation)	7
Prudent use of resources (having less of the following: paternalism, developmental training, and use of contract workers)	14.5

The replication of the results from the 2000 European HCI, when the stock markets reached their zenith, shows that good and bad human resources practices associated with higher and lower shareholder value respectively continue in bear as well as bull markets. Steven Dicker, study co-author, claims that 'great people management is linked with a 90 per cent increase in shareholder value. It is an amazing figure at first sight. As well as highlighting the gulf between the best and the rest, we believe it reflects the growing emphasis on people management within businesses as other sources of competitive advantage prove increasingly difficult to sustain'.[5]

'Being the custodian of the employer brand is often a challenge for 'new economy' Human Resources leaders', suggests Doug Ross, the other co-author. Much of the challenge comes from the need to work closely with marketing, HR, measurement and the leadership team to ensure the facilitation of good people management throughout the business. The glue that holds much of this interaction together is the employer brand. So how does the employer brand work? Watson Wyatt typically open with these questions:

1   What are the reasons for shareholders to invest in Organization X and what are the reasons for an investor to believe that these expectations will come true?

2   What are the reasons for customers (often need to link to marketing to understand the segmentation and buyer behaviour) to invest their money in Organization X as their preferred supplier and what are the reasons (proof statements) to support this statement – the commercial brand?

3   What are the reasons for working at Organization X and the proof statements that demonstrate that this is a good organization for high performers to invest their careers in?

As with the work undertaken at Unilever, Watson Wyatt supports the concern with aligning the three brand equity perspectives: shareholders, customers, and employees. Furthermore, they believe that leadership communication and action must be linked and mutually supportive to drive value to all stakeholders.

The process of employer branding is by nature holistic. It is not about tinkering with terms and conditions or corporate colours in the workplace, but about the total employment experience. Brand equity is synergistic, greater than the sum of its parts, and based on core values. If an organization increases its employer brand equity, it increases its high performing employees' barriers to exit. Employer brand commitment can be seen as a ladder:

1   Employees will change brands, especially for reward reasons. No brand loyalty.

2   Employees are satisfied. No reason to change the brand but no reason to excel.

3   Employees are satisfied and would incur costs by changing brand. Co-dependent on the brand.

4 Employees value the brand and see it as a partner to achieving their goals.

5 Employees are devoted to the brand. Need to manage brand erosion and keep performance standards (brand equity is highly related to the number of employees who are in the 4 or 5 areas).

Watson Wyatt believe that a strong employer brand can also create competitive advantage:

1 Reducing recruitment costs because of higher level of awareness, loyalty, and commitment.

2 Increasing bargaining leverage with unions and individuals since employees expect then to deliver on the brand.

3 Demanding a higher level of performance than competitors because the brand promise has a higher perceived quality.

4 Offering some defence against fierce high performer poaching.

Providing excellent and consistent performance from leaders and custodians of the brand may be the single most important characteristic in building a strong employer brand. And within brand management the most critical measure may be loyalty and commitment that comes from meeting and shaping expectations through the employee experience. Although speculative, Watson Wyatt has sought to attribute the improvements in shareholder value to specific attributes of good HR practice (Table 7.3).

Table 7.3 ◆ Contributions to shareholder value

HR element of employer brand	Shareholder value contribution %
Providing integrated leadership	5.5
Enabling employees to manage 'Me Plc' (the ability for employees to maximize their own potential)	5.2
Ensuring two-way communications	3.2
Providing flexibility in the workplace	1.6
Creation of a secure work environment	1.0
Encouraging employee involvement	0.14
Total potential value	16.64

We now move from the broad picture across employers in general to a very specific example of leadership in one, relatively small, European company. In presenting a case study, summarized below, on linking customer and employee focus, Sean Meehan and Pius Baschera noted that the CEOs of high and low performing UK companies spent about the same amount of time (18 and 15 per cent respectively) with customers. The way that time was spent, however, was very different. High performers prioritized individual issues whereas low performers were less focused, e.g. cultural or sporting events. So measuring the time spent with customers or employees may not provide useful metrics. We need to distinguish individualized from generalized time (*see box*).

Hilti

Hilti is a Liechtenstein-based business specializing in power tools and equipment for the construction and building maintenance sector. In 1996, they developed a Champion 3C strategy around three key principles:

◆ Working directly with customers, seeing how they work, understanding their issues and responding

◆ Paying close attention to employees as individuals, ensuring they understand the strategy and how it fits together

◆ Accept that you can't be smart enough to have all the answers

Since the early 1990s, Hilti had been biennially measuring employee morale. Post-1996 they found high satisfaction by employees who also understand the Champion 3C strategy. Morale was linked with confidence and respect for their immediate bosses.

Most significantly, customers who were Hilti 'fans' (brand advocates) were serviced by high-morale employees and both were significantly correlated with profitability. This is the classic service chain win-win-win. These metrics provided management at all levels with the tools to identify areas for improvement and some of the ways that can be done.

At the practical level, Hilti senior management now plan their customer visits to listen and learn with more care and put as much effort into planning the internal side of the visit. These visits are no longer sales calls, in the traditional sense, so much as building the culture in which customer and employee relationships can thrive.

Source: S. Meehan and P. Baschera (2002)'Lessons from Hilti: how customer and employee contact improves strategy implementation', *Business Strategy Review*, 13 (2), 31–9

Employee buy-in

Strategic marketing consultancy Marketing & Communications Agency (MCA)[6] specializes in helping companies to align staff with business goals. MCA proposes that only two indicators are needed to assess employee 'buy-in': understanding of, and commitment to, the company's business goals and brand values. Staff need to be aware of key business strategies and the difference they can make. The other, equally valuable, side of the coin is the need for commitment and engagement in the achievement of goals. Emotion (passion) fuels an organization like gasoline fuels a car.

To understand the components and value of buy-in, MCA commissioned Market & Opinion Research International (MORI) to conduct a nationally representative quota sample of 350 managers and staff from British organizations employing 1000 or more people within a cross-section of industry sectors.[7] About 60 per cent worked in organizations with 5000+ employees, and 41 per cent were managers.

To compare the levels of intellectual and emotional buy-in and to understand the areas for improvement, respondents were asked about their level of agreement with key benchmarking statements based on MCA's work with some of *The Times* 100 companies. The results are summarized as Table 7.4. Only 14 per cent strongly agree with all five intellectual benchmarking statements. When asked about overall awareness and understanding of key business goals, less than half (48 per cent) of respondents rate them as high.

On the emotional side, 51 per cent of respondents rated their overall level of commitment as high. Nonetheless, the responses to the emotional benchmarking statements show a noticeable drop in levels of agreement overall: for example, Table 7.4 shows that only 9 per cent of those interviewed felt their views and participation were valued by their organization. And only 15 per cent strongly agreed that they have confidence in their organization's leadership. Only 5 per cent of the respondents strongly agreed with all six emotional benchmarks.

Managers are being demotivated by excessive change, which may explain their disappointing levels of understanding and commitment. About 40 per cent say a restructuring or merger/acquisition has directly affected them in the last 12 months, compared with 29 per cent of non-managers.

Table 7.4 ◆ Indicators of buy-in

(Note: Intellectual indicators are in italics and emotional in plain text)	Strongly agree %
I understand what I need to do in my own job to support organizational aims and goals	39
I feel I play an important part in meeting our customers' needs	38
I have the knowledge/skills to do my job in a way that supports organizational goals	37
I can see how my job performance affects my organization's success	34
The people in my team/work area know how we contribute to organizational goals	28
I have a clear sense of my organization's vision and direction for the future	27
I am committed to giving my best to help my organization succeed	27
My organization's culture encourages me to work in innovative ways	17
I believe in my organization's vision for the future	16
I have confidence in my organization's leadership	15
My views and participation are valued by my organization	9

Levels of communication and internal marketing during periods of dramatic organizational change can have profound effects on the overall effectiveness of staff. An example is provided by two Fortune 500 companies that merged in the 1980s.[8] One plant received no communication until the formal announcement; the other had received early and frequent communication throughout the planning process. The plant without communication saw a 20 per cent decrease in performance, a 24 per cent increase in uncertainty, a 21 per cent decrease in job satisfaction and an 11 per cent decrease in commitment. The plant with early and frequent communication saw no change in performance or commitment and only a 2 per cent decrease in job satisfaction.

According to MCA, the combination of intellectual and emotional buy-in creates people who are both willing and able to give their best to help their organization achieve its vision and goals, and who will act as ambassadors for their brand and/or organization. These champions are vital to overcoming the neutral or negative responses likely from others in their organization. This is, of course, a different use of the word 'champion' from the one in the previous chapter, although a champion in this sense is more likely to be a successful leader of an innovation. Perspectives, the MORI normative database, found that about one in five UK employees are 'saboteurs'. This means that in an organization with 1000 employees, there are some 200 people who would bad-mouth their organization. Figure 7.2 shows four categories of employee using data from a separate survey:

◆ Champions are the ideal group of employees who both understand and are committed to the firm's goals.

◆ Bystanders clearly understand organizational goals but do not have the emotional drive to support them.

◆ Loose cannons are highly motivated to support business goals but do not understand what they are or how to achieve them.

◆ Weak links are not aware of, or concerned about, business goals.

The 100 best US companies to work for in 1997, as voted by over 20,000 employees, showed the impact of emotional buy-in on business performance.[9] Of the 61 companies in the group that had been publicly traded for at least five years, 45 had consistently yielded higher returns to shareholders than industry averages. These 61 companies averaged annual returns of 27.5

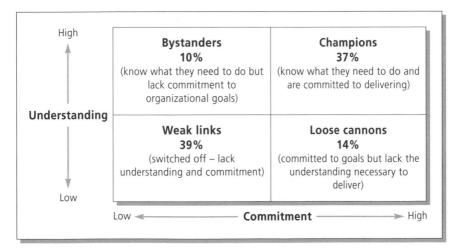

Figure 7.2 ◆ Categories of employee buy-in

per cent, compared with the typical 17.3 per cent. Although the research below imply that improved employer brand equity drives business performance, it is probably more complex; the research is mostly based on associations. In other words, the reverse is also likely: namely, better performance inspires more positive employer brand equity. Practitioners will be more concerned with the existence of the virtuous circle than the ideal point at which to enter it.

The link between company performance

and employee attitudes

The employee effect on overall company performance is especially marked in service businesses that depend on the relationship between external customers and the staff they meet.[10] Even in dot.com companies where customers interact solely with their computer screens, the understanding and motivation of employees is still important.

The starting point is for each Exec to review the impact of staff attitudes and behaviour on company performance. Hilti, in the case above, provides a good example of measuring profit performance and attitudes of customers and any employees they contact at both the micro (individually or by branch where this is possible) and macro (the firm overall) levels. Of course, correlation is not causality: working with profitable customers may improve the morale of employees rather than the other way about, but at least it is a start. If the data are available, the firm can compare staff attitudes at time t-1 with customer attitudes at time t, to get a better fix on causality but that is not essential. Correlating firm and customer performance with customer and employee attitudes and behavioural measures (e.g. staff turnover) is enough.

This is the starting point because the Exec needs to decide whether internal market metrics should be presented alongside external market metrics or whether they can be left within the HR function. We know that external metrics monitor future inward cash flow so they are vital. The issue now is whether the internal market metrics can perform a similar role. And maybe do so earlier because if the internal really do cause the external, then fixing internal problems cures any sickness sooner.

As noted in Chapter 5, Insead's Professor Larréché has been developing measures of the competitive fitness of global firms. The internal market metrics were integrated with the external but, for the purpose of this book, I have teased them apart. The main point here is that the natural assumption was to take them together. The key internal metrics, ranked out of a total of 134, are shown in the box below. Note how highly they rank.

Indicators of corporate competitive fitness

Ranking	Internal market metric
4	Monitoring of results relative to plans
6	Employees proud of products offered
10	Demonstrated ability to adapt
14	Exciting workplace in future
14	Clear firm objectives
18	Confidence in actions for improvement
21	Employee commitment
25	Shared mission
25	Shared drive for improvement
25	Targeting of profitable segments
25	Passion for work
25	Marketing actions in line with strategy
31	Focus on key products
31	Commitment to budget targets
31	Coherence of strategy/planning budget
39	Confidence in firm's ability to improve
39	Care of employees
39	Effective internal communication network
44	Teamwork between marketing and sales
44	Open communication
44	Understanding corporate challenges

Source: Larréché, J.-C. (2002) *The Competitive Fitness of Global Firms 2002*, London: Pearson Education; also *www.corvaltec.com/2002report/Appendices.htm*

Many and perhaps most large companies formalize their internal market metrics, e.g. through regular employee surveys. The missing link, however, is to see customers and employees as two sides of similar coin or, more accurately, as two components of the same brand equity. The separate sets of data are not presented as parts of a single business model, marketing techniques are not adopted internally nor HR methodologies externally. The reporting of external and internal market metrics is not integrated. The issue can be illustrated with a few examples (*see box*).

Compaq

This case study immediately precedes Compaq's 2002 merger with Hewlett-Packard.

Deanna Graham, now Total Customer Experience Research, Hewlett-Packard, sat down with colleagues across Compaq to review how the customer and employee satisfaction linked together with brand perceptions ('brand equity') to drive the financial performance and thence shareholder value. Prior to this cross-functional initiative these indicators were retained within separate departments, namely sales, HR and marketing respectively.

Taken together, the three drivers explained 77 per cent of the variance in gross market and 33 per cent of the variance in market share. Within the three, the strongest links were employee satisfaction on customer satisfaction and the latter on brand equity. Brand equity had positive feedback effects on customers and employees. Most impressively of all, brand equity alone explained 76 per cent of the variation in shareholder value.

This model enabled the team to identify how improvement in each element of non-financial performance would impact the bottom line. They were also able to track customer satisfaction back to the three main components of their product mix: access (gaining entry to systems is usually the starting point), enterprise and service products. As the relationship grows so, typically, does customer satisfaction.

Three main conclusions came from this initiative. The first concerned more integrated management of the customer experience. By looking at the relationship from the customer's viewpoint, as distinct from the three internal functions, resources might be differently allocated. Second, the same holistic thinking could be applied to measurement and accountability. Third, the limited headroom for improvement *directly* in customer and employee satisfaction implied that relatively more investment should be given to brand equity.

Source: Deanna Graham presentation at MSI Marketing Productivity Conference, Dallas, 3 October 2002

Maryland's Professor Ben Schneider has a framework not dissimilar to MCA's.[11] The three parts are foundation issues (like fairness and trust); how well employees think they are treated; and service climate (emphasis on quality, training and adequacy of resources). Schneider also finds the positive internal/external customer performance link.

In 1997, the Institute of Work Psychology conducted a study of 100 single-site, single-product-operation manufacturing companies with fewer than a thousand employees.[12] According to the study: '12 per cent of the variation between companies in their profitability can be explained by variations in the job satisfaction of their employees. Moreover, 13 per cent … can be explained by the differences between companies in organizational commitment'. Company performance is measured by relative labour productivity (relative to the industry in which the firm belongs) and real profits per employee both before and after the measurement of human resource management practices, culture and attitudes.

More recently, MORI showed that dealings with staff ranked third after price and quality in terms of repeat purchase.[13] Of the younger, more affluent consumers 23 per cent are put off by the treatment they receive. Fewer than 50 per cent of all customers felt that staff showed a genuine interest in helping and fewer than 20 per cent claimed that staff showed appreciation for interest or purchase. Fewer than 33 per cent of customers saw employees' commitment to doing their best and only 10 per cent saw pride in goods or services.

Cranfield's Professor Adrian Payne researched the linkages between attraction, satisfaction and retention across the three key stakeholder groups: customers, employees and shareholders. While the majority of the large companies in his and his colleagues' samples collected customer and employee data of these types, their investigation of about 600 UK companies found no examples of British companies linking this information to understand what drives what.[14] The Nortel example of best practice is taken from their paper (*see box*).

Nortel Networks

Nortel Networks is a Canadian telecoms company employing 80,000 staff worldwide, with revenues of $18 billion. It benchmarks leading organizations such as Disney and emphasizes quality. It has won US Baldrige and European EFQM awards. Extensive research led the company to its own model, the Nortel Business Value Cycle, which explicitly

▶

links resources (people, financials, knowledge, partners, etc.) with customers and ultimately shareholder value. Importantly the feedback loop
from shareholder value to resources is labelled 'leadership'.

Establishing such a multifunctional database across a large global
business was a major task. On the other hand it has created global organizational learning. A manager in one country, for example, can track the
data for a better performing but otherwise comparable unit elsewhere.

Nortel found that leadership accounted for 31 per cent of employee
and 18 per cent of customer satisfaction respectively. The required leadership behaviours are clearly identified and monitored. They found that
employee satisfaction accounted for 52 per cent of customer satisfaction
and are now working on the links between customer metrics and shareholder value.

Source: Payne, A., Holt, S. and Frow, P. (1999) 'Relationship value management:
exploring the integration of employee, customer and shareholder value',
7th International Colloquim in Relationship Marketing, Strathclyde University,
7–9 November.

The US retailer Sears provides the classic case study in this area. They
turned their business around by changing the marketing strategy and the
nature of the relationships between staff and external customers. The virtuous circle produced increased employee and customer satisfaction and
higher profits.[15] The CEO and a group of top executives developed a business approach for the company to track success from employee attitudes and
behaviour through to customer satisfaction and financial performance – an
approach they called the 'Employee–Customer–Profit Chain'.

This model represents a new inside-out approach to relationship marketing, as well as a management information system and self-assessment tool.
According to Sears executives: 'Our model shows that a 5 [percentage]
point improvement in employee attitudes will drive a 1.3 [percentage] point
improvement in customer satisfaction, which in turn will drive a 0.5 per
cent improvement in revenue growth' (p. 91). These results are even more
compelling when considered against national norms:

*Independent surveys show that national retail customer satisfaction has fallen for
several consecutive years, but in the course of the last 12 months, employee
satisfaction on the Sears TPI (Total Performance Index) has risen by 4 per cent
and customer satisfaction by almost 4 per cent … an improvement that translates
into more than $200 million in additional revenues in the past 12 months … It is*

our managers and employees who, at the moment of truth in front of the customer, have achieved this prodigious feat of value creation. (p. 97)

Problems at Sears since the time of this study do not, in my view, undermine its validity. Retailing in the USA is a tough environment.

For comparison, it is interesting to note the approach taken by BP in 1997, before they merged with Amoco and subsequently took over Arco, Burmah Castrol and Veba Oil of Germany (the latter in early 2002). One point of interest is the way in which the group today reflects the intentions then.

BP

The insight was the way BP researched brand matters with its own staff. They discovered managers had a sophisticated understanding of the BP brand model, audiences and financial objectives. Managers at all levels were constructive on how the presentation of the model could be improved and used to manage their external relationships.

The attributes of BP as a brand were tested on four bases: BP then and in the future as an oil company, BP with a new central purpose and the BP they wanted to work for. These four were tested with 28 attributes (plus others) ranging from agile, ambitious and arrogant through to successful, sustainable, technology led and vibrant. Respondents were asked to circle the five most relevant attributes for each of the four versions of BP.

Finally they were asked some quite direct questions, e.g. whether the company should invest more in the brand. The results were reported back by e-mail as follows (but the attachments are not shown here):

To: BP Global Brand survey participants

Your participation in the Brand survey is appreciated. The survey results helped shape an understanding of the role Brand plays within BP and provided a very useful basis for continuing discussions. Some of you will have seen the survey results presented in Group Leadership meetings. The following is a summary of the key results from the survey:

◆ People within BP demonstrated a good understanding of Brand and agree with the hypothesis that Brand = behaviour.

◆ There is a widespread awareness of, and commitment to, the importance of Brand.

◆ There is a thirst for a clearer expression of BP's Brand and a simple communication of it to all employees.

▶

◆ Emotional content of the Brand is missing.

◆ Financial objectives drive the culture of the company. We are proud of the fact that we have exceeded challenging targets quarter after quarter. We do not want to lose that part of our identity.

◆ However, BP is viewed as cold and matter of fact. There is a desire to see a balance with more human/emotional values in the future.

◆ Attachment 1 illustrates the attributes most associated with BP today.

◆ Attachment 2 portrays the results when respondents were asked which characteristics they would like to have associated with your BP.

◆ Attachment 3 illustrates those attributes which are most different in the portrayal of BP today and your BP.

◆ There is a hunger for action.

The survey results have been used along with the work of the Global Brand Team and discussions with senior managers to form a characterization of BP as embodied in the BP Brand. This characterization is being honed and validated through external research and internal leadership meetings. It is anticipated that this work will culminate in a 1998 Brand Plan resulting from discussions with the Group Executive in New Orleans and the Main Exec at the end of this month.

Thank you again for your help and support in this effort.

Source: Duncan Blake, Group Brands Manager, BP, January 2000 and October 2002

Even today, the detailed results of this research are confidential, but the quotation illustrates the imaginative way that BP used employee data both as a proxy for consumer research and as a way to establish the directions needed for internal and external marketing.

My final example is from the UK retail banking sector. We all know retention is important, but why do some customers stay and others leave? Moira Clark, also of Cranfield, investigated the relationship between employees' perceptions of organizational climate and customer retention.[16] Five dimensions emerged: structure, rewards and recognition, cohesion, warmth and support and customer care. Some of these, unsurprisingly, echo the Watson Wyatt analysis noted earlier. Although leadership is not specifically mentioned, much of the first dimension revolves around communications (open) and clear roles. The rewards and recognition is similar to 'money still matters' in Watson Wyatt and cohesion is team-ness which was included in integrated leadership practices in the earlier study. Warmth and support could be described as morale but the key point here is that only one of the five specifically refers to customers even though she is explaining why customers stay.

In summary, the evidence is that, for a wide cross-section of firms, employee-based brand equity is likely to be such an important driver of overall business performance that it should be included within the marketing metrics review process. We turn now to the question of what metrics should be used, first in the simple unitary firm and then the variations required for multiple brands and business units.

The unitary brand and business unit situation

These perspectives bear a striking resemblance to the measurement of innovation health in the last chapter. 'Staff awareness of vision/direction' and 'staff commitment to vision/direction' formed the first two metrics under the leadership heading. But the awareness and commitment applied specifically to the corporate innovation goals, whereas we are now dealing with the overall business goals. Nevertheless, it is worth looking back to see which of the nine innovation metrics in the last chapter (Table 6.2, p. 172) could apply to employee-based brand equity more generally. The nine were:

◆ Awareness of goals (vision)

◆ Commitment to goals (vision)

◆ Active innovation support

◆ Perceived resource adequacy

◆ Appetite for learning

◆ Freedom to fail

◆ Number of initiatives in process

◆ Number of innovations launched

◆ Percentage of revenue due to launches in last three years

An alternative approach is to follow the 'employee as customer' logic and adapt the proposed consumer general brand equity list from Table 5.3 (p. 136) as follows:

1 *Familiarity*: in this case we are considering the salience of the firm's goals. This issue comes through much of the research reported earlier.

2 *Penetration*: this measured the size of the customer base and although tracking the number of staff is something the Exec may wish to do, it seems less relevant to brand equity.

3 *What they think of the brand*: in the customer case, the proposed metric was relative perceived quality. The calibre of the employer needs to be benchmarked against the calibre, as perceived by their employees, of comparable firms.

4 *What they feel about the brand*: this was measured as relative satisfaction that can be translated directly to the employee situation.

5 *Brand loyalty*: in Chapter 5, this was measured attitudinally as commitment (the determination to achieve the marketing goals as understood) and behaviourally as retention.

6 *Availability*: how easy is it to get to work? Are there opportunities for work sharing/telecommuting?

The fit is not close, with only two (familiarity/awareness and commitment) appearing in both lists, but these are also the two that emerge from the MCA analysis. That could be important. A prime example of a company that involves employees in its goals and keeps them posted on progress is the TNT distribution company, where the link between employee and customer satisfaction is closely monitored (*see box*).

Combining the innovation and general customer brand equity measures therefore leaves 13, which is rather too many, or 14 if employee retention

TNT

Founded in 1978, TNT UK Limited is a subsidiary of the Dutch TNT Post Group (TPG) and describes itself as 'a dynamic international transport organization operating within a fast moving, highly competitive marketplace and with a strong focus on quality'. TNT UK has two principal business units – TNT Express Services and TNT Logistics and employs some 16,000 people at over 400 locations. The company's annual turnover is almost £1 billion and it is established as leader in its market.

▶

Our key measures of success are Customer Satisfaction, Employee Satisfaction and Financial Performance. Customer Satisfaction is actually measured by quarterly 'customer dissatisfaction' surveys in which 5000 customers are asked to provide specific details on problems they have experienced and how they were dealt with rather than how happy they are generally. Customers are encouraged to be frank and honest to explain the whole experience from their point of view.

Employee Satisfaction is monitored and measured by means of People Surveys. Every employee in the organization is surveyed for their opinion on the company, their remuneration, working conditions, how they feel about the company image, training and development knowledge of the company strategy and their views on the effectiveness of company communications and the management.

From a financial perspective the company measures performance by weekly profit and loss reports. Economic profit brings capital and profit factors are combined to produce the ultimate financial measure of business success. In the longer term an economic value measure will be used which is much more closely focused on cash generation.

Additional marketing metrics are: top of mind and spontaneous brand awareness in our target markets compared with competitors, recall of sales contacts and direct marketing, penetration of key messages in target media resulting from the PR programme and share of voice.

Internal metrics include the measurement of response levels and revenues generated by direct mail campaigns and the measurement of Return on Investment of marketing activity.

The TNT name for the principal, intangible asset built by marketing is 'Brand Health'. 'Brand performance' is tracked against competitor performance via a bi-annual commissioned survey. Factors including awareness, knowledge of business and services provided, usage and preference ratings, associations with the brand, propensity to use and willingness to recommend are weighted to provide brand health scores, a measure of brand performance.

Source: Interview with Steve Doig, Group Marketing Director TNT, 7 October 2002

(clearly a key metric) is separated from commitment. The three specific innovation performance metrics can be dropped and active innovation support can be merged here with freedom to fail. Penetration (size of work-

Table 7.5 ◆ Provisional shortlist of employer brand metrics

Awareness of goals
Perceived calibre of employer
Relative employee satisfaction
Commitment to goals
Employee retention
Perceived resource adequacy
Appetite for learning
Freedom to fail

force) and availability can probably be discarded, which brings the list to a more manageable eight as shown by Table 7.5.

The five dimensions in Watson Wyatt and the other five in the Moira Clark analysis actually embrace a wide range of specific measures, so the question here is whether this shortlist, which should also cover innovation other than performance, provides a reasonable sampling of their frameworks. Relative satisfaction should pick up the hygiene factor of rewards and recognition or 'money still matters' and probably also the cultural aspects. Resource adequacy should reflect perceived support at least in the practical sense. Paternalistic environment was the big negative in the Watson Wyatt analysis and this would be sampled by freedom to fail. Indeed, as Southwest Airlines have discovered, freedom is a powerful motivational concept for employees (*see box*).

Southwest Airlines

Hewitt Associates assisted Southwest Airlines with its effort to adapt and extend its external 'freedom' brand to its employees. In 2000, Southwest reversed the usual employer–employee relationship to say 'It's up to you to exercise the freedoms our benefits can bring you'.

'Freedom begins with me' became the slogan of the internal branding programme which teased out eight specific and measurable dimensions:

◆ Freedom to make a positive difference

◆ Freedom to create and innovate

◆ Freedom to learn and grow

▶

◆ Freedom to work hard and have fun

◆ Freedom to create financial security

◆ Freedom to pursue good health

◆ Freedom to travel

◆ Freedom to stay connected

Employee retention had proved a problem but the programme reduced the turnover and the company was now on track to achieve a 90 per cent retention rate. Net income rose 31.8 per cent in 2000 and the stock price rose by 107 per cent. For the fourth year running, Southwest was in the top five of Fortune's best places to work.

Source: Jill Elswick (2001) 'Conveying freedom', *Employee Benefit News*, 15 (10), 1

So far we have considered the unitary situation where the employer, or corporate, brand is the only one sold to customers by the employees. Unitary brand companies have an advantage in aligning the interests of consumers, trade, employees and shareholders. Ideally, the employees are the ambassadors for the brand. The multi-brand situation is more complex.

The multi-brand situation

Where a business unit markets many brands, as is the case in Unilever or Mars, each member of staff cannot simultaneously be an ambassador for all the product brands and also the corporate brand. The consumers may not even be aware of, still less care about, the corporate brand and shareholders may care little about some of the product brands. Measuring employee awareness of, and commitment to, just the top brands risks telling employees that the others do not matter. Alternative solutions to this conundrum of how the employees' share of the intangible marketing assets can be estimated include the following:

1 Loyalty to the employer, i.e. the corporate brand, matters most. We should therefore measure just employer brand equity, as in the section above, and disregard the product brands, be they goods or services.

2 Conversely, we could take the view that, from a market perspective, only the product brands matter. The equity of the corporate brand has no

commercial significance. For example, when International Distillers and Vintners Ltd was formed as a quoted company in 1962, the directors chose the name precisely because it was undistinguished and unmemorable. They did not want any corporate name that would distract attention from the product brands like J&B Rare, Gilbeys Gin and Smirnoff Vodka.

3 As a mid-position, one could decide that the corporate brand is just another brand and add together what is in the employees' heads about all these brands.

None of these solutions is wholly satisfactory and, as the next section shows, the last solution risks consolidating apples and oranges. The corporate brand is a different kind of fruit. In practice, the short list of metrics suggested above brings its own solution. Reviewing the eight short-listed employer brand metrics in Table 7.5 shows that none needs to be changed in principle, even though the details may be more complex. The goals, for example, are likely to be more diverse in a multi-brand unit but awareness of, and commitment to, those goals remain paramount. The cultural metrics (appetite for learning and freedom to fail) are unlikely to vary much by product brand. Similarly relative employee satisfaction is corporate not product branded. In effect, this eliminates the second of the three options above.

How then do we deal with the product brand issues? Suppose the employees now think that Product A is wonderful but that B is abysmal, whereas one year ago they were both thought to be equally moderate. If the two brands have really performed equally well, the (internal) marketing of A has been better than B and this, especially in a service business, would impact consumer brand equity in due course. Assessing internal marketing purely in terms of the corporate brand, and ignoring product brands, would entirely miss these key facts.

You may have noticed that the metrics in Table 7.5 failed to cover the 'customer care' dimension in Moira Clark's analysis. The various metrics that would identify staff concern with the many consumer-based equity considerations would be too many to cover here, but at least we can include one indicator of how well employees see the business from the customer's point of view. For example, the same consumer research questions could be given to employees asked to complete it as if they were customers. The correlation between the two data sets would give an index of 'customer-brand empathy'. How many brands are covered by such an index, or how the results are weighted between brands, is a practical matter that should be determined by what gives the best answer; i.e. which methodology gives the index that best predicts future performance. Naturally, this has to be tested with old data.

In other words, we are adding a metric that encourages the employees to see things from the customer's point of view across the portfolio of brands. We are asking 'Does the employee truly care about what the customer cares about?' The metrics now become the nine in Table 7.6.

Table 7.6 ◆ Employee-based equity metrics

Awareness of corporate goals

Perceived calibre of employer

Relative employee satisfaction

Commitment to corporate goals

Employee retention

Perceived resource adequacy

Appetite for learning

Freedom to fail

Customer-brand empathy

Can business units be consolidated?

While multi-branding is a complication, the existence of multiple business units is a boon, because units can be compared internally with each other, e.g. branches of a fast food retailer. Cross-learning can be provided internally and the need for external benchmarks is reduced.

Although aggregation always loses information, the average for the internal metrics for the firm as a whole provides the internal benchmark for reviewing individual business units at the appropriate level of management. A 3000-branch chain may have four layers of management between the outlet and CEO, and the Exec would not normally involve itself with the data of any particular store. On the other hand, briefing the Exec on the metrics for the best and worst performing branches relative to the firm-wide averages is an important contribution to understanding and testing the firm's overall business model.

Whether the data for separate business units can be sensibly aggregated depends on how similar they are. For example, if employees asked to name

'the boss' always name the group CEO, then aggregating leadership perceptions is fine. If, however, the names range up and down the hierarchy,
leadership metrics take on a different character.

One could be scientific about this. Business units could be clustered into
like groups and metrics only aggregated up to cluster level. But, of course,
the likenesses may not continue from year to year and reporting is conventionally according to the management hierarchy. In any case, scientific
analysis of this type is rare and, because the clusters often prove to be spurious, requires extreme care.[17]

Theory will not supply the answers here but data analysis may. Just as for
the external market metrics, the Exec really need to discover which metrics
work. Maybe the list should be the nine above, maybe different ones. Are they
sensitive but not too sensitive? Are they reliable? Do they predict future performance? Do they add new information or merely duplicate existing
information? If metrics work at the corporate level, then the lower levels can be
left as diagnostics. If adding results from unlike businesses ends up as pea soup,
the Exec will have to consider the metrics for each major business separately.

As in the case for innovation, Execs should consider an occasional major
audit using many more indicators than the nine or so suggested here for
regular review. That audit should help determine which employer brand
metrics are the most appropriate for that particular business.

Just as the provision of metrics for the Exec presents an opportunity to
rethink the relationship between marketing and finance functions, so
employer brand equity provides a challenge bridging marketing and HR
skills and information. The first relationship should lead to linking the external market metrics with shareholder value. The second relationship, as we
saw in the Compaq case study, should link employee and customer satisfaction. To do that, HR need marketing skills and marketers need to
understand and work with HR. Too often, internal communications are
seen as simply passing down information, and too little concern is given to
how or if these messages are received and what effects they have. Periodic
surveys of staff morale are unrelated to marketing goals, communications or
employer brand equity.[18] Furthermore, excessive surveying produces fatigue
and a reluctance to participate thereby reducing the quality of the data. For
many large companies, finance, HR and marketing operate as separate functions, perhaps even silos, communicating internally but barely with each
other. Marketing metrics at Exec level can unite the three.

Executive minutes

1 Chief Marketing and Chief Human Resources Officers (CHROs) to report on the relative importance of employees as drivers of business performance. To what extent do employees create immediate customer and end-user brand equity?

2 CHRO director to report on specialist firms available to measure employee indicators, costs and experience, on what benchmarking would be available against which peer companies and historical data, and which indicators each firm would recommend.

3 CHRO to review staff surveys to link more closely with employee-based brand equity and optimize both the number of questions and the frequency of surveys.

4 HR, Marketing and Finance to analyze and test candidate metrics at firm-wide and business unit levels and report on metrics suitability and aggregation levels. They should especially comment on the suitability of the nine metrics suggested in this chapter.

5 Exec to resolve the optimal set of internal employee metrics. Note should be taken of external specialist recommendations (item 2 above) and measurement feasibility.

6 CFO to include employee-based brand equity metrics with external market metrics for the Exec review.

Notes

1 For example, Heskett, J. L., Sasser, W. E., Jr. and Schlesinger, L. A. (1997) *The Service Profit Chain: How Leading Companies Link Profit and Growth to Loyalty, Satisfaction, and Value*, New York: Free Press.

Schneider, B., White, S. S. and Paul, M. C. (1998) 'Linking service climate and customer perceptions of service quality: test of a causal model', *Journal of Applied Psychology* 83 (2), 150–63.

2 Ambler, T. and Barrow, S. (1996) 'The employer brand', *Journal of Brand Management* 4 (3), 185–206 defined it as 'the package of functional, economic, and psychological benefits provided by employment, and identified with the employing company'. 'Employer brand equity' is the intangible corporate asset created in the minds of employees by leadership, culture and employment practices.

3 Survey Findings: *Emerging Trends in Internal Branding 2000/2001*, Lincolnshire IL: Hewitt Associates LLC.

4 Brooke, J. (2002) 'The brand inside', London: Maritz, 2 July.

5 Email to Tim Ambler from Doug Ross, Watson Wyatt, 9 October 2002. Steven Dicker and Doug Ross, the co-authors of the study, are both Watson Wyatt partners. Steven is a research statistician and Doug is a marketing strategist. The next quote is from the same source.

6 Most of this section is taken, with permission, from Thomson, K. and Arganbright, L. (1999) 'The buy-in benchmark: how staff understanding and commitment impact brand and business performance', CIM seminar on Measuring Marketing Performance, May.

7 Arganbright, L. and Thomson, K. (1998) 'The buy-in benchmark', London: Marketing & Communication Agency and Market & Opinion Research International.

8 Schweiger, D. and Denisi, A. (1991) 'Communication with employees following a merger: a longitudinal field experiment', *Academy of Management Journal* 34, 110–35.

9 Grant, L. (1998) 'Happy workers, high returns', *Fortune*, 12 January, 81.

10 Heskett, J. L., Sasser, W. E., Jr. and Schlesinger, L.A. (1997) *The Service Profit Chain: How Leading Companies Link Profit and Growth to Loyalty, Satisfaction, and Value*, New York: Free Press.

11 Schneider, B., White, S. S. and Paul, M. C. (1998) 'Linking service climate and customer perceptions of service quality: test of a causal model', *Journal of Applied Psychology* 83 (2), 150–63.

12 Patterson, M. G., West, M. A., Lawthom, R. and Nickell, S. (1997) *People Management, Organisational Culture and Company Performance*, Institute of Work Psychology, University of Sheffield and Centre for Economic Performance, London School of Economics.

13 MCA/MORI (1999) 'The brand ambassador benchmark' – reviewed by Mitchell, A. (1999) 'Customer satisfaction is earned by loyal staff', *Marketing Week*, 10 June, 38–9.

14 Payne, A., Holt, S. and Frow, P. (1999) 'Relationship value management: exploring the integration of employee, customer and shareholder value', 7th International Colloquium in Relationship Marketing, Strathclyde University, 7–9 November.

15 Rucci, A. T., Kirn, S. P. and Quinn, R. T. (1998) 'The employee-customer-profit chain at Sears', *Harvard Business Review*, 76, 82–97.

16 Clark, M. (2002) 'The relationship between employees' perceptions of organizational climate and customer retention rates in a major UK retail bank', *Journal of Strategic Marketing*, 10, 93–113.

17 Bottomley, P. and Nairn, A. (2002) 'Statistical syrens: can managers be lured onto the rocks by CRM analytics?', Cardiff Business School working paper, May.

18 For examples and substantiation, see Thomson, K. (1998) *Emotional Capital*, Oxford: Capstone.

Brand transparency

HOW MUCH SHOULD A COMPANY REVEAL about its marketing and brand equity to shareholders? On the one side, shareholders are entitled to know about its assets and how they have been stewarded since the previous year. But

> ## Some mystique is essential for successful marketing

a range of arguments supports the opposite position. Competitors will take advantage of transparency and maybe customers should not be shown too much. Some mystique is essential for successful marketing. Most companies believe their shareholders do not have the motivation, time nor expertise to understand market metrics and prefer to leave that to management.

This chapter draws on UK research into company annual reports that included interviews and surveys of chairmen, senior executives and analysts.[1] The recommendations from that research report form Appendix B. Informal reviews across the Atlantic indicate a similar picture although Form 10K requires rather more disclosure in the USA than in the UK. Although each company must decide for itself how many veils it wishes to remove, the pressure for transparency is slowly increasing, notably following financial scandals such as Enron. What was right ten years ago may not be right today and yet we found many annual reports well anchored in the past.

The impact of this issue also works the other way: management needs to see the business through the eyes of shareholders and other outsiders. Active management of investor relations is another branch of marketing that requires empathy with the 'customer', in this case the investor. Over-hyping the brand has much the same longer term effect in stock markets as in product markets. The internet companies around the millennium, or WorldCom, maximized share prices in the short-term which in turn magnified the failure when the truth was exposed.

Transparency, the 'sunlight test', is a useful way to distinguish the virtuous circle of honestly promoting the shares, with its knock-on goodwill effects with employees and customers, from the vicious practice of misleading impressions. Disclosing a representative cross-section of professionally gathered marketing metrics meets the sunlight test.

At the same time, candour has its limits, as Judith Martin put it: 'Blurting out the complete truth is considered adorable in the young, right smack up to the moment that the child says, "Mommy, is this the fat lady you can't stand?"'[2]

Various accounting regulators, such as the Canadian and the British, have asked for company annual reports to share their management's historical and prospective analysis of the business as candidly as possible with investors.[3] In the event, this proposal is heavily qualified. Companies are not expected to reveal confidential matters and the limits on how much shareholders need to know are recognized. However, the guidelines are quite specific that brand equity should be reported along with marketing investment in that brand. This chapter charts a course through this minefield by discussing:

◆ Balance sheets. Why balance sheets are published. Contrary to widespread belief, the UK does not allow the values of brands to be put on balance sheets although, exceptionally, the costs of acquisition may be. We need to be clear why the balance sheet is not the right place for reporting brand equity even though other parts of the annual report are.

◆ Historical data versus expectations of the future.

◆ The arguments for more, and for less, disclosure.

◆ Investor relations. Does the shareholder view of the company matter? If so, should it be managed? How the executive committee should determine which metrics should be tracked.

◆ Deciding which marketing metrics should be routinely shared with the outside world.

Although the focus here is on investors, many other interested parties such as analysts, suppliers and the media use annual reports and other investor communications to inform themselves about the company. Their interests are not separately considered but it is presumed that companies will also take them into account.

Balance sheets

The long-term trend is for greater disclosure. Balance sheets were first required to be published at the beginning of the twentieth century.[4] Directors grumbled at the time and one agreed only on the condition that the accounts would not be seen by tax inspectors. In the UK, companies were not required to provide profit and loss accounts until 1928, but succeeding Companies Acts have each required more information to be divulged. Company annual reports have doubled in size and then doubled again. The irony is that so much information is now dumped on shareholders that they are even less likely to read the metrics that matter. WorldCom did inflate profits by charging costs to capital in its 2001 accounts but the cash flow, or lack of it, was there for all to see.

By the end of the twentieth century, the assets on balance sheets accounted for a declining share of companies' market values as shown for the UK by Figure 8.1.

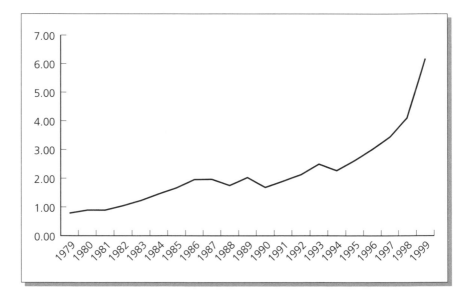

Figure 8.1 ◆ Aggregate price to book ratios for all UK quoted industrial and commercial companies

Source: Ambler, T., Barwise, P. and Higson, C. (2001) *Market Metrics: What Should We Tell the Shareholders?*, London: Centre for Business Performance, Institute of Chartered Accountants in England and Wales

This led to suggestions that brand values, along with other intangibles, should be disclosed in balance sheets in order to give shareholders a better view of the overall worth of the business.[5] The debate was fuelled by some companies in the 1980s, such as Ranks Hovis MacDougall in the UK, Lion Nathan in New Zealand and Pacific Dunlop in Australia deciding to do so. Other UK companies, such as GrandMet and Guinness, put the cost of acquired brands on their balance sheets. Had they not done so, those companies would have been technically insolvent.

The case against was made by a monograph sponsored by the Institute of Chartered Accountants in England and Wales.[6] It argued brand valuations are not sufficiently reliable to justify balance sheet recognition. The report considered that the major problems of brand valuation are inherently intractable and apply equally to acquired and to home-grown brands:

> *First, there is the difficulty of reaching agreement on a sensible and useful premise of value. Second, there is the problem of separability. And third, placing a value on a brand (however defined) involves many subjective judgements about the future of the brand and the importance of marketing factors.*[7]

Eventually the UK Accounting Standards Board decided that, subject to various technical factors, the *cost* of acquired brands could be included, but the stated figure should be reduced for any 'impairment'; i.e. if the current valuation was less than the original cost. This was consistent with the long-standing treatment of goodwill.

Two important considerations arise. First, shareholders see (usually) the original cost, not the current value. Second, home-grown brands are excluded. With hindsight, this long debate was a dead end. The balance sheet provides at best only a partial view of the company's assets and no evidence of management's performance in building brand equity. This is hardly surprising: the balance sheet was a solution to a nineteenth-century problem. At that time, long-term stability and the tangibility of assets made the balance sheet an admirable medium for disclosure. A century on, it is about as useful for disclosing a full picture of the business as the tele-graph is for transmitting films. It is not suited to the twenty-first-century dominance of intangible assets. Experiments with inflation accounting got into a similar tangle and have since been abandoned. The Accounting Standards Board, and others, have realized that the balance sheet is only part of the information provided to shareholders and that other parts of the annual report, and the Operating and Financial Review (OFR) in particular, should explain what the balance sheet does not. So far as the UK is concerned, we can expect the next Companies Act, perhaps in 2006, to formalize these requirements.

So, putting the balance sheet aside, the questions remain: why should the company disclose its marketing performance to shareholders and especially its stewardship of brand equity? What metrics are candidates for exposure? And how should members of the board decide the appropriate degree of transparency?

Historical data versus expectations of the future

One of the themes of this book is that managers would be well advised to give less time to speculating about the future, and transfer the saving to understanding the current status of the market, of competition and brand equity.

Some of the pressure for disclosure, however, is for directors to give more information about forecasts. The exposure draft guidelines for the OFR, for example, asks companies to give their 'prospective analysis' as well as the historical information. Analysts and investors would like companies to provide future cash flows, and to do so with certainty. Management would dearly like to know them too! In this utopia, markets would have perfect information and shares could be bought and sold with risk, if any, being quantifiable. No doubt those pursuing this ambition hang stockings up for Santa Claus.

The objections to the disclosure of market metrics apply much more strongly to future estimates than the actual data at the year end and in the past. Shareholders may be entitled to know the company's broad strategy but the specific marketing tactics, and the changes in metrics likely to follow, would give too much information to competitors as well as being intrinsically unreliable.

Similarly, some companies are reluctant to supply 'soft' metrics, by which they mean marketing, and prefer to disclose only 'hard' (financial and internal such as the number of employees) numbers. This hard–soft distinction owes more to convention than objectivity. Professionally gathered market research can be just as hard as some accounting ratios. Future estimates are indeed 'soft' but market share or penetration or retention ratios or awareness, if the data have been thoroughly collected and analyzed, are both reliable and important.

The proposals in this chapter refer only to the disclosure of current and past data, professionally gathered and interpreted. They do not include subjective estimates.

The arguments for more and for less disclosure

In our research, 85 per cent of chairpersons and senior executives agreed that shareholders were entitled to be informed about the company's main assets including brand equity. At the same time, levels of disclosure in annual reports were low. About 40 per cent of the sample gave up to five indications of market performance but the average number of quantitative metrics was only two. Sales volume and product distribution (availability) were the most frequently reported, with new products launched in the year being the only other indicator reported by more than 50 per cent of the sample.

Confidentiality was the most frequent reason for these low levels but when we probed, they agreed that competitors already had access to most of the individual metrics in which they were interested. Only 22 per cent would not disclose relative price for competitive reasons and no other metric scored higher than 17 per cent for this reason. Of the 15 or so metrics seen by top management, only 20 per cent could not be disclosed for competitive reasons; 60 per cent were not disclosed for other reasons.

Confidentiality is a genuine reason for non-disclosure but also a cloak for an understandable reluctance to reveal more than one has to. Some of the objections are valid but first we should dismiss the weak ones. The first was the level of detail and the amount of extra space it would take in an annual report. The modern annual report for a large public corporation is over 50 pages, glossy and with plenty of large photographs, many given over to pictures of men in suits. The space needed for ten market metrics and comparatives is about a paragraph plus a table. Compared to the report as a whole, the increase would not be significant. Furthermore, these metrics, such as market share, are not fine detail relative to much of the material to which space is given. Market metrics are the key determinants of future cash flow.

> Confidentiality is a cloak for an understandable reluctance to reveal more than one has to

Second, we were told that shareholders did not want this information and would not understand it. It is true that shareholders do not demand this information, even the large institutional investors, and also that small shareholders give scant attention to annual reports. The argument works both ways: if they would not read that section, then revealing it can do no harm. The realities are that shareholders have very little power over what they see in annual reports and that responsibility lies with the company. Without market metrics, an annual report is at best partial. The more substantial objections are:

◆ Snapshots from a moving train.

◆ Problems with consistency.

◆ Irresponsible use by analysts and media.

◆ Hostages to fortune.

Businesses are complex, dynamic and multi-faceted entities moving through an ever-changing environment. Senior executives find it hard to keep on top of the situation; analysts and shareholders cannot be expected to do so. A few blurred images of the situation at a certain moment in time cannot portray the realities of the business. The difficulty should be recognized but it is not fatal to the case for transparency. Metrics are no more than milestones along the strategic route. However blurred the images of them may be, management needs to interpret, at least for themselves, where they are at.

Consistency is more tricky. It is one thing to remove the veils when the underlying figures are attractive, quite another when they are not. A company that reveals comprehensive metrics one year will be expected to do the same the next; and comparative figures are not always flattering. This problem is minimized by disclosing the least that is consistent with one's public image. Some Muslim women argue that their traditional dress is liberating in the sense that they escape the fashion of tyranny and cosmetics. And consistency is not a problem.

The opposing argument is the growing demand for openness that is accentuated by disasters such as Enron. Rightly or wrongly, outsiders have the impression that secrecy allows top executives to profit at the expense of employees and shareholders. They may be culpable either because they do not know the company's vital signs or because they know them and fail to act or to reveal the truth. Shareholders may not need to know the individual market metrics, but at least they need to be reassured that the members of the board know them. Exposing the key metrics implies that the management has a business model that works. Shareholders would like to know that management has a marketing dashboard and that they use it.

The penultimate concern is with irresponsible use of data by analysts and the media. The nature of their business calling requires them to be selective. The sales side analyst may ignore the bad and the media may put the one bad number ahead of the nine good ones. Disclosing market metrics enhances their ability to misrepresent, or partially represent, the company position.

The hostage to fortune argument may seem superstitious but not disclosing more than one has to in good times certainly improves one's ability to fudge through the not so good. Many a marketer has refused to enter for an award on the grounds that winning will provoke nemesis. But this is just a plea for caution and to slow down the rate of disclosing new information. It is not a valid reason for refusing any more information. The irony perhaps is that

> **Shareholders would like to know that management has a marketing dashboard and that they use it**

this objection underlines that market metrics matter; if they had no significance, there could be no objection to disclosing them.

On the other side, the main arguments for providing more market(ing) information are:

◆ Pre-empting legislation.

◆ Shareholder and analyst respect leading to higher share prices.

◆ Entitlement.

◆ Professional investor relations.

The UK is not alone in the continual increase of company regulation, much of it requiring more disclosure. If the spirit of government and also popular intentions is realized through voluntary publication, then the pressure for mandatory, and probably more burdensome, rules should subside. Implementing the new Accounting Standard Board's (ASB) guidelines for the Operating and Financial Review (OFR) is a case in point. The previous guidelines were endorsed by the CFOs of Britain's largest corporations back in 1993 but our research revealed that those same companies had mostly not followed the guidelines, so far as market metrics were concerned, in the following eight years.

The new guidelines place more emphasis on shareholders seeing the business 'through the eyes of management' (p.7). The previous emphasis on financial figures has been broadened to a range of financial and non-financial measures (e.g. customer satisfaction). Companies are now specifically invited to report 'corporate reputation and brand equity' (p.16) and on their 'investment in brand equity, through advertising and other marketing activities' (p.18).[8]

On p.10 the ASB reminds readers of the listing rules for quoted companies: 'Information and analysis contained in the OFR should be neutral, free from bias and complete, dealing even-handedly with both good and bad aspects.' Companies should 'not omit anything likely to affect the import of such statement, forecast or other information'. It is perhaps surprising, in the light of these strictures, that market metrics, which address the sourcing and harvesting of the company's cash flow, should have had so little attention.

If legislation is the stick, shareholder and analyst respectively provide the carrot. Our research showed that those companies that did disclose more were also more respected by both analysts and their peer senior executives. We do not have data from institutional shareholders but similar reactions could be expected. The thesis that more disclosure leads to stronger share prices needs research, but there may be too little disclosure to be able to test variance. The effects are also likely to be small relative to cash flow itself and market sentiment. At the same time, Standard & Poor, report that disclosure is positively correlated with share performance.[9]

The third argument cuts little ice with companies who recognize entitlement but are not moved by it. Perhaps institutional investors and the representatives of small investors will demand this information but, until that happens, the shareholders' right to know will remain a small factor. The Prudential provides an example of a company that formalizes its internal metrics across its key stakeholders in a consistent fashion (*see box*).

Prudential UK (Insurance)

Prudential plc is an international financial services group headquartered in the UK and operating since 1848 predominantly in insurance and assurance. The US namesake is completely independent although the business is similar in many respects. In the UK, 'The man from the Pru' epitomized door-to-door insurance selling but that model is no longer used. This business division covers three channels: consumers, IFAs (independent financial advisers) and business to business. The same branding operates across all three.

▶

Top UK management uses six KPIs to assess the overall business effectiveness including marketing department performance but the marketing specialists, under Marketing Director Roger Ramsden, also look at success in terms of penetration, customer penetration, value and volume sold, retention rates, reputation and people's willingness to deal with the Pru.

KPIs split evenly between financial and non-financial. The financial are sales revenue (adjusted for comparability), contribution to shareholder value and cash flow for the year. These may be fairly standard but the non-financial KPIs importantly and unusually link three groups of stakeholders: customers, staff and the regulator, primarily the Financial Services Authority. The 'happiness' of each group is assessed with an index number. The Happy Customer Index, for example, is based on brand tracking research conducted by the Pru and also whether the brand retains an industry quality mark for clear and consistent products and literature, and quality of service.

The staff index is based on regular staff surveys and the percentage of job offers accepted. Reports from and visits by staff from the FSA and other regulators are content analyzed to provide that index.

The brand is recognized as a vital asset by top management but the word 'equity' is not used as it would be confused with shares. The brand is currently being formally valued.

Marketing is now firmly at the heart of the company because it is becoming customer-centric but such a fundamental change in such a large company takes time. The sales force used to be the conduit to the consumer; now the entire company is.

Sources: Tara Macleod, Director of Brand Marketing, Prudential UK, 10 June 2002 and Mike Paice, Market Research Manager, 4 November 2002

We have been looking so far at the passive supply of market metrics, mostly through the medium of annual reports. The last argument is directed to any company that seeks to manage its investor relations professionally. Communications, of which market metrics can be a part, should influence investors in much the same way that advertising influences consumers. The next section considers marketing the corporate brand to the investment community.

Investor relations

In this segment like all others, marketing begins with listening to, and understanding, the customer's point of view. This particular customer buys and sells shares rather than company products but the influence of brand equity on behaviour is likely to be much the same. We might therefore expect better known brands to have higher price/earnings ratios than similar, but less well-known, companies.[10]

The linkage of brand equity with customer and employee satisfaction discussed in the last chapter should logically extend to investors and create the virtuous circle in Figure 8.2. Whether they drive each other in practice is an empirical question each firm should discover for itself. In any case, it makes sense to keep the messages to these three stakeholder groups as similar as possible. Bragging to shareholders about high margins or low wages may prove expensive with the other groups. That in turn should require marketers, human resources and investor relations managers to work closely together and even report performance metrics to the Exec in the same package.

Investor relations managers should be concerned with what is in the shareholders' heads, why they stay and why they leave, in the same way that marketers and HR managers think about their components of brand equity. Just as with the other stakeholders, retention is usually more cost effective than acquisition. Few things rattle the target market than non-delivery, be that by the product or a profit warning.

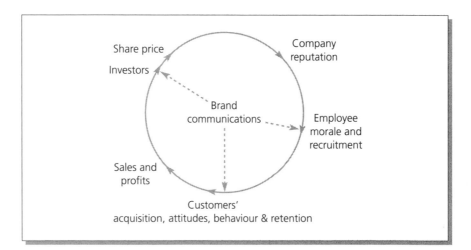

Figure 8.2 ◆ The stakeholder virtuous circle

Thus much of the investor marketing business, like any marketing, is the avoidance of negatives rather than the active selling of positives. Relationship marketing is relationship marketing and almost all the key metrics translate from one segment to the other. The nuance here, however, is how the attitudes and behaviour of investors are likely to be influenced by the provision of market metrics both in terms of the metrics themselves and the way they are presented. For example, many companies told us that they provide analysts with almost any data that the analysts request. The data are not included in annual reports but made available on the company's website for the small shareholder. That serves the rulebook against insider information but it

> **If a metric deserves the CEO's attention, then it is a candidate for the investor's**

presupposes the small shareholder knows that the data are out and knows where to find them. Nevertheless, the web will be an increasingly important part of both marketing and providing information to investors. It would be logical to reduce expenditure on paper annual reports and provide more signposts to the electronic equivalent.

This section has put the disclosure of market metrics into a slightly different context, namely that it is part of the professional marketing of the corporate brand to investors. Building corporate brand equity and trust in the company requires at least some degree of transparency and continuity. Key within that is communicating that management knows the most important market metrics and is watching those dials on the marketing dashboard.

Assessing which metrics should be disclosed

Ultimately, the disclosure of metrics, be it in the annual report or otherwise, is pragmatic. Which individual metrics should be revealed and which should not be? The starting point should be with the metrics, internal and external, that the Exec itself reviews. If a metric deserves the CEO's attention, then it is a candidate for the investor's.

The second stage is to agree the tests for non-disclosure. From the considerations above, some typical tests might be:

◆ Would publication of this metric damage us in the eyes of customers?

◆ Do our competitors already have this information and, even if they had not, would it damage our competitiveness?

◆ Is this metric likely to be used consistently into the future?

◆ Would we be able to live with the publication of this metric in bad times as well as in good?

◆ All metrics are open to misinterpretation but is this one particularly subject to negative connotation?

◆ Do similar companies that we admire provide these kinds of metrics?

Enthusiastic application of these tests will reduce the candidates for disclosure substantially, and perhaps too substantially. If so, put the process into reverse by asking which metrics not already on the surviving shortlist would help investor-based corporate brand equity. This takes us back to the basic questions of what investors think and feel about the company and the experience they have had with it. How do new investors, who are likely to be the most enthusiastic, compare with the disaffected ones who seem to be leaving or have just sold their shares?

Another key resource is the company's audit team. The OFR and other parts of the annual report outside the formal accounts are not the subject of the formal auditors' report. Nevertheless auditors are expected to read the whole document in draft and confirm to the board of directors that it appears to be consistent with their understanding of the business and reasonably based on the evidence available. Formal or informal, and practice varies across countries, such assessments are merely sensible due process. This means that the auditors are in a good position to comment on the Exec's own list of metrics and the ones they plan not to disclose to shareholders. They may be able to suggest from their experience, and the practice of other companies, additional metrics to consider, confidentiality permitting. Diageo provides an example of how a complex global organization informs its shareholders, through its annual report, about its marketing performance (*see box*).

Diageo

Diageo markets a large portfolio of premium beers, wines and spirits worldwide. For management purposes but also for reporting to shareholders, the drinks are classified into global priority brands, local priority brands and category management brands. The eight global brands account for 61 per cent of volume sales with the other two categories

▶

being 13 and 26 per cent respectively. Marketing investment is reported for the global brands together and in total but not brand by brand. Brand profitability and market shares are not given.

However, the report also analyzes the business across the leading four countries, key markets and venture markets which account for 57, 29 and 14 per cent of sales respectively. Volume and value sales increases are cross-analyzed for brand and market categories. Operating profits and marketing expenditure are also given for the four major markets, key and venture markets.

This brief summary does not reflect the very considerable amount of factual marketing information given in six pages of the Operating Review. By way of comparison, the Financial Review covers five pages. The information explains the profit and loss account but does not address consumer or brand equity issues.

Source: Diageo Operating and Financial Review, Annual Report, 4 September 2002

One can no more ask shareholders what metrics would enhance the reputation of the company they have invested in than one can ask consumers what advertising they would like to see, but one can experiment. The profiles of similar companies with different disclosure practices can be compared. Qualitative research, both in the worlds of consumers and investors, is not, by definition, definitive but it can provide insights for the better management of corporate brand equity. It can also stimulate top management with new ways of thinking about the relationships of customers, employees and investors.

At the end of the day, whether a firm is providing metrics to investors because it has an obligation to do so or because it is seeking actively to manage those investors, the issue remains the same: a healthy relationship requires good two-way communication and market metrics are part of that. If a firm has an investor relations function at all, then it should be considering how the disclosure of marketing performance and brand equity information, and especially quantified information, can strengthen both the acquisition and retention of investors.

Executive minutes

1 Board of directors to consider the importance of investor relationships and the role of market metrics within that.

2 Company secretary or general counsel to report to the board on the development, both regulatory and best practice, of the disclosure of market metrics and key performance metrics and the implications for the company over time.

3 Head of investor relations to report on how the company is seen by its shareholders, how it would like to be seen and how metrics disclosure may contribute. In particular, is management seen as being on top of the key strategic and market numbers?

4 CFO to report the auditors' suggestions about which metrics could be added or deleted from both the Exec and investor lists.

5 Board of directors to decide which of its own external and internal market metrics should be shared with investors.

6 Board of directors to consider the extent to which the interests of other parties, such as analysts suppliers and media, should influence the considerations above.

Notes

1   Ambler, T., Barwise, P. and Higson, C. (2001) *Market Metrics: What Should We Tell the Shareholders?*, London: Centre for Business Performance, Institute of Chartered Accountants in England and Wales.

2   Martin, J. (1984) *Miss Manners' Guide to Rearing Perfect Children*, New York: Atheneum.

3   Accounting Standards Board (2002) *Guidelines for the Operating and Financial Review – Exposure Draft*, London: Accounting Standards Board.

4   1906 in the UK.

5   Perrier, R. (ed.) (1997) *Brand Valuation*, 3rd edn, London: Premier Books.

6   Barwise, P., Higson, C., Likierman, A. and Marsh, P. (1989) *Accounting for Brands*, London: London Business School and Institute of Chartered Accountants in England and Wales.

7   Barwise, P., Higson, C., Likierman, A. and Marsh, P. (1989) *Accounting for Brands*, London: London Business School and Institute of Chartered Accountants in England and Wales, 77.

8   Accounting Standards Board (2002) *Guidelines for the Operating and Financial Review – Exposure Draft*, London: Accounting Standards Board.

9   Corporate governance evaluation tools, 15 October 2002 (*www.standardandpoors.com*). Also reported in *Financial Times*, 16 October 2002.

10   The share price literature provides thin support for this claim although it is a logical extension from the branding and purchasing literature. One slight exception is Kirschenheiter, M. (1997) 'Information quality and correlated signals', *Journal of Accounting Research*, 35 (1), 43–59, which showed that more information about share values, e.g. the brand being well known, was positive for share prices even though the information was not supported by the balance sheet. The issue was more directly addressed in Bowd, R. and Bowd, L. (2002) 'Assessing the financial value of corporate reputation: suggestions for a proposed formula', Manchester Metropolitan University Business School working paper WP02/01. From a literature review and a small empirical study, they concluded that reputation accounted for a significant amount of market valuation (share prices) and proposed a model for valuing reputation.

Assessing the performance of the marketing mix

FEW COMPANIES ARE CONCERNED with assessing marketing performance as a whole. Much more often, the horns are locked over the marketing budget, or some part of it. The marketers have decided, for whatever reasons, that they want to spend $1 million on, say, advertising and they look to academia for a silver bullet to justify their decision and to measure the return on investment (ROI) on the expenditure. If that is your perspective, you may have skipped all preceding chapters and come straight here.

If so, go back to the beginning. Asking only about the performance of some element of the mix is about as sensible as asking for directions when you do not know where you are going. The marketing context is crucial. Chapter 3 showed why estimating the ROI for marketing, or any part of it, is a flawed concept. The better approach is to identify the cost of achieving the firm's goals and then tinker with the mix to reach them more economically. Discounted cash flow (DCF) is a valid comparative technique; ROI is not.

> Asking only about the performance of some element of the mix is about as sensible as asking for directions when you do not know where you are going. The marketing context is crucial

Effectiveness precedes efficiency: efficiently doing the wrong things is more wasteful than inefficiently doing the right ones. 'Effectiveness' is defined by the extent to which the programme meets its intended goals. If there are no even implicit goals, then effectiveness can be judged by the extent to which the programme improves the firm's competitive position; e.g. relative profit or market share is improved. If the competitive position is also impossible to judge, the third test of effectiveness is whether the results of the programme were 'better' than those from the previous year's equivalent.

Theory differs from practice. Marketers most often use prior year for the comparative figures, as advertising effectiveness awards in the USA and UK show. It is the weakest test because it allows the performance indicators to be selected after the event. Suppose a promotion in year one scored well for increase in share and awareness but badly for profitability and perceived brand quality. Suppose further that the equivalent promotion in year two reversed the dimensions of success and failure. The brand manager would present both as successes and use the two 'better' results in each case. Marketers' reputation for moving the goalposts is well earned.

The prior year basis for evaluating performance cannot be dismissed but it should be recognized as soft. In our UK research, we found large companies looking for both effectiveness and efficiency but shifting toward effectiveness. The US picture is more balanced. Table 9.1 shows the Marketing Leadership Council 2001 survey responses. Interestingly, no one answered 'don't know'. In practice, 'efficiency' usually refers to profitability as distinct from a formal ratio.

Table 9.1 ◆ Efficiency vs effectiveness in the USA

How do you see the focus of marketing performance measurement evolving?	Responses %
Increasingly focused on marketing effectiveness	16
Increasingly focused on marketing efficiency	17
Both remain equally important	67

n = 86

The remainder of this chapter is structured as follows:

◆ General process for evaluating any component of the marketing mix.
◆ Advertising.
◆ Web/internet and direct marketing.
◆ Events and public relations.

◆ Loyalty programmes.

◆ CRM and customer service.

◆ Sales promotions.

◆ New product development.

◆ Modelling the marketing mix.

Note that trade spending is excluded. The marketing mix (and budget) is here defined to be all expenditures intended to strengthen brand equity. In that sense they are investments to build the asset and thereby profit. We all know that, in practice, heavyweight customers bully sales management into providing funds that are truly discounts from the sales price. Commercially necessary and profitable as these may be, they are not there to build the brand even though the senior sales manager may in turn bully the junior brand manager into taking the hit on the brand budget.

This chapter covers a lot of ground and yet this list of topics is only a fraction of the ways in which marketers can spend money. In the 1960s a large marketer would have perhaps two ad agencies and a small handful of other marketing suppliers. Today they have tens of suppliers and consultants in each major country. Therein lies much of the problem: in a large company, hardly anyone has a firm grasp of the complete marketing mix.

General process

This section covers:[1]

◆ The separation of individual elements of the mix from the rest of marketing.

◆ Key steps in campaign assessment.

◆ Payment by results (PBR).

Separation of the marketing mix

The first issue is whether the campaign under assessment can realistically be separated from the rest of the marketing mix or marketing as a whole. If it costs more than 90 per cent of the total marketing budget, and if the product and pricing are virtually unchanged, then the campaign is probably too mingled with the whole marketing performance to separate. At the other extreme, if the cost is a very small part of the whole, the effects may not be worth separating, even if one could.

A separated campaign still needs to be evaluated in the context of the rest of the programme. One way of doing this, the auction technique, is not much practised but has much to commend it. The first draft marketing plan with quantified overall objectives is shared with the partner agencies; e.g. the advertising agency if advertising is likely to be a major part of the budget. Then the agencies bid for the resources they could best use towards those goals and the results that could be expected. Then the plan is finalized, and payment by results benchmarks established, on the basis of the most credible and attractive bids. One attraction of this internal market is that the agencies are fully in the picture. They can improve the plan with suggestions from or outside their special expertise. However it is achieved, let us now assume that the budget allocations and the goalposts have been established. Assessing the major components of the mix matters because of the following:

◆ The client and its agency will not have the same goals for each campaign so at least they need clarification.

◆ Clients are increasingly pressed on accountability.

◆ It provides learning at the firm level. Doing better in future depends on knowing which past campaigns worked best, worst and why.

◆ It also provides learning at the individual level. Marketers move frequently and formal evaluation helps successors learn from the experience of predecessors and their peers.

◆ Sharing improves measurement methodology and data.

On the other hand, formal assessment rarely happens in practice because of the following:

◆ Many activities are seen as low-budget items of low interest to top management.

◆ Lack of relevant research data.

◆ Isolating results is difficult and time consuming.

◆ There are too many different, even conflicting, objectives for each campaign.

◆ The drive is to get the next job done, and move the game on.

◆ Junior marketers move on too quickly to make evaluation worthwhile for them.

◆ Competitive orientation (fill the campaign slot, never mind how much it improves profits or brand equity).

◆ Data deluge: large companies have more information than they can use.

◆ Lack of clarity about agency and client roles and relationship.

◆ It is difficult to do.

One company that takes the assessment of advertising performance very seriously is the UK technology giant BT, which has developed radically since the government monopoly was privatized in the 1980s (*see box*).

BT Retail

BT Retail was formed about two years ago as the customer facing part of the organization. The four channels (large businesses, SMEs, government and consumer) account for £14 billion turnover from 19 million customers. Since being denationalized, market share has dropped from 100 per cent to 73 per cent and it has been a significant achievement to stabilize it at that level over the past 18 months. BT positions itself as an ICT (Information, Communications and Technology) supplier as distinct from just another telco. Of the FTSE 100 companies, 93 rely on BT's infrastructure to run their companies whatever telcos they may think they are using. (The FTSE 100 are the 100 largest companies by market capitalization on the London Stock Exchange.)

Success at BT is defined financially in the first instance. Pierre Danon (BT Retail CEO) said in spring 2001 that he would take £850 million costs out of the business over the three years and that is on track. Thereafter innovation and market share are important and also growing new markets. Broadband is crucial.

BT is the UK's largest single brand advertiser and third largest overall with a reported £90 million expenditure in 2001. Marketing is tracked by a wide range of measures including market share linked to ROME (return on marketing expenditure), usage by segment, profitability by product, effectiveness of spend in driving branded advertising awareness, image drivers of customer satisfaction, and customer dissatisfaction. Managing down levels of dissatisfaction is very active in BT but this is done primarily by improvements in the service experience. Marketing in this area is aimed more at increasing the image drivers of overall BT satisfaction.

Since 2000, BT Retail has developed advanced models for assessing ROME on advertising, direct marketing and account management. The intangible marketing asset concept is implicitly understood in BT as 'the value in the brand' (brand equity). In all, BT is a successful but large and complex business in a dynamic market.

Source: Interview with Amanda MacKenzie, Director of Marketing Services, BT Retail, 6 June 2002

Key steps in campaign assessment

In principle, assessing a programme is blindingly simple: how well did it deliver what it was supposed to deliver? Only two things need to be constructed: the goalpost and the result. Yet such formal comparisons, as noted above, are rare in practice. As a quick study of any of the 12 volumes of the UK Institute of Practitioners in Advertising Effectiveness Awards[2] will reveal, few record quantified objectives agreed with the agency, assuming there were any. Post-campaign advertising assessment, however, is routine.

Sales promotions are usually the other way about: goals are set but the post-campaign evaluation does not take place. In UK research, we found that, although between 16 and 25 per cent of promotions agencies claimed that full comparison did take place, about the same proportion did not know.[3] Closer examination of the comparison methodology indicated that their self-assessments were overstated. The main problem here seems to be the shifting of objectives between briefing and campaign implementation. The revised objectives are not usually recorded and unexpected outside factors intervene.

Client and agency should jointly establish the goals as part of their mutual briefing process. Too many creative presentations are rejected due to inadequate briefing; a waste of resources for both sides. The agency needs to know the context, e.g. the brand positioning statement, and the no-go areas. The agency should thoroughly understand what the campaign should achieve, as distinct from how to do it (which is the agency's job). Too often the client turns creative in the course of briefing.

How will they recognize 'success'? A very small number of goals, ideally just one, should be quantified. If there is more than one, an importance ranking will help the overall assessment. Astonishingly, most standard format agency creative briefs give no space to this most crucial item.

Inevitably and perhaps rightly, the goals will be bargained. However self-confident the agency, common sense dictates that they should maximize their chances of 'success'. Effectiveness is not a matter of reaching any old benchmarks: they should be relevant (to the overall marketing goals), difficult but reachable.

Finally, the goals may need revision before the campaign is implemented to take account of changes in the current environmental and competitive context, and the new thinking that has arisen during the development phase.

Now we switch to the second, post-evaluation, phase. This has three stages: ensuring the data is comparable, testing effectives and the efficiency. Comparability requires the outcome to be teased apart in three ways:

1   Distinguishing the baseline (what would otherwise have happened) from
    the campaign uplift.

2   Isolating the campaign from the rest of the marketing mix.

3   Separating the target segment from the other consumers. (The creative
    target (e.g. 25–30-year-old homemaker in Milwaukee with two kids and
    a 4x4) should not be confused with the measurement target segment dis-
    cussed here, i.e. the one used in goal setting.)

The output from this data cleaning, or separation, exercise should then be
immediately comparable with the original or revised goals in order to establish effectiveness.

So far as efficiency is concerned, as discussed in Chapter 1, it is simply
wrong to look at profit effects without considering whether brand equity
shifted. A further question is how the profit return on this campaign compares with other [similar] campaigns, after adjusting for any brand equity
changes. Where efficiency is not part of the agency brief (profitability is
often confidential), that part of the evaluation is likely to be internal, for the
client only. In practice companies rarely have the data and the time to do all
this analysis but payment by results (PBR) provides a solution.

Payment by results (PBR)

PBR is the most effective guarantee that results will be assessed against expectations because otherwise the successful agency will not be paid. It also focuses
agency efforts on what matters. Creative awards are nice but not primary. To be
usable as the bases for payment, the goals need to be few and precise.

On the other hand, PBR can only operate within a strong and continuing relationship. It can maximize learning and promote transparency, but
only when trust exists. Within this context, challenge becomes productive.
The agency will want to negotiate the goals down, and the client up, but the
expectation of continuity should make the bargaining more educational and
less a demonstration of power. PBR is the developing trend: 33 per cent of
the UK sales promotions respondents saw PBR as the way forward, and it is
an increasing part of advertising agency rewards.[4]

PBR in practice raises more behavioural than theoretical issues. Payment
should be an honest sharing of the benefits from success, or lack of it. It is neither a device for the client to cut costs, nor just a gracious tip to a worthy
agency. As part of annual agency–client mutual assessment, it should be a
small component until both sides are happy with the way results are evaluated.

Then ratchet the PBR component up to replace the agency profits, i.e. all their profits ride on PBR, leaving the base remuneration to take care of costs. In the harsher economic climate of the 2000s, agencies can live with that and, in the UK at least, PBR is now usually two-way. In other words, PBR is no longer just a one-way bonus opportunity: their fees can go up or down.

Finally, PBR means payment by *results*. These may be intermediate (awareness, attitudes, likelihood of next purchase) or behavioural (sales, share) or both. Some companies base all or part of PBR on client service. That may improve the relationship but it rather misses the point. After these general issues, the chapter now considers some key areas of the marketing mix beginning with advertising.

Advertising

Table 9.2 shows the main metrics used for advertising assessment according to the 72 per cent of survey respondents who measured this aspect of the mix.[5]

Table 9.2 ◆ US advertising metrics

Advertising metric	Respondents %
Recall	76
Reach	72
Frequency	68
Cost per 000	53
Gross rating points	47

Source: Marketing Leadership Council survey (2001)

Interestingly, these all refer to the technical performance of the ads as distinct from the effect on brand equity or the bottom line. The highest results metric, purchase intent at 37 per cent, failed to make the top five. In the UK, the main metrics for advertising assessment the most frequently used metrics at the pre-testing (UK) or copy testing (USA) stage are shown in Figure 9.1.[6] In theory, the metrics used at this mid-term stage of the advertising process should match up with those agreed with the agency in the brief and then with the metrics used in the post campaign evaluation. We did not find that to be the case.

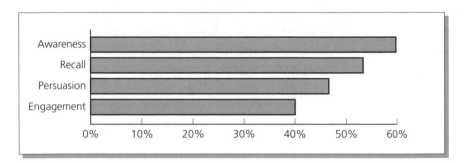

Figure 9.1 ◆ Most frequently used pre-testing metrics (UK)

Source: Ambler, T. and Goldstein, S. (2003) 'Copy testing: Practice and Best Practice', Accounting Association Monograph, London

Of UK respondents 33 per cent neither specified nor implied any metrics in their briefs to advertising agencies. The reasons for this remain unclear. On the one hand, it could indicate a respondent's own uncertainty about how they expect their ads to perform. On the other, this may reflect an advertiser's fear, expressed by one market research manager, that including quantitative metrics in the creative briefing will 'turn off' its ad agency.

The sample base was smaller in the UK but included major advertisers. Clearly awareness is important for brands at the early stages of development but, once they are well known, awareness is significant only in the relative sense (saliency). Recall features in both lists and persuasion is similar to the shift in purchase intent. 'Engagement' refers to the extent to which the ad holds the attention of the audience.

Compare this with the metrics provided by the 24 ad-tracking research companies in Table 9.3. Only awareness and recall carry across. Although these are UK data most of the agencies are linked into US and international networks with similar measures.

Some tracking agencies stress that they tailor the measures to the needs of each client, but production economics militate against that. Indeed the most remarkable feature of the Admap survey was that 13 of the 24 agencies offer the same nine measures.

Readers of this book are probably more interested in how to set ad budgets and how to assess whether advertising delivered the required bottom line or could have delivered more profit with less expenditure. Today quite a few computer models are available, and the California-based Market Innovations Inc is one such (*see box*).

Table 9.3 ◆ Ad-tracking measures, UK

Effects tracked on a routine basis	Number of agencies
Brand awareness:	
Prompted	24
Unprompted	23
Ad awareness:	
Prompted	24
Unprompted	23
Consumer purchases	23
Brand images and attributes	23
Recall of advertising content	23
Brand preference/ranking	22
Advertising 'vividness' measures	18
Purchase-related promotions	10
Prices	5
Sizes/varieties	5
Distribution	4

Source: Admap Ad-tracking Users' and Buyers' Guide, September 2002

Marketing Decision Science (MDS)

John Cripps's MDS is focused on improving the efficiency of advertising spending and creative testing through the application of 'marketing science'. A marketing science approach to ad spend optimization uses routinely available historic data. Allocating a budget across media, geographies and months is based on historic spend, impression, campaign creative and sales data, together with sophisticated quantitative models.

A budget reallocation for a mid-sized financial services company produced the following impacts from the current total budget:

◆ 15 per cent decrease in customer acquisition costs

◆ 60 per cent increase in unit sales

▶

- ◆ 70 per cent increase in revenue
- ◆ 300 per cent increase in campaign ROI

Typically the entire Ad Spend Optimization platform can be developed and put into use within a two-month period, and the platform can be reused and updated on a quarterly basis thereafter to help guide ad spend allocation decisions in an ongoing way. The platform is developed specific to each client's needs and available data, and is delivered as a simulator that runs on a PC desktop in Excel. The platform is very user friendly so that it may be used by both executives and media planners as an advertising planning tool.

Source: Extracted from standard letter supplied by Dr John Cripps, MDS

Even though they are valuable aids to judgement and should be used, I have a number of reservations about these types of model. In particular, advertising builds brand equity and only brand equity. Yes, the consequential increase in brand equity may raise revenue and/or the acceptable price level, but the increase in brand equity itself, if there is one, is at least as important as the conventional financial numbers. And if there is no change in brand equity, then (direct response advertising aside) the link with sales is probably spurious.

The next difficulty is linking changes in advertising allocation with the rest of the mix. Practitioners know that direct marketing and promotions are more effective with air cover from advertising. A direct marketing campaign for cars, for example, saw a 30 per cent increase in areas covered by advertising.[7] These difficulties do not detract, however, from the wisdom of using metrics, and some model of this type, to give structure to debates during the budget setting process. The only real danger lies in assuming that the computer knows best.

Web/internet and direct marketing

The new electronic media have brought a Noah's ark of new measures, or at least language, but we need to make the same distinction as above. Are we measuring the medium or the customer? In other words, are we measuring the efficiency of the medium, with indicators such as cost per thousand readers, or the effects on the consumer, e.g. change in perceived brand quality. This issue runs right through measuring all aspects of the mix. The technical measures change radically from medium to medium but customer effectiveness measures remain much the same. Never mind how, did the campaign cause a change in buying patterns, or price sensitivity, or intermediate measures such as perceived quality?

The web's new measures can be confusing, especially when the new jargon is used inconsistently by experts.[8] And some measures, such as the number of 'hits', may not indicate anything useful, or so says the Interactive Advertising Bureau.[9] Nevertheless, the number of hits is the most tracked measure in the above-cited Marketing Leadership Council survey at 85 per cent. The other measures ranged from 39 to 52 per cent and referred to customers: unique visitors, registered users, new and repeat customers, and sales conversion rate. Compare this with the data from NetGenesis in Table 9.4.[10] They interviewed 20 US and UK cutting-edge web practitioner companies about the e-metrics they use now and expect to use in the future.

Table 9.4 ◆ E-metrics usage

E-metric	Use now %	Expect to use in the future %
Page views	47	13
Visits	37	27
Users	32	40
Conversion/revenue	16	27
Hits	5	0
Other	10	20

Note the lack of interest in hits. On the other hand, what emerges clearly from the report is the potential for tracking customers through the acquisition, retention and attrition life cycle. Chapter 3 examined flaws in an overly financial approach to CLV but no such objections arise with behavioural tracking. In particular note that they are tracking individual customers, not segments. The difficulties here are practical: managing and making sense of the huge volumes of data available to e-marketers. Table 9.5, again from NetGenesis, shows the levels of their respondents' tracking of these stages.

'Reach', as in advertising, is the number of people who had the opportunity to see the website, i.e. the number of visitors. 'Abandonment' however is a specialist e-marketing term that refers to the number of visitors who started a shopping cycle but left the website before completing a transaction.

Table 9.5 ◆ Customer life cycle tracking

E-metric	Use now %
Reach	61
Conversion	63
Retention	68
Abandonment	47
Attrition	50
Recency of purchase	39
Frequency of purchase	56

Related measures include churn, duration, clicks and the value (sales revenue or profit) of the customer to the company. The 'churn ratio' is the loss (attrition) of customers divided by the current customer base. For example, if one started a period with 2800 customers, gained 230 and lost 30, the churn ratio would be $30/(2800 + 230 - 30) = 1$ per cent.

'Duration', or stickiness, refers to the time the visitor spends on the website. However some distinguish the two terms and Net Genesis suggests that stickiness should be measured as Frequency, Duration, Total, Site Reach.

'Clicks' are a useful diagnostic of how customer friendly the website is, particularly when investigating high levels of abandonment. Ideally, the customer should be able to complete a purchase, or achieve the desired information, with the minimum number of page visits and mouse presses (clicks). Companies can benchmark the performance of their site against peer companies.

The other main distinction in e-marketing is between those who are using the web, interactively or not, as an information medium, e.g. Shell, or as a sales channel, e.g. Amazon. This takes us back to the setting of objectives. What we expect the expenditure to be buying for us should determine the relevant measures to use.

Web advertising is perhaps separated from conventional media by the greater precision available in analyzing, for example, page or ad impressions by viewer. In principle, we can establish exactly who the viewers were and separate those in the target segment from other viewers. In practice, such sophisticated analyses belong mostly to the future as the above survey indicates, although some companies, albeit reluctant to share their methods, are using these measures today.

The web hysteria of the late 1990s has now subsided and few today see it as a revolution so much as simply another medium. Life is becoming more complicated both for marketers and consumers, but they are using the same brains they always had to make decisions in much the way they always did. And therefore much the same metrics reflect the changes in brand equity.

E-marketing, CRM (see below) and direct marketing now overlap. Direct marketing grew out of direct mail via the telephone and sometimes is closer to selling (securing orders) than marketing in the broader sense (creating demand). One of the main attractions of direct marketing, relative to advertising or PR, has always been its measurability. The individual can be tracked through the stages of suspect, prospect, customer and repurchaser. The costs and conversion rates of each stage are easy to calculate. The e-metrics in Table 9.5 can be adapted for other forms of direct marketing, whether in person door-to-door, by mail, or by phone. We can move along.

Events and public relations

If the effects of advertising are hard to measure, most practitioners give up on publicity oriented events, sponsorship and PR. If the event is a discrete business getter, such as a stand at a trade fair, the incremental revenue can be traced, but the general goodwill from sponsoring, say, a horse race is another matter. Although the UK's business magazine *PR Week* tried to persuade agencies and clients to set aside 10 per cent of each budget to monitor PR performance, most preferred to spend the money on the campaign itself.[11]

The PR industry was originally invented, or formalized, as a means to persuade the USA to join World War I. Edward L. Bernays, one of the founding fathers, later defined public relations as:

(1) information given to the public, (2) persuasion directed at the public to modify attitudes and actions, and (3) efforts to integrate attitudes and actions of an institution with its publics and of publics with that institution.[2]

This gives us more than a clue as to how PR effectiveness should be measured. Bernays's item (2) is no different from advertising, even though the section of the medium (editorial) is separate from paid space. PR practitioners like to distinguish themselves from advertising as being subtle influencers rather than crass sales people. The reality is that advertising is also a weak and subtle medium and PR has to be opportunist to make the most of the accidents that happen. Once again we are less concerned with media efficiency than the effects on customers.

Bernays's item (3) is more interesting: it suggests that the gap between internal (employee) and external (customer) perceptions of the brand should be tracked. Maybe the customer attitudes are fine; it is just the company that needs to get real in its relationship with its customers.

The UK's Institute of Public Relations (IPR) has produced a 'Toolkit' for planning, research and evaluation of campaigns.[13] They suggest that between 5 and 12 per cent of budget should be reserved for these items. Their principles closely follow the general guidelines at the beginning of this chapter and are not repeated here. The main advice is to agree clear and quantified objectives and then use them to assess performance.

According to the MLC survey referenced above, the two main sponsorship measures were the cost (75 per cent) and reach (64 per cent) per event. Public relations measurement was dominated by the number of exposures (90 per cent) with the cost per exposure (29 per cent) and keynote speeches (22 per cent) trailing behind. A number of firms track the number of events (24 per cent) and the number of public service activities (17 per cent).

Trade shows were evaluated using the cost per event (70 per cent) and number attended (37 per cent) versus the number of leads generated (57 per cent), cost per lead (27 per cent) and lead conversion rate (20 per cent).

Other popular measures are the volume and favourability of coverage and advertising value equivalents (AVEs). The idea that PR can be evaluated by totalling the number of column inches which refer to the brand has never been sound but used just the same for practical reasons. If you cannot measure what matters, measure what you can measure! AVEs build on this ground by estimating what it would have cost to reach a similar audience, with similar frequency and opportunities to see. The outcome is usually to show that PR is much better value for money than display advertising. The IPR rightly challenges AVEs but on the wrong grounds:

To attempt to value PR in terms of the equivalent bought space makes little sense. AVEs continue to be used because they are perpetuated by PR practitioners willing to accept a client's misguided perception that PR results can be expressed in a similar manner to advertising.[14]

The techniques of PR differ from advertising but the objectives of persuading and getting closer to customers are the same. Accordingly, the measures of PR and advertising effectiveness can indeed be the same.

The PR ideal is to create such interest for the brand that word of mouth (WOM) takes on an independent life of its own. Following the metaphor of the living virus spreading by contagion, this is sometimes called 'viral marketing'.[15] Jean Harrison-Walker of Houston-Clear Lake examined multiple measures for WOM and concluded that the levels of activity and praise (or complaint) were the two key dimensions.[16] She used a survey with 13 items, e.g. 'I mention this service organization to others quite frequently', as the data for her analysis. She also reviewed ways to create WOM but that is clearly difficult and beyond the remit of this chapter.

The last activity falling under the general PR heading is sponsorship. By this stage, you will not be surprised, if you did not already know, that sponsorship measurement specialist firms exist alongside the agencies that supply the events. Sara Vickers and Ian Thompson deal with hygiene factors of reach and frequency, in much the same way as advertising, before moving to the more delicate issues of the fit between the brand and the event sponsored and the sponsorship effects.[17]

The higher level of brand awareness by those also aware of the sponsorship compared to those who missed it is not, as the authors rightly show, a valid effect since those already brand aware will be biased towards noticing the sponsorship. Tracking awareness over time, as they suggest, is not all that much better as the bias still exists. If one can achieve a clean matched sample, i.e. two markets similar in all respects and with no overlap where one has the sponsorship and one has not, then all kinds of comparisons are possible for this and most other elements of the mix. Few marketers have that luxury. Martell cognac sponsors the UK Grand National horse race for the whole country, if not the world.

That said, they are right that time series are useful for picking up the impacts of PR activity, such as sponsorship, and it is useful to research the appropriateness of the sponsorship and improvement in impressions of the brand. In theory, these should correlate.

Loyalty programmes

If I carry a dozen loyalty cards from competing stores, am I more or less loyal? This conundrum lies at the heart of measuring loyalty programme performance. The first major player gains from the others. Retention rates improve and probably acquisition too. The share of current purchases also improves but the market as a whole is not significantly expanded. The other main competitors have to join in, either individually or as part of some network. Their aim may be defensive and simply seeking to stifle the gains of the first mover. If the cost of the schemes was negligible, we would have a zero-sum game. In the days of Green Shield stamps, i.e. before 1970, this was how it was. As the gains were negated, everyone would progressively become bored with the programmes and they would fade away.

Loyalty cards today, however, have a new role. They are the pathways to customer databases such as that provided by dunnhumby for UK supermarket leader Tesco (see case in Chapter 3). In the ideal, the loyalty programme at least breaks even in terms of customer retention, acquisition and purchase frequency whilst providing the raw material for better targeted marketing. This saves time and money for marketer and customer alike as waste is reduced.

But can the operators of loyalty programmes expect them to break even? Professors at two Australian business schools rather doubt it.[18] Dowling and Uncles begin their article in MIT's *Sloan Management Review* by saying:

> *Given the popularity of loyalty programs, they are surprisingly ineffective. To stand the best chance of success in tough market conditions, programs must enhance the overall value of the product or service and motivate loyal buyers to make their next purchase.*

Of course, the odds against winning a horserace have not deterred owners from investing in thoroughbreds. Against this somewhat negative background, Table 9.6 notes the measures reported in the above-cited MLC survey.

The Dowling and Uncles challenge to the loyalty business may have been overstated. Any business engaging in relationship marketing, and that is most businesses, is automatically involved in some form of loyalty programming. Attracting, keeping and developing the business with customers lie at the heart of almost all forms of marketing. Perhaps the most interesting feature of Table 9.6 is that most of the measures are actually total market metrics. A 'loyalty programme' is marketing by another name.

Table 9.6 ◆ US loyalty programme measures

Measure	Use %
Participation	64
Customer satisfaction	54
Relative purchase frequency	54
Programme costs	46
Relative purchase volume	43

Of course any marketing programme can be well or poorly formulated; Dowling and Uncles must be right when they suggest that marketers look more to the value added for the customer than to a simple discount off purchases. Future free flights for the family may well be attractive for frequent flyers but private airport lounges provide more immediate benefit.

Similarly, the value of the database triggered by the use of loyalty cards depends on how well the data can be converted into savings for the company and consumer. For example, a supermarket should read my loyalty card when I enter and give me a shopping list of the things I usually buy in the sequence in which the goods are displayed. If they also suggest a few extras that others in my affinity group have purchased, or some relevant to me special offers, so much the better. Today they do not offer this service but they will before long. Those who use the internet for supermarket shopping already have this service.

These thoughts bring us back to the importance of establishing the objectives for the loyalty programme before we can hope to assess its effectiveness, still less its efficiency. A pre-emptive major new initiative should give increases in customer acquisition, retention and relative purchase frequency and volume. If, however, it is a defensive reaction to such a move by a competitor, one may still track those metrics but one would not expect them to change. Similarly, if the database is being actively employed to provide more value or better service for the customer, one would expect that to be reflected in customer satisfaction.

The business of this chapter is not to prescribe how loyalty programmes should be designed or implemented. The selection of relevant metrics, however, does turn on seeing these programmes in the context of customer relationships as a whole. Where a formal programme exists with only part of the customer base, then the analysis should compare metrics for those within and outside the programme, after allowing for the differences in customer profile.

CRM and customer service

CRM here refers to customer relationship management, not cause related marketing, i.e. linking the campaign for your brand with benefits for a charity or other good cause. This is now so widespread that most of us are likely to have bought something with a link to a charity in the last year. CRM in the charity sense needs to be treated at two levels: the assessment of the mix element in the conventional way and then the added costs and benefits from the linkage with the cause.

With CRM in the customer sense, we move from the mix elements one would expect to find in the marketing plan to the infrastructure of sales and customer relationships. Many companies would not consider that to be marketing at all. And that is exactly why their CRM systems fail. We have all heard large numbers for these failures and they depend on what one means by 'failure' but about 75 per cent of CRM projects miss their targets one way or another.

On the one side, 'customer relationship management' is just a fancy title for one of the world's oldest professions, selling. On the other side, the term has been adopted by the IT industry to refer to technical solutions to individual communications with customers. In particular, the search has focused on saving costs through telephone and web-based technology. Technology has dominated customer understanding. Customers do not belong to the firm and therefore they are not assets of the firm; nor do customers want to be managed. Some retain the traditional notion that the business exists to serve the customer and not the other way about.

The Conference Board found that 52 per cent of the 96 global firms they asked had installed CRM in order to increase customer retention/loyalty (94 per cent), react to competition (77 per cent), and differentiate their customer service (73 per cent).[19] Cost factors did not appear in the top three and one can wonder about differentiation if so many are doing the same thing and mostly from the same source (Siebel). In this survey, the preferred metrics were customer satisfaction (72 per cent), customer acquisition (65 per cent) and communication and administrative costs (47 per cent). Ah, there they are!

The same article in the *Journal of Business Strategy* reported that, according to Gartner Group in 2001, 45 per cent of CRM projects fail to improve customer interactions and more than half (51 per cent) generate no positive returns within three years. Most businesses underestimate the CRM introduction costs by between 45 per cent and 75 per cent. Meta Group claims that up to 75 per cent of CRM initiatives do not meet their goals.

In 2002, a US independent research firm, Nucleus, contacted the customers listed on the Siebel website (and therefore presumably well disposed) and found that 61 per cent had not achieved a positive ROI from their CRM deployment.[20]

Major new technologies often have teething problems and it is early days for CRM. My purpose is not to criticize the technology but to suggest that customer empathy has proved, so far, too small a factor in its deployment. Just consider your own satisfaction with your experience as a customer. The fundamental CRM mistake lies in trying to control the customer as distinct from putting the customer in charge of the relationship, as supermarkets do, for example. Safeway do not programme the trolleys but encourage customers to push them where they wish. From this we can deduce the metrics that matter.

Technical CRM issues revolve around functionality (effectiveness), costs and efficiency. They are also very similar to web-based measures. Traditional accountancy costs belong here (costs and profits per transaction, ROI on the CRM investment) but so do measures of time. More 'stickiness' (time online) is a useful but negative indicator: both customers and company prefer to complete transactions quickly. So we need to compare time per transaction and time spent to abandonment (uncompleted transactions). Browsing should be separated from transactions, or obtaining the desired transactions, but it should still be measured by satisfaction, not elapsed time. And we need to measure system failures, e.g. premature disconnection, percentage of transactions where help, or more senior intervention, is required.

Customer relationships can be monitored using the now customary relationship marketing measures, e.g. familiarity/knowledge, relative satisfaction with the customer brand, customer loyalty/retention and perceived quality of goods/services. Do customers recommend the brand to others?

The most important CRM measures are the synergy (or friction if all is not well) between the technical and relational aspects of CRM. Simple measures include relative (to competition or peers) satisfaction with the CRM system. More subtle measures are as follows:

- Is this the first site/call centre they contact in the category?
- Perceived time online/actual time (less is better).
- Turnover of front-line staff.
- Elapsed time taken to resolve complaints.

Note that all these measures should be taken separately for each main customer segment, both for comparison across segments and like-for-like segments across countries. Where possible, metrics can usefully be benchmarked against peer companies.

Table 9.7 summarizes a simple evolution in the way metrics are likely to move. Note the consistency between those applying to customers and front-line staff. I suggest that commitment should be the primary focus, even though the bottom line remains the goal.

Table 9.7 ◆ CRM metrics

Metrics	Customer	Front-line staff	Company
Old	Retention	Turnover	CRM costs
Better	Satisfaction	Satisfaction	CRM ROI
Best	Commitment	Commitment	Shareholder value – including brand equity

Sales promotions

Sales promotions fall into two groups: those that seek to build customer value, i.e. brand equity, as well as increasing sales and those, typically coupons or price-offs, that are purely directed at short-term sales gains or defending the brand's position with retailers. In a controversial but much-cited paper, Notre Dame and Columbia Professors Mela, Gupta and Lehman concluded that consumers become more price and promotion sensitive over time because of reduced advertising and increased promotions.[21] In other words, price promotions are less attractive for brand equity, and ultimately profitability, than advertising.

Professor Andrew Ehrenberg has long argued a stronger view, namely that price promotions are generally unprofitable, even in the short term, once shifts in purchasing patterns are taken into account.[22] Of course, not undertaking price promotions when competitors are doing so may be even more unprofitable. Others take the opposing view that sales promotions can increase category size and therefore have a positive effect, perhaps even on brand equity. One such study for 173 brands across 13 categories found that 25 per cent of the gain came from category growth leaving 75 per cent to brand switching.[23]

Once again we need to understand the objectives for the sales promotion. The leading sales promotion metrics according to the MLC survey are shown in Table 9.8.

The main surprise in Table 9.8 is the omission of the measure most often associated with promotions, namely the sales uplift due to the promotion. Another popular indicator is the percentage of sales made on promotion as distinct from sales on regular terms. Comparing these sales with the proportion of the year (and customer base) that promotions are available, indicates the strength or weakness of brand equity. For example, if promotions are available 50 per cent of the time but sales on promotion account for 80 per cent of the total, the company will have a problem kicking the promotion habit.

Table 9.8 ◆ US sales promotion measures

Measure	Use %
Cost per promotion	73
Coupon redemption rate	49
Channel/vendor participation	32
Number of promotions conducted	32
Number of samples dispensed	24

This choice of language is deliberate: retailers, especially in the USA, depend on suppliers' promotions for much of their profitability. In other words, some of the brand marketer's promotional money never makes it to the consumer. Whether suppliers are addicted to promotions due to retailer or competitor pressure, does not matter. They know, like taking heroin, that they should not do it and that profits are damaged, but they cannot give them up. Sales promotions can be beneficial, especially when they build

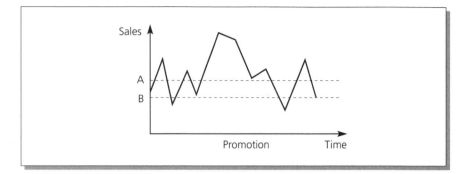

Figure 9.2 ◆ Establishing the baseline

brand equity, and they can be defensive ways to avert worse alternatives. With the pressure on quarterly reporting, marketers simply cannot take time out for kicking the habit and rehabilitation, but reality should still be measured. In particular, they should take a hard look at the sales uplift data. This is usually measured as the difference between actual sales and the 'baseline', namely what sales would have been without the promotion.

The Ehrenberg thesis would lead one to expect a peak in sales due to the promotion to be offset by a subsequent trough, plus, if the promotion is flagged head of time, a trough before the promotion. In practice, sales graphs rarely look like that. Figure 9.2 shows the difficulty: is the baseline something like line A or line B? The ACNielsen baseline usually tends to the lower level which flatters the promotion uplift. If one takes a level nearer the yearly average sales, the incremental profit probably goes negative. Where a firm is in regular promotional mode and where there are no control figures, e.g. comparable hold-out areas without promotion, one cannot be sure where the baseline is.

Sales promotions cover a wide variety of activities and are often linked with other mix elements that are likely to make them more effective but also more difficult to disentangle for evaluation purposes. Payment by results is arguably the best means of ensuring that the results are compared with intentions. Where multiple mix items are involved, there is likely to be a lead agency (the one with the biggest budget) which can also take lead responsibility for post-campaign assessment.

New product development

Returning to the more classical mix, the traditional indicator of NPD performance deployed by 3M, for example, is the percentage of revenue due to products introduced in the previous three years. Not all companies are that fast moving but the metric is tried and reasonably true. The main problem is that it gives a rear view and only operates some time after the event. Companies would prefer metrics that can give a more current assessment. The measures arising from the MLC survey are given in Table 9.9.

Looking at the pre-launch measures, defining how niche the new products are, or how strategic, is sensible but not a topic that yields easily to a single metric. Belief in the new products and the number of ideas generated will have less credibility with experienced new product managers in some sectors. One great idea is more valuable than a mass of dreadful ones and radical ideas tend to research badly. Baileys Irish Cream, now the brand leader in liqueurs, failed all market research tests but, fortunately for Diageo, the brand champions persevered nonetheless. The cycle time, however, is a useful check on the NPD process: most firms have discovered that speed is of the essence. Better 90 per cent right than 100 per cent late. Again this depends on the sector: Boeing will not wish to launch a plane that nearly flies.

The post-launch measures are less questionable although awareness should appear in this category. Awareness is a stage one metric and crucial for most new concepts.

The topic of innovation was extensively discussed in Chapter 6 where it

Table 9.9 ◆ NPD metrics

Pre-launch	Usage %	Post-launch	Usage %
Size of target market	74	NP sales (volume)	73
Belief in NP concept	46	NP revenue	69
Awareness of NP concept	30	Penetration	53
No. of ideas generated	24	NP margins	49
Cycle time from concept to launch	24	Level of cannabilization	36

was argued that establishing the innovativeness of the company was more important than tracking individual innovations, or, by implication, even groups of NPD activity. At the same time, a company will want to monitor the performance success rate. Projects that abort before launch and failed launches are not necessarily waste, if the learning is employed in future successes. Assessing this area, as in others, calls for a level of sophistication not represented by simple numbers, and especially not by financial numbers.

Modelling the marketing mix

There are many possible elements of the marketing mix beyond those explicitly covered above, notably pricing. Indeed planning and assessing pricing performance is a huge topic that deserves a book of its own. It also defies ROI-type thinking. Short-term gains by increasing price (margins) or reducing it (sales) may very well be reversed in the longer term and competitive reactions need to be taken into account. Tracking the key relative price metric has been covered in earlier chapters. Many practitioners consider pricing to be fundamental to the whole company concept of marketing rather than a detail of the marketing mix. One widely touted metric is price elasticity but in practice this has a number of problems:

- ◆ It is not a fixed number at any point on the price quantity curve but depends on the amount of change being considered.

- ◆ Short-term elasticity differs from the long term.

- ◆ It ignores brand equity.

- ◆ It ignores interaction (synergy) in mix.

- ◆ It also ignores the changing environment, and especially how competitors may react.[24]

Rather than take the other elements of the mix one by one, this chapter will conclude with an overview of the mix as a whole and some thoughts on how companies, such as the US grocery products giant Kraft, bring the elements together through modelling (*see box*).

A number of firms now offer marketing mix modelling, Mindshare (WPP), BBDO and Commetrix (Publicis) being examples.[25] They can operate with or without databases. The first stage is to estimate the response curves for each element of the mix. Figure 9.3 illustrates a typical response curve.

Kraft

Kraft, like other US highly developed packaged goods businesses, has developed a comprehensive database that enables it to carry out sophisticated modelling and assessment of payback for elements of the mix. In other words, the models sought to optimize the mix for each brand.

More recently, in recognition of the fact that the minority of its brands were driving the great majority of its corporate growth, Kraft set out also to optimize mix across brands. The process takes each element of mix across all brands. For example, the brands are first ranked by return on investment (ROI) on their advertising element. Funds are reallocated from low returns to high and the process is repeated with the next element of the mix. Ultimately it reviews all mix elements across all brands.

The technical tools applied to the database include clustering, multivariate regression and rules-based analytic techniques, but the real strength comes from the process being conducted with the full management team of the relevant business units. In this way, their experience and intuition can be combined with the models.

The process has five steps. First, the database is updated and the model reconfigured. Second, the model is run several times with 'what if' alternatives. The third stage checks back with the suppliers (internal and external) of the data to validate the data outputs. The fourth stage 'triangulates' the output against other means of establishing optimal budgets and mix. This is one of the strengths of the Kraft system: to ensure convergence across alternative approaches.

Finally the management team gets to work with the models synergistically: their knowledge improves the model and the analysis from the model enhances their ability to manipulate all the variables.

Source: Marketing Leadership Council (2001) *Stewarding the Brand for Profitable Growth*, Washington DC: Corporate Executive Board, 77–83

Where the data is available, then the curve can be derived using multivariate methods. Otherwise the first stage involves the key executives pooling their experience. In the model developed as an Excel package at London Business School, the executives are asked to estimate the sales at each of five points: if the budget is set at the previous level, at 50 and 150 per cent of that level, if there is no expenditure and if the advertising is set at a level beyond which sales will not increase (saturation).[26]

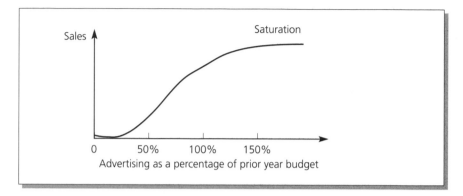

Figure 9.3 ◆ A typical sales response curve

This model has two advantages over most commercial models: the curve is not symmetric around the midpoint and brand equity is taken into account. The output from these types of models usually takes one of two forms: optimizing the profit return from a fixed total marketing budget; and determining what the optimal budget should be. The portfolio optimization can be for the mix across different brands, or brands across different markets (e.g. countries) or both. In most models the variety of the mix is limited (e.g. above and below the line and fixed costs) not so much to simplify the model as to minimize the data input required.

The Kraft case above underlines the importance of using these tools interactively with management to support their decision making. It is very unlikely that any model will outguess management planning but a combination of quantitative techniques, taken together with management judgement, should converge on the 'best' answer; i.e. the one management is most prepared to go with. The other main advantage is that the tools enable managers with very different expectations to exchange their experiences in a structured manner. Consensus should emerge with less heat and more light.

The importance of metrics in these models lies in the first stage of developing the response curves. The more robustly these emerge from the firm's business model, the more reliable the outputs from the second stage. In other words, the metrics serve to link the relationships between the input variables (expenditure on the mix) with sales and brand equity consequences.

Executive minutes

1 Before evaluating the need for, and the performance of, any element of the mix be sure the context (the firm's business model and goals) are explicit.

2 Check sales support expenditure that does not build brand equity is not charged to the brand budget.

3 Consider payment by results, if not already in place, for the major items of marketing expenditure but ensure that they are really for results and not good service. If PBR is not appropriate, ensure that goals are validated and compared with profits and brand equity effects on a like-with-like basis.

4 Ensure that performance is measured by profits and the shift in brand equity.

5 All elements, and potential elements, of the mix should be considered firstly for their ability to deliver the marketing goals. Only then should efficiency be considered, not as ROI but by asking whether the goals could be achieved with less expenditure or even better performance with more.

6 After a first cut plan focusing on each element of the mix separately, the Exec should use portfolio analysis, possibly modelling, to determine optimal expenditure across the mix, brands and markets.

Notes

1 This section is based on separate research funded by the UK Sales Promotion Consultants Association during 1999 and 2000, and on a review of the UK IPA Advertising Effectiveness Awards for 1998. The promotional research is reported in the Sales Promotion Consultants Association White Paper on promotional assessment that may be downloaded from *http//www.spca.co.uk*.

2 The award winners are published every two years since 1981 by WARE, Henley on Thames.

3 Research conducted by Tim Ambler for and with the UK Sales Promotions Consultants Association 1999. See website above.

4   Lace, J. (2000) 'Payment-by-results: is there a pot of gold at the end of the rainbow?', *International Journal of Advertising*, 19 (2), 167–83.

    Lace, J. (2000) *Paying for advertising*, London: Incorporated Society of British Advertisers.

5   Marketing Leadership Council (2001) *Measuring Marketing Performance*, (supporting data), August, Washington DC: Corporate Executive Board, 5.

6   Ambler, T. and Goldstein, S. (2003) 'Copy testing: Practice and Best Practice', Advertising Association Monograph, London.

7   Madden, R. (2002) 'I'll tell you what I want, what I really, really want', presentation to Marketing in the Interactive Age conference, London, 16 October.

8   See *www.abce.org.uk* for one organization seeking to standardize terminology and measures.

9   Interactive Advertising Bureau, UK (*www.iab.co.uk*) 'Jargon Buster': 'When users access a website, their computer sends a request to the site's server to begin downloading a page. Each element of a requested page (including graphics, text, interactive items) is recorded by the site's web server log file as a "hit". If a page containing two graphics is accessed by a user, those hits will be recorded once for the page itself and once for each of the graphics. Webmasters use hits to measure their servers' workload. Because page designs and visit patterns vary from site to site, the number of hits bears no relationship to the number of pages downloaded, and is therefore a poor guide for traffic measurement.'

10 Cutler, M. and Sterne, J. (2000) *E-Metrics: Business Metrics for the New Economy*, Cambridge MA: NetGenesis and Santa Barbara CA: Target Marketing.

11 *Marketing Week*, (2001), 1 February 2001, 51–3.

12 Bernays, E. L. (1952) *Public Relations*, Oklahoma: University of Oklahoma Press, 3.

13 Fairchild, M. (2000) *The IPR Toolkit*, London: Institute of Public Relations. See also *www.pre-fix.org.uk*

14 Fairchild, M. (2000) *The IPR Toolkit*, London: Institute of Public Relations, 37.

15 Goldsmith, R. (2002) *Viral Marketing: Get Your Audience to do Your Marketing for You*, London: PrenticeHall.

16 Harrison-Walker, J. (2001) 'The measurement of word-of-mouth communication and an investigation of service quality and customer commitment as potential antecedents', *Journal of Service Research*, 4, 60–75.

17 Vickers, S. and Thompson, I. (2002) 'Sponsorship: the real deal', *Admap*, 432, 19–22.

18 Dowling, G. R. and Uncles, M. (1997) 'Do customer loyalty programs really work?', *Sloan Management Review*, 38 (4), 71–82.

19 Anonymous (2001) 'Does CRM pay?', *Journal of Business Strategy*, 22, 3.

20 Campbell, I. (2002) 'Assessing the real ROI from Siebel', Nucleus Research Report C47, Wellesley MA, September.

21 Mela, C. F., Gupta, S. and Lehmann, D. R. (1997) 'The long-term impact of promotion and advertising on consumer brand choice', *Journal of Marketing Research*, 34, 248–61.

22 Ehrenberg, A. S. C., Hammond, K. and Goodhardt, G. J. (1994) 'The after-effects of price-related consumer promotions', *Journal of Advertising Research*, 34, 11.

23 Bell, D. R., Chiang, J. and Padmanabhan, V. (1999) 'The decomposition of promotional response: an empirical generalization', *Marketing Science*, 18 (4), 504–26.

24 Hardie, B. and Ambler, T. (2002) 'Improving marketing productivity: introducing the HAMRAT process', London Business School working paper no. 02–901.

25 For further comments on this approach, see Dyson, P. (2002) 'Setting the communications budget', *Admap*, 433, 39–42.

26 Hardie, B. and Ambler, T. (2002) 'Improving marketing productivity: introducing the HAMRAT process', London Business School working paper no. 02–901.

10

Getting the right metrics to the top table

GROUCHO MARX, not for the first time, put his finger on the problem: 'I didn't like the play, but then I saw it under adverse conditions – the curtain was up.' Exposing the harsh reality of the firm's business model in its competitive context may be just as ugly. And yet this play is the thing: how and why does cash flow from customer to shareholder?

Simple as it may seem in theory, stepping back from the business, assembling a clear business model and putting numbers on the key drivers defeats most top executive teams. Successful businesses, obviously enough, have perceptions that work but full clarity is rare. A complete understanding of the firm's [marketing]   performance and brand equity requires considerable organizational skills and energy. This chapter reviews the idealized information supply situation and then some of the real-world difficulties. Getting the data is only a start: marrying it together is the challenge considered in the last section.

> Stepping back from the business, assembling a clear business model and putting numbers on the key drivers defeats most top executive teams

As every experienced marketer knows, large company life is complex. Meeting follows meeting and new initiatives rain down on top of initiatives devised at lower levels. Managerial time is in such short supply that companies would probably do better if they outsourced accountancy services and replaced the CFO with a chief of managerial time whose approval would be required before any new project was agreed. When mid-level marketers were asked, in the course of our research, what they considered to be the single largest impediment to better marketing performance, we received a wide variety of answers. Money, perhaps surprisingly, was not high on the list and nor was the shortage of information. The most frequent response, in large companies, was the difficulty in gaining cross-functional support. Lack of conceptual understanding of marketing, and brand equity in particular, was part of that.

Reviewing and choosing the metrics, gathering them from diverse sources and running them in will take many months in a large company. Marketers have neither the manpower nor the muscle to draw the data from other departments and present them consistently. Recent years have seen support staff stripped from marketing, especially from junior levels. When did you last meet an assistant brand manager? Furthermore, senior marketers, with an in-post expectation of 18 months, do not plan to be around as long as creating a metrics system would take, nor can a market research firm supply a complete package. Some research firms have many different customers within a single large corporation, each interested only in their particular needs. With marketers not falling over themselves to be measured, and perhaps found wanting, our research reveals a big gap at the top. No one is championing the metrics needed to give an overall picture.

There are stories, apocryphal or not, of consultants being hired by the Exec to gather the measures from the market but then collecting them from the company's own management silos. This is not as foolish as it may seem: numbers from external consultants carry more credibility than the same metrics from the internal marketers. Consultancy services have been one of the fastest growing sectors, mainly because middle management use them as conduits to the Exec and, vice versa, Execs use them to get things done that their own management are too busy to do.

Figure 10.1 gives an overview of this chapter, which covers the following key points:

◆ *Auditing the company's marketing information needs*: it is one thing to identify the metrics needed in theory, but quite another to source and pay for them. The resources allocated to metrics have to be kept in proportion to the marketing they are helping to assess.

◆ *The state of the market research supply business*: tidy it is not.

◆ *Alignment*: when reality takes over, metrics will not be perfectly aligned. Segments and time periods, in particular, are likely to be inconsistent.

◆ *Packaging metrics for the Exec*: one of the many paradoxes in this metrics game is that the larger the company, the more simple presentation has to become. The problem is not that the Exec is dumb (they are likely to be smarter than anyone else in the company), but that they have too little time. Messages have to communicate instantly.

◆ *The role of the CFO in overseeing information supply*: metrics come reluctantly and unaligned from many quarters. Chief marketing officers (CMOs) would be wise not to take a turf stance on this but instead to ask their finance colleagues to take over marketing metrics, including Exec presentation. This section shows why.

Auditing the company's marketing information needs

Market research accounts for between 2 and 5 per cent of total marketing expenditure.[1] Attempts have been made to assess scientifically how much each firm should spend on information, and in what circumstances, but such studies are unconvincing. The installation, or revision, of Exec-level marketing metrics should prompt a market research audit to answer these questions:

◆ Do we already have, somewhere in the company, the data to support the metrics now selected?

◆ Do we also have the more detailed data that will be needed to answer questions about variances in the metrics (diagnostics)?

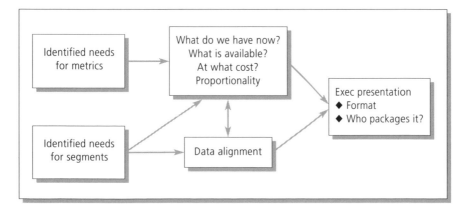

Figure 10.1 ◆ Getting the right metrics to the top table

◆ What other information do we regularly receive through tracking studies or surveys?

◆ What are the lowest costs to obtain what we now need?

◆ How does the resulting overall cost compare with whatever yardstick the company deems appropriate and with the cost of providing the internal (financial) metrics?

The third question should prompt two subsidiaries:

◆ What do we now get that can be culled?

◆ If it cannot be culled, should it be reconsidered for the metrics list, i.e. what is its purpose? What does it add?

Most large companies are buying research that serves no apparent purpose, but they hesitate to cull. Top management questions once asked may be asked again. In-house market researchers accumulate reports like books in a library but, corporate life being what it is, the unceasing stream of newly hired marketers commission new work from ignorance or time pressures or because new work is more credible. Driven by the problem of the week, marketers need information tightly tuned to that particular topic. Academic marketers are no different. Old databases are rarely used for new research.

The data or information warehouse has long been regarded as the answer to all this. Marketing information, internal or external, should be stored on the mainframe in some logical order and be available to any manager on a terminal or PC. Those responsible for adding new research or statistics should then ensure that they are accurate and consistent. For example, the 'month' for accounting should be the same as the 'month' for measuring consumer sales. The segment used for measuring awareness should be the same as the segment identified for advertising.

The warehouse could supply top-level information (metrics) with analysis by time, region, stock-keeping unit (individual product pack), customer, etc. Software could generate graphs, pie charts and histograms and run regressions. Data mining could, in theory, help target mailings to ever more tightly defined groups, as Tesco is demonstrating with its Clubcard data by sending over 60 segmented mailings to identified groups of customers.

However, this ideal of a single global and comprehensive marketing database has rarely, if ever, been implemented outside the e-commerce, high-tech world of Amazon and Dell. It is especially difficult across national boundaries. Nevertheless it is an ideal worth holding on to as companies move in that direction. The Shell example shows a major trader developing an increasing range of marketing measures worldwide. In 2002, Shell extended the Tracker by commissioning a further piece of work to understand the key drivers of reputation among a wider range of stakeholders (*see box*).

Shell

Shell's 'Global Brand Tracker' provides metrics and diagnostics for their brand versus competitors since 1997 across 70 countries. A very wide range of interview questions includes:

◆ Spontaneous awareness

◆ Trial

◆ Purchase

◆ Loyalty

◆ Avoidance

◆ Preference

◆ Image

◆ Formula 1 (racing)

◆ Familiarity

◆ Favourability

As trends emerge, the database is proving increasingly useful. Preference and convenience interact, for example, to provide insights into loyalty. The data is used to provide scorecard measures, marketing planning, portfolio decisions (extend/cull) and broad insights at the macro level.

The scorecard shows, for Shell and competitors, the key brand image (intermediate) and behavioural indicators, market and store share, pricing and composite ratios.

Source: Simon Saville, Global Brands Standards Manager, Shell, presentation to the Centre for Marketing workshop at London Business School, 24 November 1999

The reality of data supply

This section makes the point that the market research industry is complex, untidy and geared to supplying detailed figures for particular problems. They are more interested in the technicalities and efficiencies of their own production process than in providing an overview of the client's marketing. Ironic as it may seem, the market research industry is not market, or at least consumer, oriented. Few are particularly concerned, according to Robert Heath, then Managing Director of Icon, with their customers' needs. They are reluctant, for example, to interpret the data they provide. If you agree with this paragraph, skip the rest of this section. If not, read on.

The data warehouse ideal organizes information coherently but it does not address a key difficulty for modern marketers in large companies: data glut. In reality, marketers are not chained to their PCs scanning the real time data and acting on what they see. They are much more likely to be in a meeting discussing the current fire which needed quenching yesterday. But research is used, perhaps sensibly enough, on a problem-by-problem basis. The issue is formulated, research commissioned and presented. Other research, such as tracking studies, rolls in according to the annual timetable. In all cases, information is process, not market, driven.

So to portray the data warehouse as a single coherent information iceberg with metrics being the 10 per cent visible to the Exec and the submerged 90 per cent being readily available diagnostics is a nice metaphor, but far from reality. The process-driven nature of the market research business can be seen from the way they interact with clients. For example, since the 1930s ACNielsen has made a good living out of supplying marketers with, essentially, sales diagnostics. Shortfalls in sales performance could be pinpointed back to the sales person responsible without the need for internal statistics. ACNielsen, then and increasingly now, supplies more market information than this, but its early success was due to the routine need to explain sales variances to top management.

The specialization is both vertical, i.e. according to industry sector, and horizontal, according to the type of research technique employed. Examples of vertical specialization include research agencies – or divisions of agencies – that are entirely devoted to studying the automotive market or the pharmaceutical market. Specialization can pay off handsomely. The world's second biggest research agency, after ACNielsen, is IMS Health, which concerns itself mainly with the pharmaceutical industry and monitors global sales of medicinal drugs. Other agencies concentrate wholly or partly on media research, which has become a highly complex and technical field of study, particularly as far as the measurement of television audiences is concerned. In the USA, Nielsen Media Research, now entirely independent of its progenitor ACNielsen, is a giant in its own right, and part of an even bigger group, Dutch publishing house VNU.

In Britain, such leading agencies as Taylor Nelson Sofres, which for many years handled the Broadcasters' Audience Research Board (BARB) TV contract, and Ipsos-ASI, which has done likewise for the National Readership Survey, owe much of their income to their expertise in this area. Examples of horizontal (technique) specialization include, again, Taylor Nelson Sofres and ACNielsen. The former has huge experience of using consumer panels to measure brand shares of markets; the latter, like its great rival, Information Resources, is best known for the collection and analysis of retail data.

Some agencies, such as Research International which is part of WPP, pride themselves on the methods they have developed for assessing the potential size of the market for new products. They have also invested in new thinking and models relating to brand equity (understanding what comprises brand equity and tools for tracking it) and customer loyalty (what builds customer retention and what reduces it). Others, such as Millward Brown (also WPP) and Hall & Partners, are known principally for their continuous tracking of public awareness of brands and advertising.

Several, including MORI and Gallup, have won fame through conducting political opinion polls, though that is usually only a small part of their business. Very many, often quite small, agencies concentrate on so-called focus groups to produce hypotheses about public attitudes to different questions.

Big or small, most agencies have imitated their clients to the extent of offering branded 'products', which more often than not are essentially similar to services available from their competitors. Branding of research services does not, incidentally, save the agencies from having to compete fiercely on price when pitching for new business. The paradox is that, while market research has been steadily growing as an industry over the past 30 years, and greatly expanding the range of its clients, market researchers have been losing influence as a source of business advice.

The sales growth is real and impressive. World expenditure on market research is estimated to have totalled $11 billion in 1997, of which 37 per cent was spent in the USA itself and 10 per cent in the UK, which has a large research industry relative to the size of its economy. According to John Kelly, President of ESOMAR, the global turnover by 2001 reached $15.9 billion, with over 650,000 employees.[2] Over 80 per cent of turnover is in the top 10 countries, 39 per cent in the USA, and 60 per cent is with the top 25 companies.

The advertising and marketing services group WPP consistently reports that its research subsidiaries are among the fastest growing parts of its business.[3] Diversification of the client base in the industry is likewise impressive.

Whereas in the 1960s research clients were mainly manufacturers of packaged goods, they now comprise companies and non-commercial organizations of all types, from charities to tour operators.

As for the decline in influence, one reason is that there are now so many more research agencies, busy with so many more tasks than 30 or 40 years ago, that individual research experts no longer wield the clout that some – a George Gallup or an Ernest Dichter in the USA, a Mark Abrams or a Harry Henry in the UK – once did. Another reason is that much research is today commissioned on a project-by-project basis, with rival agencies tendering for each project rather than being hired as long-term business partners.

Then again, it is hard to give sound advice if you do not know the full picture, and it is hard to get the full picture if you are unable to talk directly to senior management. Indeed market researchers have long bemoaned their lack of access to top management and the way they have been pushed down the reporting line. Where large client companies are concerned, research agencies commonly deal with research managers, who themselves are not Exec members and are considered by their own CEOs as organizers and suppliers of data rather than as business decision makers.

The CMO who attends research debriefs, or focus groups, has become a rarity. Cause and effect are hard to separate. The question is whether declining Exec-level interest resulted from the researchers' obsession with their own methodology or whether researchers have been pushed back into low overhead data production by lack of senior managers' attention.

Or is it that researchers, like advertising agencies with similar complaints, have been upstaged by management consultants? This is more discussed than real with strategic marketing forming a small share of the major consultants' businesses. More likely is that the Exec listens to those they commission to address the problems they define and these problems are rarely seen by the Exec as marketing, or market, issues (*see box*).

Gaining ground but losing influence

Nevertheless, research agencies can take comfort from a survey carried out in the summer of 1999 among large British companies in which 77 per cent considered that the agencies they used made a significant contribution to their marketing strategy.[4] However, this finding was not quite such good news for the agencies as might be at first supposed.

▶

The same survey, found that, while 73 per cent of respondents expected to make greater use of market research in future, they did not necessarily expect to buy it from research agencies; 28 per cent expected research agencies as such to lose ground against consultants. Only 21 per cent expected the research agencies to gain ground. Reasons for losing ground were most commonly the greater effort made by consultants to understand their clients' business and their ability to offer a wider range of services.

When it came to comments on particular research agencies, the survey threw up some interesting material. For example, 24 per cent of clients of one very large agency thought it showed very good knowledge of their business sector, 24 per cent fairly good but 24 per cent showed poor sector knowledge.

Asked about the level at which they communicated with the same very large agency, 60 per cent of clients answered senior management and 10 per cent said the marketing director. Another 30 per cent said it depended on the project. In no case was the managing director of the client company involved in dealing with the agency.

In the USA, there has been discussion of the market research industry meeting clients' needs better by packaging data in models for each marketing usage. In other words, a research company would supply one package for overall marketing assessment, another for pricing decisions and so on. This would respond to the problem-driven nature of marketers' research needs and it would syndicate the costs not only of the data but of the expensive and rare technical modelling skills.

The global amalgamation of research companies with each other and with other large groups, such as London-based WPP and Paris-based Ipsos, is likely to encourage this development. Marketing mix models, as noted in the last chapter, are now available and Ipsos, for example, offers integrated research and analysis across ad concept development, copy testing, tracking and brand equity assessment. Their two key metrics are relevance and differentiation both in terms of how the consumer understands the ad and the effect on brand equity. Ads are researched in the traditional ways outlined in the last chapter, but also for the three other metrics in the Ipsos view of brand equity: familiarity, popularity and consistent quality.

Even this level of integration, however, does not provide metrics for assessing marketing as a whole and nor does the information arrive for the same time periods. Some research is commissioned by marketing managers but others, such as customer satisfaction and complaints, may be purchased by logistics or sales. The customer segments and competitive benchmarks they specify may differ from marketer perceptions.

On the face of it, no such difficulty should exist with internal data, largely financial and under the control of the firm itself. In practice it is not so simple. Internal monthly cut-off dates do not correspond with calendar months or the rest of the market. Cost allocations change as well as the level at which the 'bottom' line is taken. The treatment of allowances, discounts and rebates changes from year to year. And the list continues.

Many of these details are not significant and may best be ignored. Where they do intrude, Execs need to think about the extent to which variances are questioned and who has to separate the technical glitches from the real (market) ones. The final section here takes us back to process: who should package and, where necessary, unravel the metrics?

Alignment

The selection of the audiences, or segments, to be measured can be a more subtle business than selecting the metrics themselves. Comparability requires consistency from year to year. As noted above, it is the change, not the absolute number, that is important. Yet circumstances will change. One solution to this is to collect all possible metrics for all possible segments, including not just customers but also employees, influencers, shareholders, etc. This provides diagnostics for middle management who then select the metrics to present to the Exec. This process, however, risks bias and non-comparability. Our research did not find examples of that in practice and it may be more theoretic than real. Quite apart from straining the market research budget and IT system, managers might not be able to cope with the ensuing information avalanche.

In practice, it is hard to align the units (brand market segments) from goals through plans to assessment, with year-to-year continuity. Even where all internal and external metrics are available at segment level, the exact boundaries differ from metric to metric and unit to unit. Firms can only buy the market research that is available, and internal figures only record what trade sales are made, not the sales made by customers. Retail businesses aside, the differences can be crucial. As markets and marketing develop (or managers change or their minds change), target segments are redefined.

One year may prioritize customer retention, widely seen as the most cost effective form of marketing, whereas another year may target new customers and increased market share.

Full formal segmentation will thus be seen as an expensive luxury for most companies, which are still wrestling with integrating marketing as a whole. The more important aspect of segmentation that applies to everyone is alignment. The goals, the target market, the research and the results should all be focused on the same group of people. At the very least, make sure that you are not advertising to one group and measuring another.

> At the very least, make sure that you are not advertising to one group and measuring another

Global companies are seeking to harmonize measurement systems and metrics worldwide and the amalgamation of the market research industry is facilitating this. Flexibility of the marketing mix to adapt to local customers is one thing, but localizing measurement is another. The industry shows a trend towards reconciling market research standards and measures worldwide. The reason is simple: a global firm suffers greater overheads, but those should be offset by greater organizational learning opportunities. What works in one market can be tried in another.

But for this learning to operate, comparisons need to be made, i.e. measures need to be comparable. Recognizing that compulsory standardization may inhibit innovation and stifle development, the term 'harmonization' is preferred, which implies some flexibility, as Nestlé and others permit, but not to the point that communication is obscured.

Packaging metrics for the Exec

In our interviews with large, cutting-edge companies, we expected respondents to agree that Execs should create the climate for effective marketing, but leave variance chasing to others. This was rarely what we heard. Obviously the Exec of a small company must be hands-on, but the Execs of multi-divisional companies were expected by their senior managers (our respondents) to dive into detail too.

Not only should Execs seek answers for marketing variances, we were informed, but they should do so promptly. Our suggestion that large companies should apply the learning to next year's plan was also rebuffed. The majority message was 'think small and think for today'. Some respondents, however, did report greater empowerment with regard to which detail was delegated, and the Exec used information to determine how well the system worked.

If marketers' perception is that Exec information will only be followed by demands for detail and double-guessing, then the lack of enthusiasm that we have witnessed for metrics makes sense. Information will only make trouble. Marketers know overall marketing assessment is important but they are reluctant to create rods for their own backs. 'Like turkeys voting for Christmas', someone noted at one seminar. Maybe they should: Christmas is the reason turkeys exist.

Perhaps this section should be retitled 'Packaging the Exec for metrics', as the emphasis thus far is on the need to use them responsibly. Where a specialist marketing function exists, the role of the Exec is to encourage it to be more effective by removing road blocks, not to create new ones. And still less to ask about the variances the marketers will, or should have, already addressed. How can that happy state of trust come about?

We are now moving from best current practice to speculation about the future. One of our most encouraging findings was the extent to which internal finance and marketing functions have moved closer. Marketers have learned, and use, financial language and disciplines. Accountants are now keen to understand marketing. They certainly recognize that everything cannot be explained by financial numbers. The UK guidelines for companies' annual operating and financial reviews in 1993 assumed that all metrics would be financial, but by 2003 the Accounting Standards Board recognized non-financial market metrics and brand equity in particular.[5]

The Institute of Chartered Accountants of England and Wales (ICAEW), as another example, commissioned London Business School to report on brand stewardship: in other words, how companies report on marketing performance and brand equity otherwise than in the formal accounts. Sir Bryan Carsberg, the Secretary of the international accountancy rule-setting organization, said: 'We do not account for intangibles very well and perhaps cannot do so under traditional accounting.'[6] The widely adopted Balanced Scorecard was devised by two professors of accounting.[7] The ICAEW, when making proposals for reporting on shareholder value, recommended that five of the nine metrics be what we would recognize as non-financial marketing metrics, and the financial metrics largely coincided with those proposed in this book (Table 10.1).[8]

It is a small step from here to integrating the informational roles of the finance and marketing chiefs. I have written elsewhere about the difficult

Table 10.1 ◆ Performance indicators recommended in the ICAEW report

Non-financial	Financial
Market share	Revenue growth
Market growth	Economic profit
Customer retention	Return on capital
Customer satisfaction	Market/customer profitability
Price premium	

role of internal market research departments: their crucial independence of mind sits uncomfortably with being part of the team and justifying what that team wants to do.[9] Some firms, e.g. Unilever and Mars, already have marketing information and science reporting independently of the marketers. Every Exec needs someone to package and present metrics in a coherent fashion. Where a separate market information function does not exist, there is much to be said for giving the job to the CFO:

◆ It integrates Exec information.

◆ Finance can iron out inconsistencies between and within external and internal information.

◆ To present the market data, the CFO will have to understand more about the market and marketing.

◆ Finance, through market research, will be more engaged in planning, and better marketing plans, with non-financial goals, should result.

◆ More objectivity. Even post-Enron, CFOs are credited with more integrity and objectivity than marketers. When the metrics are presented to the Exec, the CFO is more likely to be believed than executives looking for budgets to spend. Many Execs, and not without foundation, believe that marketers sometimes move the goalposts.

◆ Finance is better trained to distinguish purely technical variances from the substantive. Discussion between finance and marketing should eliminate the technical and illuminate the substantive before the variances get to the Exec.

◆ It creates a better balance between the presentation of non-financial and financial metrics.

◆ Market research costs will be treated similarly to internal information, i.e. not included in marketing investment, but allocated in the same way as other information costs.

◆ The CFO is best placed to assess proportionality in allocating resources to information of all kinds.

◆ There will be a larger market research budget, or at least one less likely to be cut mid-year. Impartial as they are of course, CFOs also have a natural reluctance to cut their own.

The idea of integrating internal and external information is not new. IT functions were made part of the CFO's remit with mixed results. More recently firms have been creating chief knowledge officers (CKOs) whose role is to provide, group-wide, the total knowledge held in any part of that group, be it stored electronically or in the heads of the staff. Not too many CFOs are lining up for this responsibility. Some are secure in their traditional mindset but discussions with more progressive CFOs indicate some enthusiasm for closer integration with, and understanding of, marketing.

Few firms will, in practice, reassign market research and marketing information from the marketing department to finance. But it should at least be discussed. Better to have marketing metrics presented to the Exec by a keen CFO than a reluctant CMO. Whether these functions are merged or not, a single marketing metrics document needs to reach the Exec in a timely fashion and with a complete explanation of how the metrics are arrived at as well as the metrics themselves.

Early on, a target for a manageable set of metrics was set, arbitrarily but consistently with respondents' views, at 20 or fewer. The generalized set (Chapter 5) suggested three profit and loss accounts plus six covering brand equity. If you add four to tailor the metrics to the firm's unique strategy and nine for innovation and employer brand equity, this gives a total of 22. A single page can accommodate up to 30 if necessary. Compromise will be needed to reconcile a complete overview with focus.

In a unitary company (one brand in one market), the metrics should occupy a single page and adopt the traffic light system (red, green and amber for worsening, improving and static metrics) for short-term changes. Exceptional longer term trends can be shown as charts on back-up pages. Alternatively, arrows can be added to the traffic lights to indicate the direction of longer term changes or double derivatives (rate of change of the trend). Consideration will need to be given to the number of benchmarks for comparison. The best two are plan and the key competitors, but prior year and the total market are alternatives.

A large multi-brand, multinational company will have to be selective about the brands and brand market segments it wishes to review at Exec level. The balance between consolidation and retaining the precision of brand market segment analysis is an empirical matter, about which the Exec must make hard choices.

Executive minutes

1 Exec to appoint CFO, senior executive or external consultant to recommend process for integrating external and internal information for routine Exec assessment. This should include the timetable for the production of the first marketing metrics report, taking data availability into account, and frequency thereafter.

2 Unless there is a senior information specialist or CKO, the CFO should take charge of metrics processing and Exec presentation.

3 Marketers and finance team to audit market research in the light of the new metrics specification and report on additional costs and savings (as a result of culling redundant research).

4 IT executive to report on the marketing data warehouse concept, how closely it matches the ideal for the company and what progress has been made towards it. If the warehouse concept is not appropriate, he or she should report on how diagnostics will be produced and how the whole system will retain consistency and integrity.

5 Metrics team and other research users to review expectations from suppliers. Are they just buying data or is the supplier communicating intelligence and implications? Should certain suppliers occasionally report on key metrics directly to the Exec?

Notes

1   The Marketing Forum (1998) Research Report (16) reports 5 per cent but their respondents were from larger companies with bigger marketing budgets; 1997 figures from the *NTC Market Pocketbook* show 4 per cent of total advertising expenditure or, by inference, 2 per cent of all marketing expenditure.

2   Kelly, J. (2002) 'View from the bridge', *Admap*, 429, 44–6. ESOMAR website (*www.esomar.nl*). The European Society for Opinion & Marketing Research now operates in 81 countries and markets itself as 'The World Association of Research Professionals'.

3   For example, 18 per cent in the first quarter of 1999 against 5 per cent for advertising and 5 per cent in the first three quarters of 2002 against 2 per cent for advertising.

4   Carried out by FDS Market Research International for Market Research News (*www.mrnews.com*).

5   Accounting Standards Board, *Operating and Financial Review: Statement*, London, January 2003.

6   Carsberg, B. (1998) 'Future directions of financial reporting', *Performance Measurement in the Digital Age*, London: Institute of Chartered Accountants of England and Wales, 36–40, 37.

7   Kaplan, R. S. and Norton, D. P. (1992) 'The balanced scorecard: measures that drive performance', *Harvard Business Review*, January–February, 71–9.

8   ICAEW (2000) *Inside Out: Reporting on Shareholder Value*, London: Institute of Chartered Accountants of England and Wales (January).

9   Ambler, T. (1997) *Marketing from Advertising to Zen*, London: Financial Times Pitman, Chapter 26, 280–90.

11

The fuzzy future

THIS CONCLUDING CHAPTER provides a dash of cold water after the sauna of metrics that has gone before. A company cannot be managed by metrics alone. Furthermore, metrics can actually damage performance if used addictively. In the British National Health Service, when the length of waiting lists became the key performance indicator, targets were met by preventing patients from joining the lists. The lists were reduced, but the waiting times were increased. Worse still, non-urgent patients were seen before priority cases. So what is the answer? Fuzziness helps. Being too clinical kills off the enzymes that the firm needs for growth. Figure 11.1 gives an overview.

> Fuzziness helps. Being too clinical kills off the enzymes that the firm needs for growth

The first section of this chapter, on the misuse of performance measurement, makes two points: one should not mistake the signals for the business itself. Metrics should probably not, perhaps surprisingly, be used for management incentive schemes. What gets measured is what gets done, they say, but once bonuses ride on the measures, what gets measured is what gets fiddled.

The second section deals with complexity. Piling new metrics on top of old confuses everyone; large companies have too many numbers to review already.

Third, the chapter considers how exact the system should be. Goals and measures should be aligned, but should they be perfectly aligned? Should they be precise, unambiguous and unchanging? The answer to all these is 'no'. Perfect alignment belongs to the funeral parlour. Dynamic searching for growth, experimentation and innovation all require some degree of misalignment. Experimentation means that some parts of the business will

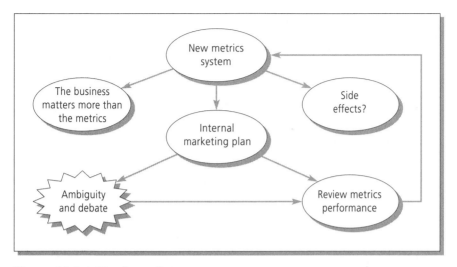

Figure 11.1 ◆ The fuzzy future

always be out of step. The metrics system should support evolution and be constantly changing as part of it. Ambiguity is not some unfortunate lack of precision but an essential ingredient of growth. The future is fuzzy.

The way the marketing metrics system is used is more important than both the choice of individual metrics and the process that delivers them to the Exec. These tools may be honed to perfection and yet the whole thing will go horribly wrong if the Exec treats metrics as mechanical levers to drive performance. They are merely crude indicators of the vital signs of a living business. As usual, the chapter concludes with some key action points.

Misusing measurement

There are many examples of metrics misuse. Lin Fitzgerald of Warwick Business School uses a classic tale of the newly privatized water industry. During successive droughts and water shortages, the public was outraged by leakages left unrepaired. The regulator introduced water leakage reduction as an incentive target. Targets were met but the rate of repairs was little changed. How come? The companies reduced water pressure to place less strain on the pipes. Fire service hoses drooped just as the drought increased the number of fires. In July 1999, the UK train infrastructure monopoly Railtrack announced that top management bonuses would be moved from train punctuality to shareholder returns: train user groups predicted worse performance from the customer's perspective. They were right. Performance deteriorated and the government closed Railtrack down in 2001.

My favourite is the Institute of Chartered Accountants England and Wales' performance metrics for main board directors.[1] Apparently, directors' attendance records provide the sole measure of directors' performance. Woody Allen seems to have been right: so far as British directors are concerned, 90 per cent of success is just showing up.

We all know the dangers of measuring what is easy to measure. A fuzzy sense of what matters is far more important than precise calculation of the irrelevant. Chapter 5 compared universal measures with developing an original set specifically to fit the firm's goals. Both approaches can be combined but there is danger in making the decision with too little debate. Installing a set of alien measures and moving promptly along to the next burning issue is not efficient management but merely creating a new burning issue for tomorrow.

Any Exec should know, worry about and constantly revise its model of business success and where the cash comes from. In other words, why do customers want to hand over their money? How can that motivation be improved? How can others be persuaded to do likewise? And how can more go to employees (including the Exec itself) and shareholders? In that cash flow, what are the key signs of vitality and growth? Never mind, for the moment, whether they can be measured or not. If you walked into your own company, knowing nothing, how would you tell which things are going well and which badly? The marketing metrics system is merely a way to maintain those eyes of innocence; it provides signals, not solutions.

The point is that any set of signals gives a partial, lopsided view of the business as a whole. Chapter 3 explored some of the dangers of excessive reliance on financial indicators and tools but the issue is wider than the conceptual or behavioural problems with any particular technique. When any metrics are given too much importance, they obscure the sense of the business itself.

A popular quick fix is to use the metrics as the base for management incentives. For example, the top five metrics can be weighted to give a single index for bonusing purposes. Kaplan and Norton's Balanced Scorecard is sometimes used as the basis for an incentives index. The system will work slightly better by insisting that a minimum improvement must be made on every one of the top five individual indicators before any bonus is paid. This at least has the advantage of stopping managers ramping up the easy ones and letting the others go.

Having been there and done that, using marketing metrics for bonusing turns out to be a bad idea. Quite apart from the need for ambiguity to which we will revert, the use of metrics for bonuses has five major flaws:

◆ They become more important to those managers than the business itself. At the very least they distort it, as noted above. The Balanced Scorecard has spawned many bonus schemes, notably in the USA, but not with any apparent success or business improvement.[2] New schemes soon follow.

◆ Metrics are only as useful as their credibility. Once suspicion arises that managers may be manipulating them for bonus purposes, their value dries up.

◆ Management incentives, at least in the west, are intended to reward individual performance, whereas marketing metrics reflect the company's performance as a whole. Metrics have more merit for the Exec itself and any company-wide scheme.

◆ For bonuses, metrics have to be boiled down to a single index. The restrictions, e.g. minimal performance on each metric, serve as negatives rather than motivation. No matter how cleverly it is done, this model oversimplifies business reality. It may be better than using the single index of shareholder value growth, but that does not make it good. When bonuses pay out against numbers, whether rigged or not, that do not reflect reality, this unfairness debilitates enthusiasm and motivation.

◆ Finally, the use of metrics for control can be demotivating. Reluctance to provide control data to the Exec is both real and understandable. It provokes criticism and demands for explanation of variances and for more data. This is especially true for innovation, where we were told that key performance indicators (KPIs) would damage creativity. Using measures for our own professional assessment differs from providing others with sticks to beat us with.

As noted earlier, most of our respondents expected top management to be primarily in control mode, even though self-control outperforms the top-down control so often destructive to fine marketing. The command and control model seems to be alive and well. Execs can exercise self-restraint at two levels: using metrics for their own information and to motivate management to do likewise. Execs of large companies should hold back excessive variance chasing but provide a culture in which middle management will balance discipline with creativity. Should managers know where they stand? Broadly yes, precisely no.

Is there a contradiction here? If payment by results is good for marketing agencies, why should it not be applied internally too? Some of the internal objections do indeed apply externally. The measures need to be chosen with care but the key difference lies in the arm's-length relationship between agency and client: the agency should not be able to fiddle the figures to the extent that the internal managers can fiddle their own. Not a complete answer, perhaps, but then the whole area is fuzzy.

Shedding the old

Some years ago, a spirits company was remunerating the sales force on the basis of volume sales. With diverse profits per case, values per case and discounting out of control, the quick fix was to remunerate the sales force on gross profit. Information was shifted from sales volume to include values and margins. The sales team grumbled about losing their familiar figures. A few years later, the process was reversed. The incoming sales director decided, now that discounts were under control, that this delegation was too sophisticated and sales value was all they needed. The same discontent surfaced. Change is unwelcome.

Metrics are merely the apex of the whole marketing information system that needs to be understood from the points of view of the various users. Metrics have little value in themselves; their effect depends on how they are used and that, in turn, will be strongly influenced by how other performance measures are used by the Exec and whether the Exec itself is changing. We were told that one of the most frequent reasons for a radical revision of metrics was a change of management: the new team uses new measures in new ways to symbolize and create the makeover they require.

At the same time, piling a new metrics system on top of the old is a mistake. As noted earlier, the key to revising the metrics system lies more in culling the redundant and unaligned than finding new ones. The process of designing a new system for one large firm I was working with proved so straightforward that I should have been suspicious. It was only when the CMO mentioned that his team would, of course, be supplying the new information for the Exec while they themselves continued with the old system, that we realized that we were still at the beginning.

The line of sight may be fuzzy but it does need to be consistent in order to integrate the business from top to bottom and side to side. Shedding the old may be complete and instantaneous and radical or evolutionary. The radical option loses continuity and the ability to detect trends; the evolutionary risks continual procrastination. Whichever model is adopted, the new system needs active internal marketing. The installation team, which preferably includes users, needs to show how the new metrics can be used to better effect. A better measure needs to prove itself in practice just as a better spade needs to be easier to dig with.

Our research routinely produced the argument that 'hard' numbers (i.e. financial) should always have precedence over 'soft' numbers from the marketplace. Some referred to market numbers as 'qualitative', omitting to notice that numbers are numbers. The arbitrary allocation of costs, overheads for example, gives data no harder than professionally garnered market research for, say, penetration, but this is a non-argument. Who cares if numbers are hard or soft if they give a more reliable picture of the marketplace and, better, predict future cash flow? An impressionist painting may seem splodgy close to, but capture the scene perfectly if viewed from a distance.

In this transition, there is no substitute for an eager and impatient CEO who is ready to take risks and accept a fuzzy version of reality rather than a precise rendition of the irrelevant.

The need for misalignment

Innovative companies, such as 3M, recognize the need for experimentation, which implies freedom for managers to explore areas beyond existing strategy. Indeed, by the time a corporate activity is officially enshrined in strategy, it is already middle aged. Recognition that businesses are now in an era of constant change is hardly new. Yet we seek to install new systems, and align policies and people, as if the firm will never change again. When thinking of changing the metrics system, we have two choices. In one, metrics are perfectly aligned with strategy, and they identify the levers that managers should operate to optimize results. The other is fuzzy: metrics are used for broad positioning rather than precision and for illumination rather than control. Table 11.1 compares the present situation, where marketing performance is rarely quantified in the full formal sense, with these two alternative future choices. Future 1 is precise with perfect alignment and may seem the goal for the quantified approach. Future 2 has the basic measures in place but it is inexact.

Table 11.1 ◆ Two future metrics scenarios

	Today	Future 1	Future 2
Goals	Mostly implicit	Clear and complete	Fuzzy and incomplete
Key performance indicators	P&L account	Balanced Scorecard with precisely identified trade-offs	Financial and market measures both seen as important but trade-offs unclear
Market metrics tied to executive bonuses	No, financial and tasks if any	Yes, as above	No, but influenced by metrics
Goals, performance and metrics	Alignment uncertain	Exactly aligned	Knowingly misaligned
Use of metrics by Exec	Personal choice	Means to direct and control	Don't know what junior management have to do but wish to provide the tools
Organizational mindset/culture	Habituation	Cognitive/logical/ rational	Affective/social/ feelings

Sharing drafts of this table provoked opposing reactions. Some saw Future 2 as common sense and rejected the rigidity of Future 1, whereas others did the reverse. In the same company, some executives are more, and some less, tolerant of fuzziness. These differences are important: the disagreement is part of fuzziness itself. But the continual tussle between alignment, or uniformity, and diversity needs to be open rather than political. It needs to be managed for performance enhancement.

While companies need both points of view, the balance may depend on the corporate life cycle. The young thrusters of a vital new business may be intolerant of the very controls they need. Conversely, the one-foot-in-the-grave mature businesses may resist ambiguity. Rigor is next to mortis.

In most companies today, the extent of goals and measures alignment is unknown. Michel Lebas, of the HEC School of Management in France, reports that managers from the same company rate their organization's characteristics across a number of dimensions with little consistency.[3] They are surprised by this but the resulting debate, while reducing the gaps, rarely brings total alignment. What the debate does, and this is important, is to stimulate fresh energy and commitment.

Alignment is another of those upside-down U shapes where too little and too much are both suboptimal. Some degree of misalignment is essential for experimentation and growth but the company as a whole will only benefit if this, and the experiments, are widely understood. This is why the debate is so important and why the imposition of any set of metrics, however well chosen, is a mistake.

The case for fuzziness is itself fuzzy and should not be wholly accepted or rejected. While fuzziness is superior to the old command and control model, your company's need will depend on the current balance between the control and fuzzy cultures and its own life stage.

Executive minutes

1 Before installing a new metrics system, the Exec should consider possible misuse and side effects.

2 The installation should itself be subject to a marketing plan to ensure that new metrics will be adopted over previous metrics as a matter of preference, not fiat. Marketers to propose how the new system can be sold in and the old discarded.

3 Although the new system will require at least enough consistency for comparative information and trends to be retained, the new system should allow for continuing evolutionary development.

4 CEO to establish the internal debate needed to implement the three criteria for assessing the firm's marketing performance measurement system: own and competitive benchmarks and brand equity measurement. Goals and metrics to be aligned, albeit fuzzily, in consequence.

5 Exec to ensure that metrics remain subservient to corporate ideology and identifying the firm's vital signs; and that self-controls are preferred to top down. Exec to monitor culture to ensure metrics make the most positive contribution to performance.

Notes

1   ICAEW (1999) *Boardroom Governance: Practical Insights*, London: Institute of Chartered Accountants of England and Wales, 2.

2   Discussion during the Theory of Measurement symposium, Cambridge, UK, 16 July 1999. None of the assembled experts could recall a balanced scorecard type of incentive scheme's surviving very long.

3   Lebas, M. (1999) 'Building the foundations of performance management: from "OR" to "AND", a diagnostic tool', paper presented to the Theory of Measurement symposium, Cambridge, 16 July.

Glossary

A marketing glossary for UK public companies' annual reports

In research for the Centre for Business Performance, 85 per cent of chairmen and senior executives of FTSE 350 companies agreed that shareholders were 'entitled' to be informed about the company's main assets, including brand equity. In January 2003, the Accounting Standards Board published new guidelines for the 'Operating and Financial Review' section(s) of company annual reports. They suggested shareholders should see the business 'through the eyes of management' and, in particular, be informed about marketing investment and brand equity.

In practice, annual reports have very limited information on these topics and part of the reason is unfamiliarity with the language of marketing. This glossary has been provided to help improve shareholder communications about intangible assets and marketing investment and has been prepared as a service for those producing and reading the annual reports of UK public companies. The project was supported by (in alphabetical order) the Advertising Association, the Chartered Institute of Marketing, the Incorporated Society of British Advertisers, the Institute of Chartered Accountants in England and Wales, the Institute of Practitioners in Advertising, The Marketing Council, The Marketing Society, and The Worshipful Company of Marketors, with financial funding by Shell on behalf of The Marketing Council. The aim remains to improve consistency in the usage of marketing terms in company annual reports. Where these terms are given different meanings, brief explanation would help the users of annual reports.

Further sources

◆ This glossary has, for convenience, fewer than 300 terms but over 2700 items are available on:
www.themarketingdictionary.com

◆ See also the Chartered Institute of Marketing glossary on:
www.cim.co.uk/cim/ser/html/infQuiGlo.cfm

◆ ESOMAR – Market Research:
http://www.esomar.nl/EGlossary.htm

◆ Interactive Advertising Bureau's internet marketing jargon buster on:
www.iabuk.net

◆ Marketing and media:
http://www.mma.com/resources/glossary.asp

◆ New product development:
http://www.pdma.org/library/glossary.html

Explanatory notes

Marketing can be defined in various ways. Non-marketers typically think of it as advertising and promotion but marketers consider that too narrow. They see marketing as a whole company activity whereby the goals of the organization are achieved through first achieving the customers' goals. In other words, profits arise from securing customer preference. An alternative, but consistent, view is that 'marketing' refers to all activities that generate and harvest an organization's inward cash flow. It is concerned with why customers spend money with the company and what would cause them to spend more and more frequently and perhaps in ways that are less expensive for the company to service. Note that this glossary is addressed to UK plcs; the word 'marketing' has a wider meaning when applied to other organizations, e.g. political parties.

However it may be defined, marketing supplies the livelihood of every business in the world, for a very simple reason: cash comes from customers. That is why shareholders in every business, not just those traditionally seen as marketers, are entitled to information about their company's marketing performance.

A 'market metric' is a quantitative, financial (e.g. sales by value) or non-financial (e.g. market share) indicator of marketplace performance important enough to be regularly reviewed by the company's board, either as a relative (to competition) or absolute number. The term includes internal marketing metrics, e.g. advertising expenditure.

Although based on a survey of annual reports, other dictionaries and authoritative sources, this glossary is by no means comprehensive. Most business sectors have some special terms and some companies coin their own. The aim was to provide a broad common denominator for most terms and users.

Terms consisting of more than one word are usually shown as they are used, e.g. 'market share', not 'share, market'. So if you cannot find a term, e.g. 'share of market', please check under the other keyword. A dominant word may be used first, e.g. an 'attribute' can be part of a product or brand; so the usage here is 'Attribute, brand/product'. Italics are used to indicate a term used as part of a definition that is itself defined elsewhere in the glossary.

above-the-line Media advertising [expenditure] in distinction from other activities like sales promotion and public relations which are 'below the line'. It originated in the nineteenth century on the basis of whether commission to the ad agency was paid by the media or by the client. Typical metric: share of voice.

advertising spend The cost of media space usually including production and agency fees. Sometimes expressed as percentage of revenue and/or percentage of marketing investment.

affinity group An analyzable set of customers with common interests. Smaller than a *segment*, the difference also lies in how the marketer treats the consumer group. If the marketer recognizes the special common needs of some customers, e.g. mothers with small children, and makes provision for them, that's an affinity group. If the subject of a separate marketing programme, the term *segment* is better.

affinity marketing Allowing a commercial business to use the membership list of a not-for-profit (NFP) organization for a promotional offer which provides some benefit for the NFP organization, e.g. a charity or a sports club.

after-sales service Provided by a manufacturer or retailer to customer some time after completing the sale. Likely to be perceived as a cost by transactional but as an investment by relationship marketers.

ARPU See *Average revenue per user*.

aspirational brand Usage of such a brand is intended to convey social status or provide a target for the upwardly mobile.

attitude State of mind reflecting a negative or positive personal view about an object or concept, measured to provide a link between marketing actions and consumer behaviour. May be emotional and/or cognitive and is a composite of a number of *intermediate metrics*. Typical metrics: rating on 'my kind of brand', intention to purchase. Counterpart of *attribute*.

attribute, brand/product The characteristics that are important to consumers. For example, aroma, flavour, caffeine content, and price are the main attributes of instant coffee. Usually limited to measurable physical (functional and economic) factors, i.e. not psychological or emotional. See *attitude*.

audience Group of people, or market segment, to whom marketing communications are specifically addressed. Also used: *target market*

average revenue per user (ARPU) Performance metric used especially by mobile and other telecom operators.

awareness Consciousness either spontaneously or when prompted. An *intermediate metric* generally linked to a brand or its advertising. Ad awareness does not imply brand awareness nor vice versa. Typical metrics are: aided/prompted – the respondent is given a list of brands to prompt recognition; spontaneous/unaided – the respondent is asked to name one or more brands in a category. *Top-of-mind* usually means the first of those named. Illogical as it may seem, total awareness is the sum of aided and unaided awareness.

baseline Used in estimating the additional sales or profits due to a promotion. Baseline is what the sales or profits would have been had there been no promotion.

below-the-line Any marketing activity except media advertising. Opposite of *above-the-line*.

benefit Additive, improvement or other advantage which makes a product more desirable.

brand Can be either: a name, term, symbol or design (or a combination of them) which identifies one or more products (mostly used in the USA); the identification plus the product itself and its packaging, i.e. the gestalt (mostly used in the UK). For example, 'A product is something that is made, in a factory; a brand is something that is bought, by a customer. A product can be copied by a competitor; a brand is unique. A product can be quickly outdated; a successful brand is timeless' (Stephen King). Not the same as *brand equity*.

brand consistency Correspondence between the brand's message and associated promotion and advertising activities and between internal (employee) and external (customer) marketing. Continuity of the brand's development over time. Inconsistency is generally held to have an adverse effect on brand equity and customer loyalty.

brand consolidation Strategy of reducing the number of brands to facilitate management and communications, e.g. British Caledonian was merged into British Airways following acquisition.

brand equity An important intangible asset for the company, it can be seen as the reservoir of results gained by good marketing but not yet delivered to the profit and loss account. Awareness, attitudes, associations, memories and habits, which cause people to choose/recommend the brand more often and/or in larger quantities and/or at higher prices than would otherwise be the case. Also trade availability and brand information stored in IT systems. 'Customer brand equity' is the part of total brand equity in the minds of customers as distinct from other stakeholders, e.g. employee brand equity which is the reputation of their employer in the minds of employees. Similar to *reputation* which is often used for corporate brand equity but excludes product availability. Can also be described as goodwill. The financial value of brand equity cannot (in the UK) be included on a balance sheet although the cost of acquired brands may be, so long as the cost is not more than their financial value.

brand equity evaluation Distinguished from *brand valuation*, this assesses all key aspects of brand equity financially, non-financially and qualitatively.

brand essence The smallest compression (six words or less) of what is special about the brand. Derived from 'interrogate the brand until it confesses its essence' (David Ogilvy).

brand experience What the consumer learns and senses from using or contact with the brand. Not the same as an *experience brand*.

brand extension Launch of one or more new products under the same brand name but in a new category, unlike *line extension* which is in the same category.

brand identity Individuality of the brand perceived from its product form, name, packaging and communications. Its unique characteristics. Important for *brand consistency* and similar to *corporate identity* since the company can be seen as a brand.

brand image Perceived impressions of a brand by its *audience*. A multidimensional concept that is hard to measure precisely but can be defined by its associations, e.g. Martell cognac is associated with expensive sporting activities. The various ways of measuring brand image, e.g. whether it has relatively high status, are *intermediate metrics*. Closely related to *attitude*.

brand leader(ship), or market leader Brand with largest share of market.

brand management Sometimes known as *product management*. A management system developed in the 1930s by Procter & Gamble, it has grown into a widely accepted method of managing individual brands in multi-product companies. A brand manager is given responsibility for a single brand and becomes the champion for that brand and its underlying products. Responsible for planning, implementation and coordination of marketing activities although the remit of 'marketing' differs across companies.

brand market unit or combination A market unit defined by one brand in one market (country).

brand perception Same as *brand image*.

brand personality Brands are often anthropomorphized and this refers to the individual character of the brand that (uniquely) identifies it. The consumer perception of the brand as distinct from its underlying products.

brand preference (preferred brand) Usually the brand the customer expects to purchase next time. Implies that the *attitude* is relative to other brands in the *consideration set*. May vary by occasion for use or price considerations. Same as *customer preference*.

brand ranking The rank order of brands by market share, i.e. the brand with the largest share is number one.

brand reformulation Changing the products and/or their qualities that make up the brand.

brand reinforcement Insofar as brand equity is a set of brand memories, this is marketing activity, typically advertising, designed to strengthen those memories rather than persuade or change them. Used mainly for mature brands.

brand revitalization Strategic invigoration of a mature brand, e.g. Lucozade. May include *repositioning* or *relaunch* and/or a much larger *marketing investment*.

brand value(s)/valuation Brand value is usually the same as brand valuation, i.e. the financial worth of the brand equity, whereas brand values refers to the principles the brand is perceived to stand for (derived from personal values). What the brand equity is financially worth depends on the purpose for which it is being valued, e.g. sale or purchase. Usually the present value of expected cash flows attributable to the brand equity. Note that the definition of *brand* is critical here, i.e. whether the profits attributed to the branding have to be separated from the profits attributed to the underlying product(s).

brand building Building the brand asset (brand equity) as distinct from *harvesting* or going for short-term profit. Image advertising is typically seen as brand building whereas discounting or price promotions are not.

buyer's market A market characterized by low or falling prices, occurring when supply is greater than demand and buyers tend to set the prices and terms of sale. Also known as a 'soft market'. Opposite of *seller's market*.

buying cycle The frequency with which a product in a particular category is purchased.

buying power Consumer's income after commitments have been met, and therefore applicable to buying in this category. Not the same as buyer's power, i.e. the buyer's strength of bargaining position relative to the seller, e.g. ability to demand discount. See *share* of wallet.

call centre Central or contracted out facility for dealing with customers, prospects and other contacts by telephone. May be linked with CRM technology. Can be inbound (customer calls) and/or outbound (call centre initiated).

cannibalization Sales gained from the company's other products, i.e. reducing the net increase.

cash cow A brand with no further investment and being *harvested*.

catchment area The district, territory, etc. from which a shopping centre and/or individual shop draws its custom. It is also sometimes known as the trade area or hinterland.

category All the brands and products which directly compete, i.e. they are sufficiently alike for customers to choose one or the other. Sometimes, imprecisely, called 'market' or 'sector' which is better seen as a collection of related categories.

category management The internal marketing process that uses the category as the management unit rather than individual brands. Especially used by some multi-brand companies when selling to retailers to help both parties maximize profit from the category.

cause related marketing Commercial activity in partnership with a charity or other good cause for mutual benefit, e.g. publicity and funding for the charity and goodwill for the company.

channels Chain through which products move from manufacture or source to end user, i.e. the distribution system. Companies may use multiple (complementary) channels to market, i.e. a network, or a single sole distributor. See *customer* and *distribution*.

churn rate Customer retention metric, i.e. percentage of customers lost during the year or other period. Useful measure of customer satisfaction, or lack of it, and behavioural loyalty.

CLV See *customer lifetime value*.

co-branding Joint venture marketing under more than one brand name and possibly from different companies, e.g. Intel and Dell computers, Haagen Dazs and Baileys. See *cross-branding*.

commercial communications Any method (e.g. advertising, direct mail, other media paid for by the marketer, and public relations) used to communicate with its commercial *audiences*. Similar to *marcoms*.

commitment One of the key measures of brand equity, it expresses the probability of consistent repeat purchase and usage. Typical metrics are purchase intent, switchability (or some similar measure of retention, *loyalty*, *purchase intent*, or bonding) and emotional attachment to the brand.

commodity A basic product which is capable of little or no differentiation and so generally sold on the basis of price in accordance with the theory of perfect competition, i.e. unbranded. Farm produce, raw materials and a number of fabricated products such as steel qualify as commodities and call for the addition of value added services if the supplier is to avoid straight price competition.

comparable sales Same as *like-for-like sales* or *same store sales*.

competitive advantage A unique, or at least distinctive, benefit or value provided by a product or company and which is attractive to some or all customers. Alternatively, the advantage may arise directly from the types of customers served and the relationships with them.

consideration set The small set of brands in any category from which the customer selects.

consumer behaviour The ways in which consumers buy and use *products*. Typical metrics: purchase frequency, *loyalty*/retention, assortment/range of different products purchased from company.

consumer confidence End-user's trust in and certainty about the *product* purchased. Brand equity metric in, for example, a financial services company.

consumer patronage Established consumers purchasing regularly. Same as consumer *franchise*.

consumer uptake Rate of the adoption by consumers of a new service/ *product*. Also called consumer take-up.

contribution, net brand contribution (NBC) A measure of brand profitability before overhead costs but usually after marketing expenditure has been allocated.

conversion rate Measure of translation of enquiries or replies or prospects to an advertising or mailing shot into customers. Some identify potential prospects as 'suspects' and track the conversion of suspects to prospects.

core brands/categories The brands and categories seen by the board as essential to the business and therefore not available for disposal or harvesting.

core competencies The particular skills and expertise that make a firm successful and, by inference, distinguish it from competitors. In theory, establishing core competencies, or competence, is fundamental to a firm selecting the appropriate strategy ('know thyself'). Sceptics allege that this self-analysis becomes circular or, like visions and missions, woolly.

core values From all the brand or corporate values that apply, these are the most central. Related to *brand essence*. See also *brand values*.

corporate identity The individuality of the company and its unique characteristics. Represented, albeit in a limited way, by its logo and communications, but also the way it does business externally and internally. See *brand identity*.

cost leader Lowest cost marketer (producer or other vendor). Usually implies price leadership, i.e. the firm also sells at the lowest price. Some advocate becoming the lowest cost producer as the start of the path to becoming cost leader and thereby market leader.

cost per contact Cost of sales call.

cost per enquiry The amount of money spent on a promotional activity divided by the number of enquiries received as a direct result.

cost per mille (CPM)/ cost per thousand (CPT) Basic approach to media costs: cost per thousand audience. CPM is American and CPT is the British equivalent.

coupon A certificate that gives the consumer a price reduction on a specific product.

cover price Normal retail price of magazine or newspaper or magazine.

CPM/CPT See *cost per mille*.

critical mass The minimum market size, or share, for cost-effective marketing or some element of the *marketing mix*.

CRM, eCRM See *customer relationship management*/marketing.

cross-sales ratio The proportion of sales resulting from the sales of other *products* from the same company.

cross-branding Brand promotion by utilizing the strength of another brand. See *co-branding*.

cross-merchandising, promotion or selling The presentation/selling of two or more distinct but associated product classes, e.g. cheese with wine, swimwear with sunglasses, suntan products and beach towels. Sometimes the two items taken together may attract a discount or other benefit.

cross-referrals Introduction of new business by existing customers. Also called cross-selling.

customer acquisition (cost) Marketing schemes designed to recruit new customers are classed as customer acquisition activity. Typical metric: prospecting costs/number of new customers.

customer behavioural scoring System examining customer's relationship with the service provider (e.g. a bank) to determine his level of risk. More generally, the likelihood of responding to an appeal.

customer footfall The number of customers visiting one or all retail units.

customer lifetime value (CLV) May also be called customer value or customer equity. CLV is the net present value of either one or all customers, that is, the discounted value of the cash flow generated over the life of their relationship with the company.

customer preference Same as *brand preference*.

customer profitability Current profit contribution from customer. This is projected into the future and then discounted to give the *customer lifetime value (CLV)*.

customer proposition The main benefit of the product for a potential customer. For example, Seven-Up's proposition to its customers is 'Drink me up and you'll feel fresh and clean'. Pedigree dogfood says to its customers: 'Buy me and you'll have a bouncy, energetic dog'. Often confused with the *positioning statement* of which it is part.

customer relations An aspect of *relationship marketing*, this seeks to build positive customer *attitudes*, e.g. through complaint handling, publicity, persuasion and aligning customer and company goals. Similar concept to *public relations* but with a different target.

customer relationship management/marketing (CRM) Activity undertaken by companies to develop and manage relationships with their customers. May be technically (call centre or IT) or marketing driven, or both. Often linked with *database marketing*. eCRM is the web-based equivalent.

customer retention Usually measured as percentage previous period's customers buying in current period. Converse of *churn*.

customer retention cost Keeping existing customers may involve formal *customer relationship management (CRM)* or loyalty programmes. Typical metrics: relationship marketing costs/number of customers retained, *churn*, *loyalty*. Retention marketing is widely believed to be less expensive and more productive than acquisition if examined as the profit from and cost of the incremental customer.

customer service The services supplied before, with or after the sale of *products*.

customer value management The marketing approach of seeking to maximize customer lifetime value by concentrating costs on high value customers and ignoring or culling low value customers. See *customer lifetime value*.

customer-facing Staff, or business units, who deal directly with customers, e.g. sales people, service engineers.

customer-focused Where all the operations of a company are carried out with the customer in mind; not just marketing activities but also logistics, R&D and finance.

customization Adapting standard goods and services to suit individual consumers, especially through the use of information technology. See *mass customization*.

cycle time The time from concept to launch, i.e. time-to-market, is a performance measure for new product development. The metric used especially by those who consider first mover advantage key.

database marketing Customer information, stored in an electronic database, used for targeting marketing activities. Information can be what is collected from previous customer interactions and what is available from outside sources. Databases are now regulated, e.g. customer permissions are required. See also *customer relationship management marketing* (CRM).

demand management Controlling the requirements for company products in terms of quantity, quality, price and timing. Hugh Davidson proposed this as a better term for 'marketing'.

demographics Analyzing consumers by sex, age, income, social class, family size and where they live as distinct from *psychographics*.

derived demand A term from economics. Without direct access to end users, the supplier has to deduce, or derive, demand from sales to intermediate customers, i.e. *channels*.

de-stocking Reduction in *channels*' inventory(ies) often used as an explanation for reason for lower sales not reflecting lower demand.

diagnostics Some firms distinguish between metrics, i.e. high-level performance measures or key performance indicators, seen by top managers, and explanatory measures, i.e. diagnostics, that account for variances in metrics, e.g. sales by channel. Diagnostics would normally be reviewed by the managers specializing in that area.

differentiation Extent to which a product/brand is not interchangeable with others in the same category. Differentiation may be real (some product characteristic) or perceived (image or perceived quality).

diffusion Process whereby a new product is taken up, or adopted, by a broader user base.

direct mail(ing) Posting promotional material to sales prospects. If carefully targeted and monitored, it may be highly productive. Not to be confused with *direct marketing*.

direct marketing Dealing directly with end users and bypassing retail outlets. May include, but is not limited to, the internet, direct mail, phone selling, mail order and advertising where a direct response mechanism is included. Direct Marketing Association definition is: 'Communications where data are used systematically to achieve quantifiable marketing objectives and where direct contact is made, or invited, between its existing or prospective customer.'

direct product profitability Profit contribution before overheads and other indirect costs. Used in retail and often applied to space occupied by those products.

discount Reduction on the quoted or list price of a product either to all customers or, more typically, for specific reasons such as prompt payment, large quantities, bulk deliveries, special sizes and deliveries in off-peak times. Should be treated as a reduction in revenue, not as marketing expenditure.

discount brand A rare entity, this is a brand, such as a discount warehouse, where its equity depends on perceived low price, i.e. good value.

distribution The term has two different meanings: the logistics involved in making the products available to end users, i.e. the physical supply through *channels*; availability to the *end user*. A typical metric is the percentage of relevant outlets that carry the brand, often weighted by the turnover of the outlets concerned.

distribution platform A media term for the ways of disseminating information, content via different media: e.g. TV, web, telephony, interactive TV. Equivalent to *channels* for disseminating products.

downmarket Lower priced segment of the market or products purchased in less expensive areas or by lower income or socio-economic status people. May be called 'downscale' in the USA. Opposite of *upmarket*.

dynamic pricing Using different prices for the same product according to the date of sale or location or other conditions, e.g. theatre seats sold late or standby airline prices. Similar to *variable pricing*.

economies of scale Reduction in unit cost from overheads being divided over a larger volume.

efficient consumer response (ECR) Co-operation along all stages of the supply chain to improve responsiveness and eliminate waste. Promoted as a win-win-win for supplier-retailer-consumer on the basis that it improves service and reduces cost all along the channel. In some people's opinion there is some doubt about that. Usually driven by strong retailers, e.g. Sainsbury, Walmart.

elasticity Broadly, the ratio of the relative change in the dependent variable (demand) to the relative change in an independent variable (price, consumer income). Inelastic sales have elasticity equal to zero. From economics, this term is not as simple or precise as it sounds. Elasticity differs not only according to where you are on the demand curve, but also according to the size of the adjustment. The exception is the demand curve $y = ax^b$ which has constant point elasticities. Furthermore, short- and long-term elasticity are not usually the same and, especially in the short term, there may be a 'zone of indifference' where demand does not seem to change. Elasticity is not necessarily symmetric, i.e. decreases may not reflect increases.

e-marketplace Internet-based enabled marketplace, where e-commerce takes place. Largely follows general market rules.

endorsement Public support for the brand by one or more [typically famous] alleged users.

end-user Usually the same as the consumer. Should be distinguished from intermediary customers (*channels*) and, where significant, from the final purchaser (e.g. the final purchaser of baby clothes is not usually the end user).

experience brand An experience brand implies that its equity or perceived quality depends on usage, i.e. experience, as distinct from inspection or advertising. Also refers to a way of marketing/advertising to consumers. Not the same as *brand experience*.

familiarity Similar to *awareness* but implies some direct or indirect experience of the brand and not just knowing the name.

features in store Very visibly displayed in a retail environment, a feature is a promotion without necessarily a price discount. The metric is usually a count of the times the brand was merchandised specially during the period.

first-price-right-price policy Used to reduce need for later price reductions. See *markdown*.

flagship Brand, business or outlet for which the business is best known or which best presents its proposition.

fast moving consumer goods (fmcg) Frequently purchased consumer products, usually known as packaged goods in the USA, e.g. food brands, beverages, toiletries and tobacco.

four Ps Shorthand term for the classic elements of marketing: product, price, place and promotion. 'Place' refers to sales and distribution and 'promotion' here includes all forms of marketing communications. For services, the mix is sometimes extended to seven Ps: people, process and physical evidence. Also known as the *marketing mix*.

franchise There are two different meanings: a licence to use someone else's brand subject to contractual conditions; existing loyal end users or customers, i.e. *consumer patronage*.

frequency Used as a measure of media performance. Number of times an advertising message is delivered within a set period of time to the average target consumer. See *reach*.

frequency of return visits/purchases Used as a measure of customer satisfaction for retail (visits) or products (purchases). The weighted average frequency of repeat purchases plus frequency of first-time purchases equals total purchase frequency, but separating the metrics may yield more information. See *repeat customer* and *customer retention*.

front-of-mind High unaided *awareness* or *salience*.

generics Commodity, i.e. unbranded products. Sometimes, albeit incorrectly, used for retailer own label, private label or own brands.

grey market See *parallel trade* (unauthorised reselling) but the term is also used to describe the over 55-year-old *demographic* group.

gross rating points (GRP) The number of exposures of a broadcast ad multiplied by the size of each audience. A single GRP represents 1 per cent of the total or target audience in a given region. The total weight of the campaign.

harvesting Extracting cash flow from brand equity without rebuilding it. Typically done before a brand or product is withdrawn from the market. See *cash cow*.

high value customers The segment of most profitable customers, typically in financial services.

high-end The most expensive items in a category. Also known as 'high-tier'.

high involvement In relation to brand or product where consumers take time and trouble to reach a purchasing decision and may shop around, comparing prices or financing arrangements. High involvement may be due to economic (high price, performance, value) and/or emotional (self-image, items we care about) factors. Cars, homes, fitted kitchens, hi-fi systems and package-tour holidays are examples of high-involvement products. Opposite of *low involvement*.

IMC See *integrated marketing communications*.

impact Force with which an advertising or promotional message registers in a person's mind; may be positive or adverse.

impulse sales Also impulse product, impulse buy(ing), impulse purchase, impulse volumes. Instantaneous decisions to buy products such as magazines and sweets. Impulse products are often merchandised beside the checkout.

innovation Usually applies to *new product development* but may be any form of new market-changing activity. Usually has three distinct phases: creation, development and implementation requiring different skills.

integrated marketing communications (IMC) As communications media diversified each with its own specialists, consumers began to hear different messages from the same brands. IMC was created to manage communications more consistently from the consumer's perspective, e.g. a single creative brief for all media.

interactive marketing Marketing where neither buyer(s) nor seller(s) are passive but both active and reactive in their dealings, particularly in business-to-business sectors. See *relationship marketing*.

intermediate metric Metrics can be grouped into at least four categories: inputs (e.g. expenditure), intermediate (what the consumer has in her head, e.g. awareness, purchasing intention), behaviour and other. Thus intermediate, in theory, provides the link between inputs and behaviour.

leads generated/enquiries Number of new prospects, the first stage in building customer relationships.

life cycle In marketing, the product or brand life cycle. Analogous to organic life, some believe that products go through a natural cycle: birth, growth, maturity, decline and death. Whilst there is substance in the early stages, decline is not certain but usually caused by the arrival of better substitutes. The brand life cycle theory is less valid as brands can be refreshed by marketing activities such as *new product development*.

life stage Demographic age group [of consumers].

like-for-like sales Sales compared to the previous period sales at the same retail space, not taking into consideration the newly opened or acquired or closed stores. See *organic growth* and *same store sales*.

likelihood to recommend Percentage of respondents who would suggest or advocate the brand to their peers.

line extension Additional product within the brand and in the same category, e.g. new flavours of crisps; not the same as *brand extension*.

logistics The parts of the business concerned with getting the goods and services to the point of sale (or front line in its military sense), i.e. purchasing, production and distribution.

logo A symbol and/or group of letters in a particular font or style that identifies a company or brand.

loss-leader Pricing a particular product at a loss in order to 'lead' customers to buy other products. Subject to fair trade legislation.

low-involvement A product that is purchased without much consideration. Also applies to advertising that barely engages the mind. The strength of product involvement usually turns on the user's interest in the category rather than the brand. Opposite of *high-involvement*.

loyalty A key concept in customer retention but measured in quite different ways; (snapshot) the share of category requirements (SCR) held by the brand in a given time period; (longitudinal) of those who bought in the last period, the percentage who bought again in this one or the proportion of repeat (versus first-time) purchasers; (attitudinal) either snapshot or longitudinal but measured as something like *purchase intention* rather than behaviourally.

loyalty programme Part or all of a marketing campaign designed to retain customers by rewarding them for continuing business, e.g. by giving air miles.

marcoms Abbreviation for marketing communications; similar to *commercial communications*.

margin Difference between sales and direct costs, i.e. gross profit, but gross is distinguished from net (after discounts and rebates). Terminology differs between companies but net margin is usually struck before marketing costs and net (brand) contribution signifies they have been deducted. May be expressed as percentage of revenue. Not the same as net income or net profit.

markdown A reduction of an established retail price.

market growth An increase in the total annual market revenue by the attraction of new customers and increased expenditure by current customers.

market price Arm's length price between a willing buyer and willing seller based on prices prevailing in the marketplace.

market(ing) metric Quantified marketing performance measure regularly reviewed by top management. Lower level measures that explain variances in metrics are *diagnostics*. Can be classified into six categories: (1) 'Consumer intermediate', for example, consumer awareness and attitudes. The word 'intermediate' is used because these measures lie between inputs (like advertising spend) and behaviour (such as sales). (2) Consumer behaviour, for example quarterly penetration. (3) Direct trade customer, for example, distribution availability. (4) Competitive market measures, for example, market share, measured relative to a competitor or the whole market. (5) Innovation, for example, share of turnover due to new products. (6) Financial measures, for example, advertising expenditure or brand valuation.

market(ing)-led Distinguishes the orientation of the firm from e.g. finance- or production-led where top management primarily considers the financial numbers or production issues respectively. Market(ing)-led organizations empathise with customers and focus primarily on how [more] customers can be satisfied [more] profitably.

marketing As noted in the preface to this glossary, the many definitions of marketing may be confusing. Ted Levitt referred to 'getting and keeping customers' but it is more than that. The AMA version below captures the classic 4Ps and the second set describes the main alternatives. The third is for those hooked on cash flow. (1) The process of planning and executing the conception, pricing, promotion, and distribution of ideas, goods, and services to create exchanges that satisfy individual and organizational objectives (American Marketing Association, 1985). (2) Three main meanings: (a) A company-wide business philosophy, which gives priority to satisfying customers' wants and needs as a means to achieving the company's goals. In this sense, marketing as a customer-orientated culture can be applicable to non-profit organizations as well as businesses. (b) What the company's marketers do, typically developing and launching products, packaging, branding, pricing, advertising, promotion, and distribution. The CIM definition is close to this: 'Marketing is the management process responsible for identifying, anticipating and satisfying customer requirements profitably.' (c) The activities covered by the marketing budget, usually just advertising and promotion. This is what people typically mean when they talk of the 'return' on marketing. (3) The sourcing and harvesting of inward cash flow.

marketing investment Marketing expenditure that builds *brand equity* as distinct from achieving short-term gains, such as sales discounts, and price promotions, and other expenditures such as market research. Image advertising is typically seen as an investment.

marketing mix The variety of marketing activities, see *four Ps*, which has been put together to form the marketing campaign. For services, the mix is sometimes extended to seven Ps: people, process and physical evidence.

mark-up pricing The (retail) sales price is calculated by adding a fixed percentage to cost.

mass customization The provision of *customization* to the mass market through modern technology, e.g. allowing the end user to specify the ideal configuration of a car or computer she wishes to buy. The production system automatically includes that specification in the next available schedule.

merchandising No longer used in the traditional sense of being a synonym for 'marketing', it now means product display, usually with added material, at point of purchase and elsewhere, e.g. on T-shirts. Essentially it means exposing products to the risk of purchase.

multi-brand Where a company is marketing several brands within a single product category, e.g. Unilever or Procter & Gamble, and their various washing detergents.

NBC See *contribution*.

new product development (NPD) New product development is the creation or reformulation of products usually under existing brand names, as distinct from new brand development (NBD). See *innovation*. Generally a crucial part of ensuring the longevity of a brand or business. It may include the launch of the new product.

off-trade Consumption takes place at home or otherwise outside the retail [food/drink sales] premises.

one-stop shop(ping) Purchasing a variety of goods and/or services from a single location, originally from a shopping mall or the equivalent. Multi-skilled marketing services companies, within groups such as WPP, seek to cross-sell the work of other subsidiaries although this is not strictly 'one stop'.

on-time delivery Market metric, measuring percentage of deliveries on schedule, a customer satisfaction or service quality measure. Whether punctuality is defined by when the customer expected it or when the firm intended to deliver it can make a big difference to the metrics.

on-trade Consumption takes place on the retail (food/drink sales) premises.

opinion leader Someone who influences the *attitudes* and especially *purchase intent* of others, often by word of mouth or example. May or may not be an early adopter.

organic growth Increase in like-for-like sales and/or profits excluding acquired brands and businesses; similar to *like-for-like sales*.

orientation Market orientation is used in contrast with financial or production orientation where management is focused on the financial [profit] figures or *logistics*, respectively. Market orientation can be further divided into competitor or customer or end-user orientation. See *market(ing)-led*.

OTC See *over-the-counter.*

out-of-home (1) In relation to advertising: advertising media viewed outside the household, which are not available in the home, such as displays on shopping carts, advertising subway. (2) On-trade or other consumption away from home.

outsourcing Subcontracting internal, usually non-core, operations.

over-the-counter (OTC) OTC is used primarily in pharmaceuticals to indicate products that can be sold by a pharmacy, or other retailer, direct to consumers, without a doctor's prescription. The category further divides into restricted, where a pharmacist has to be present when the sale is made, and non-restricted.

parallel trade In addition to the official route through which a brand is exported to the exclusive distributor in a given territory, the brand is being imported separately and, typically, sold at lower prices. May be expressed as parallel exports or imports and also known as the *grey market*.

payment by results (PBR) Form of agency remuneration normally used in conjunction with fees or commission. Increasingly used for advertising where three types of measures are used: consumer behaviour (e.g. sales or share); intermediate (e.g. intention to buy); client service. Can be used for all marketing services suppliers provided the objectives are quantified and agreed.

peer group People or companies who see themselves as having similar status or expertise. So P2P (peer to peer) marketing is largely word of mouth. See also *viral marketing*.

penetration percentage of target market that purchased the brand at least once during the period.

penetration pricing Strategy for quickly gaining share on market entry with low prices. Opposite of *skimming*.

personalized About products, services solutions. Same as customized. See *customization*.

pipeline Two different meanings: (1) new product development (NPD) – the number of new products or re-formulations that have been created but not yet launched. (2) Inventory – goods stocked in *channels*, usually measured by the number of days it will take to sell through.

point-of-sale (POS) Usually referring to retail sales outlet and also known as point-of-purchase (POP). Place at which a sale is completed, e.g. check-out or shop. Now checkouts provide a major source of customer behaviour data.

positioning Brief description of the unique identification of the brand in the consumer's mind. Similar to *brand essence*.

positioning statement Brief summary of strategy that describes the (unique) customer need that the brand fulfils. Also defines target end user, competitor, why it is different and better (*competitive advantage*) and possibly the pricing strategy.

premium brand Goods and services selling at about 10–80 per cent above the average price. Products still more highly priced are usually called 'super-premium'.

price deflation Price reduction due to economic conditions as distinct from discounting.

price point A price considered critical for consumer purchasing volumes, e.g. £1.99 compared to £2.

price sensitive A product is said to be 'highly price sensitive' if a small change in price results in a large change in sales. See *elasticity*.

procurement Obtaining supplies by various means including purchasing which implies payment.

product The physical goods and/or services intended for sale and to which branding may be applied.

product management Temporarily a successor term to *brand management*, and still used in the USA, to signify that the focus was on the fundamental product and its attributes rather than the branding or emotional aspects. In practice it is functionally similar.

product mix The variety or assortment of products offered for sale: (a) width – the total number of product lines; (b) length – the average number of brands of each category; (c) depth – the average number of products under each brand name; (d) consistency – the closeness with which the products are related.

product placement Persuading the producer to use the brand or product service within entertainment media programmes or publications, e.g. TV, radio, or film, such as the James Bond movies.

products per consumer A metric which describes the number of different products the end user buys from the range.

psychographics Consumer lifestyle, personality and psychological character- istics as distinct from *demographics*.

public relations First formalized to persuade US citizens to support their country joining World War I, Edward Bernays defined it as: '(1) informa- tion given to the public, (2) persuasion directed at the public to modify attitudes and actions, and (3) efforts to integrate attitudes and actions of an institution with its publics and of publics with that institution.' Similar concept to *customer relations* but with a different target.

pull One of the two main distribution strategies. Pull relies on creating demand directly with the end user, e.g. through advertising, so that calls are made on the retailer. The opposite of *push*.

purchase intent(ion) A measure of the buyer's claimed likelihood of pur- chasing the brand either next time or sometime in the future (the difference may be important).

purchasing on promotion Key metric for assessing robustness of pricing, it measures the percentage of sales linked with special (usually price) promotion.

purchasing power Same as *buying power*.

push One of the two main product distribution strategies. Push implies the sales force loading the immediate trade customer thereby exerting pres- sure for onward sales. The opposite of *pull*.

quality A crucial component of *brand equity*, actual quality needs to be dis- tinguished from perceived. Actual is given by objective measure(s) of the product's performance compared to some benchmark, e.g. the main com- petitor, based on a set of physical attributes. Perceived quality refers to the consumer's impression, i.e. it is attitudinal. Metrics are usually relative to the same benchmark. Perceived quality may be more influential than actual in the short term, but the two usually converge over time. Perceived qual- ity is widely thought to be a key driver of market share and profitability.

reach The percentage of the target market who (will) see any ad of a campaign. A companion measure for *frequency*. Also used in distribution to indicate coverage.

rebranding Changing the *brand* name, e.g. Andersen Consulting to Accenture, Jif to Cif, or Marathon to Snickers.

recall Aided recall measures the percentage of the target market who remember an advertisement when prompted with a set of ads including the one being tested. Unaided recall is the same except without the stimuli.

recognition Similar to aided *recall* but requires prompting with actual object, not just the name.

redemption rate Percentage of distributed coupons, or money-off vouchers or other incentives, used by customers in exchange or towards a purchase in a promotional activity.

relationship marketing Introduced in the 1990s to put the emphasis on long-term customer interaction, as distinct from concluding with the sale. Seen as a third perspective of marketing after economic (also known as *four Ps* or 'transactional') and competitive (indicated by market share being the priority metric).

relationship pricing From *relationship marketing*, it is a pricing system based on long- rather than short-term considerations.

relative price A key brand equity metric, although in some sectors, e.g. financial services, it can be hard to measure. The brand's average selling price relative to competitors, i.e. share of market by value divided by share of market by volume.

relaunch The reintroduction of an existing brand on to the market after changes have been made to it, or attempted revivification of a tired brand. Difficult to do successfully but easier if a new target market or use can be found, e.g. baking soda as a deodorizer.

relevance A brand equity metric that indicates the consumer's empathy with the brand. 'My kind of brand' but also a brand that solves the problems I have, e.g. crash helmets are relevant to bike users.

reliability Product *attribute* if, functionally, it will do the job punctually and not break down. Perceived reliability, i.e. trustworthiness, is a consumer *attitude*. Usually correlated with *quality*, but not necessarily, e.g. airlines.

repeat customers An important measure for new product launches, it distinguishes first-time sales from customers returning for more.

repositioning A strategic change for the brand, possibly in the consumer's perception of the brand.

reputation Corporate *brand equity*. Often used as a term for *brand equity*, in businesses without physical distribution, e.g. professional and financial services.

response curve The graphical or mathematical expression of the relationship between an input and an output variable, e.g. between advertising and sales. The two main forms are diminishing returns, which is also a special case of the 'S-shaped' curve in which the output is slow to take off, accelerates and then levels off again in the diminishing returns stage.

rolling launch Introducing a new product market by market. Can reduce risk and cost and progressively build learning. Against that it will take longer and may expose product to pre-emptive responses by competitors.

roll-out Two meanings: (1) Progressive expansion of distribution for a (new) brand or product (2) In direct mail, the largest mailing in a campaign.

route to market Strategy and staging posts for a brand/product launch. Provides a step-by-step programme for evaluation.

sales mix The variety of products sold to one, a group, or all customers. As the word 'mix' means 'analysis', it may also be an analysis of the customers to whom the products are sold.

sales on deal Same as *purchasing on promotion*.

sales promotion Activity to increase short-term sales, typically through a price reduction or increased quantity, e.g. two products for the price of one. Promotions may use inducements or rewards of all kinds, e.g. air miles.

salience Prominence, standout. A typical metric is the brand's *familiarity* as a percentage of the average of other brands in the *category* or *consideration set*.

same store sales Same as *like-for-like sales* or *comparable sales*.

sampling Two meanings: (1) Small quantities of the product given, usually free, to prospective buyers. Perhaps the oldest and most effective introductory marketing tool. (2) The use of a statistically representative subset as a proxy for an entire population, for example, in order to facilitate quantitative market research.

satisfaction The degree to which a person's expectations of a product, brand or employment are met by their perception of reality. Used for customers, end users and staff. Some believe that relative (to competitor) satisfaction is a more reliable indicator of *brand equity*.

scaleable The ability to increase a small sized market or marketing activity to the full size. May be the incremental cost of increasing size. If this is small, then the market or activity is highly scaleable.

seasonality Variation of sales according to the time of the year, e.g. ice cream sells more in summer.

sector Collective noun for an associated group of categories, e.g. butter and margarine are part of the yellow fats category, but both are just part of the food sector.

segment Used loosely to mean any subset of the total customer base or an *affinity group*. More precisely, a group of sufficient importance and distinction to justify a separate marketing campaign, e.g. high value customers. In theory, within segment customers are more like each other than outsiders. In practice, implementing multiple track marketing campaigns is difficult and expensive.

segmentation A means for analyzing a total market, typically *demographic*, geographic, *psychographic* or by product usage so that marketing can be more efficiently and/or effectively targeted at one or more subsets of customers. Each such subset is a *segment*.

seller's market A market characterized by a shortage of supply or unexpectedly high demand. Seller dictates terms. Opposite of *buyer's market*.

share A widely used ratio to express sales (share of market or brand share), advertising (share of voice), consumer usage (e.g. share of throat, used in drinks), retail space (share of shelf), or consumer spending (share of wallet). May be either value or volume. It is what the company/brand achieves as a percentage of the total market (category).

skimming Market entry strategy relying on an initially high price for enthusiasts and then gradually lowering the price to expand the market. Opposite of *penetration pricing*.

SKU See *stock-keeping unit*.

sourcing Identifying and choosing original suppliers – may include the supply itself.

spend per transaction Metric used in retail on-premises business to indicate average bill for each customer.

stock cover Inventory expressed as number of days' sales. See *stock-turn*.

stock-keeping unit (SKU) The atomic product level for which separate store-keeping records are needed, i.e. the unique package, colour, size, etc. which defines the single unit the consumer could buy.

stock-turn Number of times (usually per annum) that inventory is sold and restocked. This is a financial calculation, not actual physical clearance. See *stock cover*.

supply chain management Logistical process designed to get goods from source to end user as efficiently and effectively as possible. Linked with 'value chain management' which additionally seeks to build end-user value at each stage. Criticized by some marketers for working in wrong direction, i.e. it should be 'demand chain' (work back from end user).

synergy Originally just 'working together' but now taken to imply that the total (output, value or efficiency) will be greater than the sum of the parts. Often used to justify acquisition.

tactical pricing Short-term variations, usually reductions, to stimulate sales and/or discomfort competitors.

target market The particular *segment* of customers for whom the brand and its marketing are primarily intended. See *audience*.

target market fit The match between the actual and intended consumer profile (*demo/psychographics*).

telemarketing A wider term than *telesales*, it may also include use of telephone for publicity and research.

telesales Short for telephone selling, i.e. a selling operation in which potential customers are contacted by phone, or incoming sales enquiries are handled by phone. Now usually undertaken by *call centres*.

test market A small-scale version of the full market used to launch a new product or experiment with different marketing variables. It may aid the decision whether to roll out the product but also learn how best to operate in the larger market. The main problems are finding representative test markets and preventing competitors from also learning the test and responding pre-emptively.

throughput Measurement of volume of product, information, etc. Implication will differ depending on the industry. Network throughput is the capacity for data transferral. High throughput screening is simultaneous screening of large numbers of potential drug candidates.

through-the-line Where *above-the-line* and *below-the-line* activities are integrated in the marketing programme. See *integrated marketing communications (IMC)*.

top-of-mind High unprompted awareness as signified by being the first brand to be named. See *salience*.

trade-in The return of an object in exchange for a discount against the purchase. Frequently found in markets for industrial machinery and consumer durables.

trademark The legally owned device that can protect the use of the brand name and presentation. Not to be confused with the brand itself.

transactions per customer Average purchase frequency, often used in on-premise business. Number of customers × transactions per customer × *spend per transaction* = sales revenue.

transfer price The price charged by one business unit to another unit of the same firm. It may be market price or some adjustment to cost.

transition customers Those that are in the process of adopting a new stage product/service from their provider (e.g. analogue customers transitioning to digital).

transparent pricing Pricing so that the customer can see the cost components, e.g. ad agency charges to some clients.

trend How a *metric* is changing (e.g. year-on-year percentage increase in revenue if that is consistent with the immediate past). Short- and long-term trends need to be distinguished in assessing metrics.

umbrella brand Sometimes a corporate brand, e.g. Ford, but always a broadly based brand under which, in this brand 'architecture' sub-brands, such as Mondeo, shelter so that advertising, for example, can be more efficiently spent.

unique selling proposition (USP) The USP is based on the idea that advertising should communicate the logical reason to buy which also differentiates the brand from competitors (Rosser Reeves). As substantive physical differences have diminished, so has the following for this advice.

unit pricing Expressing a retail price (typically on the supermarket shelf) per each unit of weight or volume to facilitate price comparison.

uplift Increase in sales over the previous period.

upmarket Higher priced segment of the market or products purchased in more expensive areas or by higher income or socio-economic status people. May be called 'upscale' in the USA. Opposite of *downmarket*.

value added The incremental features of the brand beyond the bare functional necessities to do the job and which increase customer satisfaction.

value-for-money In principle it is quality divided by price but in practice it may be a synonym for cheap.

variable pricing Using different prices for the same product according to the date of sale or location or other conditions, e.g. theatre seats sold late or standby airline prices. Similar to *dynamic pricing*.

venture market Exploratory market to determine its future strategic importance.

vertical integration Company operating at more than one level in the *channels* of distribution, typically as both manufacturer and distributor.

viral marketing Originally *word of mouth*, the term is now used for electronic communications between peer consumers (e.g. e-mail). The metaphor arises from plotting the spread of awareness and usership on a map. The pattern that emerges is similar to that of a virus epidemic. Since the activity is primarily between consumers, the marketer has limited powers of intervention.

weight ratio The proportion of heavy (frequent or large volume) users to light users. Calculated as market share divided by {*penetration* times *loyalty* (share of category requirements)}.

wholesaler An intermediary linking manufacturers and retailers. The bulk-breaking part of the channel or distribution chain. Increasingly taking the form of cash and carries.

word of mouth Advocacy or discussion of the brand between users. If a brand has *high involvement* these consumer interactions can have a powerful effect on brand equity, whether positive or negative. See *viral marketing*.

Sources and further reading

Baker, M. J. (1998) *Macmillan Dictionary of Marketing & Advertising*, 3rd edn, London: Macmillan. Now replaced by *www.themarketingdictionary.com*.

Baron, S., Davies, B. and Swindley, D. (1991) *Macmillan Dictionary of Retailing*, London: Macmillan.

Bennett, P. D. (1998) *Dictionary of Marketing Terms*, Chicago: American Marketing Association.

Brown, A. L. (2002) *E-Commerce and Marketing Dictionary of Terms*, *http://www.udel.edu/alex/dictionary.html*

Buster, J. (2002) *Interactive Advertising Bureau*, *http://www.iabuk.net*

Doyle, P. (1998) *Marketing Management & Strategy*, 2nd edn, London: Pearson Education.

Doyle, P. (2000) *Value-based Marketing: Marketing Strategies for Corporate Growth and Shareholder Value*, Chichester: Wiley.

Hart, N. A. (1996) *The CIM Marketing Dictionary*, 5th edn, London: Chartered Institute of Marketing and the CAM Foundation.

Hart, N. A. and Stapleton, J. (1992) *The Marketing Dictionary*, 4th edn, London: Chartered Institute of Marketing and the CAM Foundation.

Jefkins, F. (1987) *International Dictionary of Marketing and Communication*, Glasgow: Blackie.

Kotler, P. (2003) *Marketing Management*, 11th edn, Upper Saddle River, NJ: Prentice-Hall.

Rosenberg, J. M. (1995) *Dictionary of Marketing & Advertising*, Chichester: Wiley.

The Economist (2001) *Pocket Marketing*, London: Profile Books.

Recommendations for marketing disclosures in companies' annual reports to shareholders[1]

We suggest that companies and their shareholders will gain from adopting the following annual reporting disclosure practices:

1 Companies should report brand equity and market performance in the operating and financial review (OFR) sections using the following principles:

1.1 The information should be in the form of market metrics, i.e. *quantitative* measures, supplemented by commentary. Text alone has little value.

1.2 Metrics should be compared, at least, with the prior year and thus need to be *consistent over time*. If the definition of a metric changes, the prior year should be restated on the new basis.

1.3 If a company has more than one brand, or metrics are otherwise not summable, the metrics should be given for the whole company (where applicable) plus a small number of brands (usually only two or three) which represent most shareholder value.

1.4 If a metric is regularly reviewed by the board, it is presumed to be a candidate for disclosure to shareholders subject to confidentiality (see below). Auditors should informally test the reasons for non-disclosure.

1.5 The metrics should be *auditable*, i.e. reliable and professionally sourced. All measures and definitions (including market definitions) should be explicit and precise. Note that only the usual provisions for the auditors' examination of the annual report outside the financial statements would apply, i.e. consistency but not full audit.

2 The metrics which present the best summary of brand equity and market
   performance will differ from sector to sector and, to a lesser extent, from
   company to company. For example, the size of the market and market
   share might be better conveyed in value terms in some sectors and in
   volume terms in others. In addition to *sales (already required), market
   definition and size*, the core metrics which almost all firms should report
   (with trends) are:

   2.1 *Market share* by value and/or volume together with a brief
        definition of the 'market'.

   2.2 *Marketing investment*, i.e. the expenditure on marketing intended to
        build brand equity. This excludes, for example, sales discounts, price
        promotions, and the cost of distribution.

3 Other metrics relevant to most sectors, and therefore candidates for
   disclosure, with trends, are:

   3.1 *Relative end-user satisfaction*, i.e. the satisfaction with this company's
        products indexed against satisfaction with competitors'.

   3.2 *Relative price*, i.e. value market share divided by volume market share.

   3.3 *Perceived product quality* as perceived by the end user.

   3.4 *Customer loyalty/retention*, e.g. percentage of start-of-year customers
        still active at year end.

   3.5 *Sales to new customers* as a percentage of turnover.

   3.6 Share of turnover represented by *products launched in previous three
        years* measured incrementally (to exclude cannibalization) by also
        showing the change in sales of products already being marketed
        three years before.

   3.7 *Availability/distribution*, i.e. the extent to which the products are
        available for purchase by final customers. The exact metric will
        depend on the sector.

   3.8 Firms should also provide a *glossary of marketing and brand
        terminology*, which should be the general (or at least industry)
        standard for annual reports. The development of standardized
        terminology would require a joint task force between accounting
        and marketing bodies. Companies would still be free to use
        alternative expressions and meanings but different usages should be

clarified where they are important. The terms used in this report are broadly defined in Appendix A but their application would need to be adapted for each sector. Note that these recommendations are not tailored to any sector, e.g. consumer goods. Business-to-business products equally have 'end users'.

4   Candidate metrics should already be reported internally. They should not increase the size of, nor the cost of preparing, printing and distributing, the annual report. Firms should have the option of *publishing and archiving full annual reports in electronic format only*, thus building on the existing trend to provide shareholders with abbreviated reports tailored to their interests. Web access to full annual reports, and analyst briefings, should be available to all shareholders.

5   Firms should not be expected to disclose target metrics, i.e. detailed future marketing intentions.

6   Most metrics are already known to competitors. Nevertheless *commercial confidentiality* is a real issue and possible disclosure should be reviewed, on a metric-by-metric basis, with the auditors. Where shareholders will gain more from discretion that should be observed.

These recommendations are proposed at this stage as non-mandatory guidelines. Some commentators on the drafts of this report pressed that at least the principal metrics should now be mandatory since similar metrics were proposed by the Accounting Standards Board, with support from the finance directors of the leading UK companies, back in 1993 but only patchily implemented, if that, since. However we believe there are good reasons why they should remain non-mandatory which include international considerations. UK companies should not be required to disclose more than foreign competitors.

Our aim is to show how annual reports could become more valuable while helping firms take a long-term view of their brands and businesses. At the same time, we have tried to avoid rigid, one-size-fits-all prescriptions, which might increase companies' reporting costs and/or fail to take account of the real issue of commercial confidentiality and the differences in the relevant metrics in different industries. By adopting these recommendations, companies should enhance performance by using clearer staging posts, without damaging shareholder interests.

Note

1   Amber, T., Barwise, P. and Higson, C., *Market Metrics: What Should We Tell the Shareholders*, London: Centre for Business Performance, Institute of Chartered Accountants in England and Wales. The research was sponsored by the Centre for Business Performance at the Institute of Chartered Accountants in England and Wales to whom the authors are grateful.

Supplement to innovation health metrics (Chapter 6)

This supplement first notes some objections to innovation health metrics, including some listed in Chapter 6. This left a long list of 38 innovation health metrics which was reduced by further discussions with practitioners to yield the shortlist in Chapter 6.

Concerns with the metrics long list

and alternatives

The boundary between culture and process is regarded as artificial and metrics are assigned to one or the other according to provenance but duplications have been eliminated. The basis for actually measuring these 38 indicators, shown in Table AC.3 below, may not be obvious since some of them are really composites, e.g. 'sociability' is an index constructed from the answers to six questions. To trace the methodology for each one will distract us from the innovation health overview we are seeking. Closer examination of each tree does not help the view of the wood.

A general point should be registered about the fact that many of the measures can come only from internal staff surveys. That is also true of employee, or internal customer, corporate brand equity. Staff will tolerate filling in questionnaires only if they believe them to be worthwhile and if they are rare events. One can stretch frequency, in large companies, by careful sampling but these points remain:

◆ Innovation health and corporate brand equity surveys should normally be combined.

◆ Even if benchmarked with other companies, they remain subjective indicators of how staff care to report their perceptions, as distinct from objective measures.

An example of the latter problem, also from Chris Voss, is the 'excellence paradox'.[1] Top companies, as professionals, know the heights they have yet to achieve. As a result, grade themselves modestly. At the other extreme, poor performers rate themselves about average because they are unaware of world-class standards. Ignorance breeds complacency. The paradox then is that self-ratings may reflect the opposite of reality.

Does this invalidate self-assessment? Not really. It takes us back to the need to compare performance both with what firms are trying to achieve (plan) and the market as a whole. Self-assessment will provide good answers to the former but not necessarily the latter. The two need explicitly to be separated by asking for assessments against what the firm's standards should be and then again the standards elsewhere. Testing the respondents' knowledge of external comparisons (e.g. did s/he work there?) determines the extent to which the external comparisons should be retained or ignored.

The positivism, or lack of it, in the responses may give a better impression of the overall helpfulness of the current culture than the individual answers. Nevertheless, surveys are a means of upward and downward communication that can be manipulated in ways which are little to do with metrics. For example, the recent idea that senior management bonuses should, in part, be tied to the outcomes of such surveys is nice but daft. It is bound to distort the responses. More subtle, non-intrusive measures should be used.

There is no complete answer to the inherent subjectivity of surveys for innovation health and corporate brand equity measurement, but the odds can be improved by using outside professionals who can provide a broad database of comparable findings.

Additionally or alternatively, companies will look to non-survey sources. Most typically, internal matters of culture and process are ignored. Quantified outcomes can be compared with quantified innovation goals. Examples are provided by Table AC.1.

Table AC.1 ◆ Examples of goal-directed innovation metrics

Innovation goals	Initiatives	Innovation performance
Customer retention	New loyalty schemes	% customers lost
Increased new product innovation	Number of innovations launched	% successful paybacks/shareholder value effects
ucts		% of turnover due to prod- launched in last three years
Differential advantage	R&D expenditure	Number of patents registered
	Specific initiatives implemented	
Market leadership	Number of new to the world concepts initiated in period	Average entry position (first, second) to market with new products and/or services
	Type of market typically entered (new, mature, declining)	

Discarded innovation health metrics

These few paragraphs record some objections to the other popular approaches encountered during our research. There is no suggestion that the methods are wrong in principle or wrong for other purposes. They are addressed here only because, in moving towards a shortlist of innovation health metrics, their omission needs some justification.

The shareholder value approach forecasts the free cash flow from each proposed initiative, subtracts the cost of capital and chooses the highest discounted cash flow (DCF). Fine in theory but dubious in practice: no honest marketer can reliably do the arithmetic until some real market numbers show up. The arithmetic is still worth doing but only to remove some no-hopers.

A similar approach is to work back from share of revenue targets by estimating the expected success rate at each developmental stage from concept to mass market to derive the required number of new concepts per annum. That helps budgeting. Adequate resources are a necessary but insufficient condition. Conversely, excessive resources replace discipline with confusion.

It is better to budget lean than fat as creative marketers are good poachers too. Resources aside, assessing innovations by their total number is plainly, in this environment of excess, counter-productive.

The most popular innovation metric in marketing is the share of revenue (or profit) represented by products launched within the last three, or five, years. This gives direction to the new product team and probably influences the approach to other marketing innovation. The two difficulties are that measurement takes place a long time after the event and the figures can be manipulated with trivial variations. Table AC.2 summarizes discarded metrics.

Table AC.2 ◆ Discarded innovation health metrics

Metric	Reasons for elimination
Shareholder value	Not enough evidence for reliable forecasts but a helpful diagnostic for spotting no-hopers.
Desired future share of revenue	Similar difficulties. More of a wish list than practical action.
Share of current revenue/profit from recent innovations	Popular and useful but lagging indicators.
Total number of innovations	Encourages quantity over quality which is the opposite of most firms' needs.
Number of innovations at each stage of the development process 'milestones passed'	A useful diagnostic to see the *flow* but not a metric of overall health.

Long list of innovation health metrics

This section gathers together a long list of metrics following the model in Figure 6.1. Table AC.3 highlights those that seem most salient for most firms. The number 38 may seem too many but it is a condensation of the wisdom from past research on innovation. Most of them have to be obtained from internal surveys and are accordingly subjective. This list was used as the base for refinement to the short list presented in Chapter 6.

Table AC.3 ◆ Generic innovation health metrics

	Metrics
Leadership	1 Staff awareness of vision/direction
	2 Staff commitment to vision/direction
	3 Level of anxiety about the state of the business
	4 Trust in the leadership, e.g. perceived competence
	5 Leadership by example, e.g. risk taking, quality
	6 Active support by the leadership
	7 Perceived control (may be the reverse of autonomy below)
	8 Focus (reverse of initiative diversity)
Goals	9 Specificity of innovation goals, e.g. quantified
	10 Awareness of innovation goals
	11 Commitment to innovation goals
Resource adequacy	12 Finance availability
	13 Time availability
	14 Staffing (a mix of clever, creative, financially aware, networkers and task-oriented people)
Culture impacts on creativity, development and implementation	15 Encouragement of creativity
	16 Autonomy/delegation
	17 Challenging work
	18 Fun place to work
	19 Workload pressure (may be reverse of organizational slack)
	20 Organizational impediments (seen as reciprocal of experimentation being expected of all managers)
	21 Learning culture, e.g. extent to which failures are celebrated, evaluated and broadcast
	22 Supplier/customer involvement in the firm's innovation, e.g. suggesting new products or problems for solution
	23 Sociability
	24 Solidarity
	25 Valence of culture for innovation (+ve / -ve)
	26 Culture style/leadership fit with sector needs
Process (better, faster, cheaper)	27 Formality of process
	28 Organizational shape
	29 Incentives
	30 Commitment to quality
	31 Relative state (to chief competitors) of technological development
	32 Fewer (rapid elimination of improbables)
	33 Stretch time targets
	34 Frequency of meetings
	35 Action-orientation
	36 Thrift
	37 Recycling
	38 Benchmarking competitors' costs

Note

1   Voss, C., Blackman, K., Hanson, P. and Oak, B. (1995) 'The competitiveness of European manufacturing – a four country study', *Business Strategy Review*, 6 (1), 1–25.

Index